HOODWINKED

How marketers use the same tactics as cults

MARA EINSTEIN, PH.D.
FOREWORD BY DOUGLAS RUSHKOFF

Prometheus Books

Essex, Connecticut

Prometheus Books

An imprint of The Globe Pequot Publishing Group, Inc.
64 South Main Street
Essex, CT 06426
www.globepequot.com

Distributed by NATIONAL BOOK NETWORK

British Library Cataloguing in Publication Information Available

Library of Congress Cataloging-in-Publication Data

Names: Einstein, Mara, author.
Title: Hoodwinked : how marketers use the same tactics as cults /
    Mara Einstein ; foreword by Douglas Rushkoff.
Description: Lanham, MD : Prometheus, [2025] | Includes bibliographical
    references and index. | Summary: "Combining industry interviews,
    advertising campaign analysis, and business and scholarly research,
    Hoodwinked offers an insider's view into how marketers co-opt our
    emotions in the name of corporate profits. Armed with this information,
    readers can learn to spot cult-inspired marketing so they can decide
    how, or if, they should engage with it"—Provided by publisher.
Identifiers: LCCN 2024020961 (print) | LCCN 2024020962 (ebook) | ISBN
    9781493086153 (cloth) | ISBN 9781493086160 (epub)
Subjects: LCSH: Marketing—Psychological aspects. | Marketing—Moral and
    ethical aspects. | Multilevel marketing. | Social responsibility of
    business. | Consumer behavior.
Classification: LCC HF5415 .E447 2025 (print) | LCC HF5415 (ebook) |
    DDC 658.8—dc23/eng/20241010
LC record available at https://lccn.loc.gov/2024020961
LC ebook record available at https://lccn.loc.gov/2024020962

♾️™ The paper used in this publication meets the minimum requirements of
American National Standard for Information Sciences—Permanence of Paper
for Printed Library Materials, ANSI/NISO Z39.48-1992.

To my husband, David.

And to my sister, Dari Schwartz Bookamer,
who gave so much and was gone too soon.

To *hoodwink*, or put something over on someone, derives from the act of thieves literally throwing a hood on victims before robbing them, thereby making them "wink," which has an archaic meaning of "to close one's eyes."

—*A Way with Words* (podcast), August 23, 2014

I was participating on a panel at the Institute for the Future, nestled in Palo Alto, the home of Stanford University and the heart of Silicon Valley. The rest of the lineup was a band of brothers—trailblazers in the creation of the internet, dressed in that "I'm-wearing-jeans-and-a-wrinkled-shirt-but-I-have-a-shit-ton-of-money" way. I was the only academic among the group of presenters.

I explained that the online space had become deceptive because it was filled with advertising that didn't look like advertising. Branded journalism was spiking—like Shell Oil paying for a story about sustainability or Discover Card touting the value of a college education because marketers wanted to sell students on credit cards with high-interest rates. This was the real "fake news."

One of my fellow panelists leaned over and whispered, "It wasn't supposed to be this way. We were trying to create community. We just didn't know. I'm so sorry."

I leaned back. "You're still going to hell."

CONTENTS

Part IV: From "Cult Lite" Influencers to Social Media Extremism

FOREWORD

Douglas Rushkoff

What if I told you I had found a book that could, quite literally, change your life?

What if all the seemingly inscrutable dilemmas of modern existence, all the intractable problems of daily living, all the challenges of establishing financial sustainability along with physical and mental health can be solved with a single insight? And what if I told you that the path to reaching this insight is in your hands right now?

Well, in a sense, it is. This book contains more than just one life-changing secret; it contains hundreds of them. Each product, system of thought, institution of higher learning, medical breakthrough, financial investment, blockchain white paper, diet drink, career coach, spiritual retreat, social media influencer, stoicism course, or hashtag campaign chronicled herein offered the One Truth needed to get from here to there.

All you have to do is believe, buy, click, follow, subscribe, and, most of all, share. For the only certain way of proving your faith and guaranteeing your own success in any system is to enlist others. And that's why, as the newest member of the Mara Einstein Hoodwinked Society, I am—for a limited time—inviting you to step up, drop in, reach high, join the team, unlock the secret, take the leap, and find yourself in the new reality you always knew was possible and right over the next horizon but always just out of reach. It's not any longer.

It's here. You've found us. Welcome. Now tell your friends.

Yes, you've joined a cult. But the cult of Hoodwinked is no normal cult. It is a meta-cult, exposing the underlying dynamics driving our culture of branded belonging and accompanying disempowerment. The experience of reading about the hundreds of cult recruitment tactics deployed by those who wish to control our beliefs, behaviors, and buying is itself like a spiritual revelation. About that part, I kid you not: coming to recognize the essential, repeating architectures of cult marketing is a bit like putting on those special glasses in John Carpenter's movie *They Live*, which allow you to see the coercive messaging embedded in every billboard. I was lost, and now I'm found.

When you have finished this book, every opportunity to achieve "personal growth" will remind you of both the Mormon church and Mindvalley; each invitation to find "community" will smack of WeWork or GaryV; the chance to get in on the *next big thing* will shout LuLaRoe or NXIVM; the words "wellness" and "spirituality" will trigger the same justified suspicion one applies to Jim Jones or even Deepak Chopra.

Welcome to the cult of those who are willing to see the sticky strings attached to the promises of nearly every invitation to belong, to learn, to improve, or to "wake up." More often than not, these pleas are to enlist you in something less a club than a war. Whether it's antivax against the government, supplement against medicine, crypto against cash, Mac against PC, or the Great Awakening against wokeness, "getting in" means learning who is *out*. For all their promise of belonging, unity, and unconditional acceptance, the cult-inflected brands and organizations described here all demand exclusion, assignment of blame, and the payment of social, spiritual, and monetary dues.

To me, that's the real crime. If someone wants to sell memberships, products, education, or enlightenment, they're welcome to use whatever methods of persuasion to convince us of the benefits. Go for it. *Caveat emptor.* But those who employ the tactics of cults do so by leveraging our healthy and essential social and emotional needs against us. And the more desocialized and emotionally alienated our world becomes, the more vulnerable we are to the painstakingly concocted efforts at answering these needs with false promises and enforced surrender.

What makes this book so crucial at this particular moment in our history is that these techniques are now migrating online. I was one of the early cyberpunks who saw the digital realm as an escape from the forces of commercial and political hoodwinkery, in which we would be able to liberate ourselves from the brand tribes and social castes of American strip mall society and forge new bonds based on genuinely shared interests and values.

As the internet pivoted from a nonprofit-funded commons to an investment pyramid and surveillance marketplace, these new avenues for human social connection were replaced with opportunities to buy and sell our friendships for profit and status. Those who weren't selling social graphs directly were selling new systems and platforms for monetizing or new systems and platforms for developing platforms and systems for monetizing and so on. Everything went, as Mark Zuckerberg would have it, "Meta."

Although most of us may recognize a selling scam when it comes from the Bible salesman at the door, we don't have the same skills to detect such appeals online. We can't look into the seller's eyes, evaluate whether he or she is triggering any of our painstakingly evolved social mechanisms for detecting duplicity, or see the personal data and algorithmic processing being used to customize the appeal to our individual psychological profile.

In a landscape characterized less by true human bonding or solidarity than by likes, retweets, and subscriptions, the tactics of cult recruitment don't seem out of place at all. In the fabricated digital world, they may as well be features of nature.

It's time we recognize the salespeople, influencers, and algorithms in these spaces for what they are: cult recruitment agents. We must learn to alienate ourselves from these entities so that we may regard them less as preconditions for social interaction and belonging than as impediments to healthy, sustainable social outcomes. The massive success of QAnon online is no more testament to the ingenuity of Incel, Russian, Gamergate, or MAGA hackers than it is to the widespread ignorance of cult recruitment techniques and even more widespread inability to recognize such techniques when they are being used in virtual realms.

It's not our stupidity that's to blame, but our longing. Just as legions of high-worth investors could be hoodwinked into losing a combined $8 billion to Sam Bankman-Fried's crypto Ponzi scheme, we can all be hoodwinked into surrendering our common sense to an appeal too good to be true—especially when that appeal has been crafted for us, individually, by an artificial intelligence that knows more about us than we can remember ourselves and more about our inner workings than our therapists.

The best defense is to learn the fundamental methods for getting people to join these cult-inspired systems, to stay in them, and to recruit others. Only then can we recognize the patterns and stand a chance of identifying them when deployed in the ever-more-automated landscapes in which we are living, working, and making meaning together.

Let this meta-cult of those of us learning from Mara Einstein's wise experience be the last one you ever need to join.

New York
April 2024

ACKNOWLEDGMENTS

Hoodwinked is the book I always wanted to write. I just didn't know it would take thirty years until I was ready to do it.

Along the way I have met and learned from many friends and colleagues about the ever-changing world of media, the tricks and tips of the digital marketing landscape, and the complexities of religion, faith, and belief in all their manifestations. I am deeply indebted to Douglas Rushkoff, Jamie Cohen, Sarah McFarland Taylor, Michele Rosenthal, Lynn Schofield Clark, Diane Winston, Sarah Banet Weiser, Brooke Duffy, and Gina Neff, in addition to Chad Boettcher, Perfecto Sanchez, and others at the Impact Guild; my friends at the Advertising Education Foundation, especially Gord McLean; reporters who shared their knowledge and insights, such as Sapna Maheshwari, Craig Silverman, and Makena Kelly; and so many others who freely gave their energy and their wisdom. I would be remiss if I did not thank the fabulous and forthright E. Jean Carroll: You have long inspired me as a writer and more recently as an advocate and a champion of my work. I am so grateful. Finally, I want to thank my students who, over twenty-five years, keep me honest and help me to continuously see the world in new and unexpected ways. If I have forgotten anyone, please forgive me and feel free to hit me up for cocktails.

Many thanks to those who graciously took the time to read drafts of this book and provided thoughtful insights that pushed me to clarify my thinking, including Katie Lofton, Lazar Dzamic, Ed Timke, Mitch Baranowski, and Bill Keep.

I owe a huge debt to those who were willing to chat with me—on and off the record—so that I could pull back the curtain on the cult/marketing phenomenon. These include William Gasner, Katie Stoller, Reilly Newman, Lauren Fiedler, and new colleagues I have met through the multilevel marketing conference, notably Roberta Blevins and Maire O'Sullivan.

Hoodwinked would not have become a reality without my agent, Marilyn Allen, who saw the value of this work when others could not, and to Jonathan Kurtz at Prometheus Books, whose enthusiasm for *Hoodwinked* very nearly surpasses my own. Thanks as well to Nicole Carty for keeping the production process moving along and doing so with much grace. For my "team" who helped get this writing project off the ground and make it the best it could be, my thanks go to Allison Lane, Alison K. Williams, and Jen Glantz. Many, many thanks to all.

Personally, gratitude goes to the friends and family who support me through life's ups and downs. To my husband, David Langer, for helping me work through my arguments (as a good lawyer does) and knowing not to ask to read the manuscript. To my mom, Barbara Schwartz, who taught me the importance of education and fighting for what you believe in. To my sister, Jan Dannenberg, who keeps me honest. To my three musketeers, Karyn Slutsky, Roni Caryn Rabin, and Vashti Bernard—you know why. And, to my daughter, Cayla, your wit and wisdom give me hope for the next generation.

INTRODUCTION
Here a Cult, There a Cult,
Everywhere a Cult Cult

Ever go to Trader Joe's on Saturday morning? Around 7:30 a.m., shoppers start lining up, grocery carts at the ready, so they can dash through the aisles as soon as the store opens at 8:00. Once through the doors, people run to the refrigerator section like it's Black Friday at Walmart. After multiple "excuse me's" as you reach past fellow shoppers for the broccoli and kale chopped salad, it is not long before you find yourself bisecting the checkout line, which has already begun to wrap around the store.

Why all the excitement over a food store? It may be because of products like Everything but the Bagel seasoning. It could be because of promotion, like a TikTok influencer giving you a store tour to find the latest keto products or an article in *Real Simple* magazine in which employees "reveal" their favorite products. Most likely, though, what draws people to the store in a cultlike frenzy is Trader Joe's use of scarcity marketing, the practice of regularly limiting the supply of products to gin up consumers' fear of missing out. A quick trip to @traderjoeslist[1] on Instagram, and you will see post after post with tens of thousands of likes, all breathlessly exhorting *"it's back"*: pumpkin cream cheese, maple oat drink, ube ice cream, and planters shaped like skeletons doing yoga. Withholding items people want or need and consciously raising their anxiety is what experts call "systems of control," an important tactic in the cult tool kit.

Lululemon uses a different cult trick to get consumers to pay the unsightly price of $98 for a pair of yoga pants. For more than a decade, Lululemon has used "brand ambassadors" or influencers to promote their products. In the early 2000s, the company gave free clothing to CrossFit trainers and yoga instructors.[2] A simple aside—"*Oh, these yoga pants are soooo comfortable when doing a downward dog*"—was enough to spark interest in the clothing, and it didn't look or feel like a sales pitch.

Today, that promotional tool has been moved online where thousands of ambassadors promote Lululemon. These multiethnic, utterly hip, ultra-fit men and women embody the company's lifestyle and its professed mission to improve the world by enabling people to live healthier lives. Ambassadors include Deja Riley, a former dancer for Beyoncé and Lady Gaga turned popular YouTube fitness instructor,[3] and Farinaz Lari, an exceedingly buff Canadian athlete who is also a consultant for Arbonne, a beauty products purveyor and a notorious multilevel marketing company (MLM), a sales structure that resembles a pyramid scheme and preys on women looking to make extra cash.[4]

After reviewing influencer posts, the company's website, and business writings about Lululemon, I couldn't shake the sense that Lululemon, too, felt like an MLM. Like those marketing companies that do business as legal pyramid schemes, Lululemon does not pay its ambassadors; influencers make money only if they make sales through affiliate links on their sites. That's standard industry practice, so that's not the problem. Then it hit me. The company expends a lot of energy promoting the idea of community, especially among its ambassadors. And for good reason. By promoting community and a sense of shared mission, Lululemon can more readily coordinate their ambassadors and save millions of dollars in advertising expenses. From April 2019 to March 2020, for example, the company amassed more than $86 million in free media exposure through the unpaid work of 5,600 ambassadors.[5]

In sum, Lululemon professes an all-encompassing ideology, a theory for how one should look, act, and engage with the world, which is a defining element of a cult. And it lures people—both prospective ambassadors and customers—through the promise of community and by restricting information about what they are signing up for. These are fundamental recruitment tactics used by cults and by MLMs.

Key to any cult is a charismatic leader. In the consumer marketplace today, there is no better example than Elon Musk. He has the power to move markets and shake up industries by simply posting a few characters on X, formerly Twitter. When Tesla, Musk's company, purchased $1.5 billion in Bitcoin in early 2021, the price of that cryptocurrency jumped 60 percent.[6] Today, when the bottom is falling out of crypto, Musk claims he never told people to invest in these currencies. Well, that's not true. He promoted using Bitcoin as an option for buying a Tesla and flouted that his SpaceX mission was paid for with Dogecoin.[7] He called Doge "the people's crypto," and he claimed to buy it for his son. To his one hundred million followers on what was then Twitter, that seemed like an endorsement, and millions of them lost money blindly following him.[8]

One of his followers is Glauber Contessoto, a man dubbed the Doge millionaire. He grew up poor but as a Gen Zer knew his way around the internet and decided to invest in Dogecoin. Initially, he invested less than $100. After Musk promoted the cryptocurrency, though, Glauber—using his life savings and borrowing still more money—went all-in to the tune of $250,000. He saw that investment grow—on paper—to more than $2.5 million. But that didn't last. In June 2022 he wrote that although his investment had been worth as much as $3 million, it was down to $230,000 at that point. He ironically notes, "if I had just held my entire original investment in Tesla, I would have had $3 million."[9]

Whether Trader Joe's, Lululemon, or Elon Musk, this behavior is not simply being a fan of a brand. Marketers have purposefully worked to generate outsized passions for products so that they become "brand cults." Positioning products in this way is good for them, not so great for you. That's because when brands become this important, purchase decisions become less mindful. Aided by capitalism and long-cultivated, unachievable standards about how we should look, how much money we need to make, and what schools properly brand our intelligence, we have internalized our own systems of control—regulating what we eat and how little we sleep in order to compete in the rat race—while social media acts as a 24/7 system of influence, shaming us into believing we can never make the grade. Underlying all this are the online algorithms written to manipulate content to produce maximum anger and anxiety.

The integration of personal, passionate connections to brands—be they physical products or social media influencers—paired with social controls and anger-inducing algorithms has created the perfect storm for cultlike strategies to permeate the marketplace.

WE'VE TRADED ADS FOR IDENTITY

Over the last decade marketers have glommed on to the idea that elevating brands to the level of cult status is the perfect strategy to retain customers. That's because getting ads in front of us—never mind getting us to watch them—has become almost impossible. Marketers can't be sure you are ever going to see a commercial or a print ad or an online post. Led to desperation, their recourse is to make damn sure that the brand is so important to your life—so embedded and ingrained—that you don't ever need to see an ad again.

Part of this results from changes in the media we use, but it is also related to broader societal changes. Institutions like religion and family and our place of employment used to help define who we are. Now, not so much. The gaping void for identity markers has been filled by the consumer marketplace via branded products touting not just benefits (we'll get your teeth whiter!) but moral values. So Trader Joe's isn't just a supermarket. It is an environmentally correct, organic-focused store with a highly selective employment standard. Fenty by Rihanna is not just a beauty brand, but a cosmetic line and lingerie purveyor that embodies inclusivity for all races and abilities. Patagonia is a company committed to sustainability that creates ads telling people not to buy their clothes. By shopping at these stores or using these brands, we communicate to the world who we are—or at least how we want to be perceived.

Connecting brands to values in this way makes them more important to us, and they instill what social psychologists call in-group and out-group dynamics. Fraternities do this; "mean girls" do this; cults do this. You're Target rather than Walmart, or Monster rather than Red Bull, CrossFit rather than SoulCycle, or iPhone rather than Samsung. This is purposeful. Creating an us-versus-them mentality is just one of the psychological methods used by cults and co-opted by marketers that we examine throughout this book.

Psychology has been used since the 1950s to design advertising that taps into our deepest desires to get us to buy. When I worked on the Miller Lite account, my ad agency boss used to say, "I want to get people to drink so much beer their livers burst." Back then, though, the best we could do was bombard people with TV ads and some billboards. Today, marketers have the ability to know on an individual basis what our needs and wants are, and personalized messages can be delivered by trusted sources—an influencer, a friend, or a family member. The ability to communicate messages this way spawned what I am calling the cult + marketing continuum.

At one end are brand companies that want to sell you a product. Some of these have a cultlike following—say, Nutella or REI. While being a passionate fan of a product is unlikely to envelop your life the way a fanatical religious cult can, there are some important similarities to be aware of. At the extreme other end of the cult + marketing continuum are multilevel marketing companies like LuLaRoe and doTERRA that combine self-help pep talks with it's-your-fault-that-you-can't-sell anxiety. In the middle are influencers, including wellness gurus selling think-for-yourself philosophies, or crypto bros telling you "buy now . . . or else," who, with the aid of algorithms, become gateways to conspiracy theories or even MLMs.

Digital technology—with its ability to bring large groups of people together while pushing us into narrowly delineated silos—has forced a re-wiring of the word cult. Eli Pariser explains in his book *The Filter Bubble: What the Internet Is Hiding from You* that we do not all experience the same internet. So whereas I might like musicals, pit bulls, and media regula-tion, someone else might be interested in space exploration, football, and politics, and the algorithms work to feed us content based on our interests and shared affinities. In doing this, the technology corrals us into groups of people who by and large think the same way we do.

At its base, a cult is simply a group of people that coalesce around an idea.[10] A brand cult, or what some might call a marketing tribe, targets peo-ple based on their beliefs and affinities, like Fenty or Patagonia. Companies do this because brands are fundamentally about ideas, not products. What differentiates a brand cult from a high-control or high-pressure cult like Sci-entology is that the shared ideology of the latter is extreme, and the group is headed by a charismatic—and typically narcissistic and authoritarian—leader. This person—usually a man—uses his powers of persuasion to cre-ate his following. It's one thing to buy $98 Lululemon leggings and quite another to leave your family for a persuasive religious leader. Cults may be groups with deceptive, manipulative, all-encompassing belief systems, but they may also be groups that share beliefs about a person or product with less nefarious outcomes. In either case, people join these groups for the community they provide, and social media spaces facilitate personal connections—for good or for ill.

Cults (and marketers) are sneaky. After all, no one raises their hand to join a cult and no one who's in one admits they are. The process of indoctrination is slow and methodical, which is why it feels like it has come out of the blue. But if you or someone you know "suddenly real-ize" that you have a freezer full of Trader Joe's sweet potato gnocchi or a drawer crammed with more Fenty foundation and mascara than you can use in a lifetime or that you have been sucked into selling Herbalife, spent too much time at CrossFit, bought into worthless Bitcoin, or paid untold sums of money to get your kid into "the right college," then you've been indoctrinated into a marketing cult.

The concern is not that you will be brainwashed into joining a reli-gious group and isolated in some remote country. The issue is that you will be hoodwinked into buying things you don't need or can't afford, or that that you will accept extreme ideologies that do not align with who you are.

Being vulnerable to manipulation is predicated on the fact that we have come to accept anxiety as our default state of being.

THE CULT + MARKETING CONTINUUM

The feeling that extremism has become pervasive is evident in the use of the word "cult" seemingly everywhere. There are books titled *The Cult of Trump, The Cult of Smart,* and *The Cult of We.* Magazines hawk "cult beauty products," like Nars Orgasm blush or Charlotte Tilbury's Matte Revolution lipstick in Pillow Talk. Go to any website targeting women, and there's bound to be the latest "cult fitness craze." Celsius, a low-calorie energy drink for women, reached cult status so quickly that the product was almost impossible to find.

I doubt twenty-first-century marketers intended for brand cults to open the door for creating an environment in which people were made more vulnerable to extreme groups and ideologies. Truth is, they didn't do it alone. This time they had the help of social media.

As we spent more time online during the last decade, we also became more adept at avoiding traditional advertising messages. To compensate, advertisers turned to more deceptive methods such as native advertising (sponsored posts you see in social media news feeds), branded content (articles that look like news but are ads paid for by advertisers), and social media influencers.[11] These techniques are intended to engage us and evoke emotion, mostly through video. Often those messages are bolstered by influencers, who don't properly label their content as advertising, even though that is required by law.

HUCKSTERS . . . CHARLATANS . . . INFLUENCERS

Hucksters, quacks, snake oil salesmen, and charlatans have existed for millennia. Whatever you call them, they are tricksters who use deception, manipulation, and exploitative tactics to gain people's trust so they will loosen their purse strings. Swindlers are so fundamental to the human experience that they appear not only in the Bible, but in popular culture like *The Adventures of Huckleberry Finn* and *The Music Man,* to name just a few. These flimflammers are the cultural ancestors to today's social media influencers.

P. T. Barnum—considered the godfather of PR—is probably one of the most famous hucksters of all time. Although he is known for the circus that bears his name, Barnum's real talent was in flimflam, promoting hoaxes and sideshows like the "Fiji mermaid," which was the head and torso of a monkey sewn to the tail of a fish, or events such as the lavish wedding of Tom Thumb, which drew crowds by the thousands. His disdain for his audiences is evident in his well-known phrase, "There's a sucker born every minute."

Today's charlatans are as creative and deceptive as their earlier counterparts. Who can forget "Miss Cleo," with the Psychic Readers Network in the 1990s, inviting viewers to "call me now"? Or Anna Sorokin, aka Anna Delvey, who posed as a wealthy socialite in New York City, ended up in jail for grand larceny, and became the subject of the Netflix series *Inventing Anna*? Corporate swindlers have become too numerous to list but include the likes of Bernie Madoff, the Sackler family, and Billy McFarland of Fyre Festival fame. Religious deceivers include the likes of Jim and Tammy Faye Bakker, Ted Haggard, and Joel Osteen. And the fakers in politics are too numerous to mention.

Although the word "influencer" is new, the concept behind it is decidedly not. Know, too, that not every influencer is a con artist or a swindler or a charlatan. However, digital media has enabled millions of people to become "content creators," so if even a small percentage of those influencers want to take advantage of others, millions can and will be affected. Add to this mix online algorithms—that is, computer code—designed to make us angry and anxious. Ramped up emotions keep us online longer. Being online longer means we see more advertising. More advertising means more money for Facebook and other social media sites. And we know that Facebook doesn't care if you are falling down the QAnon rabbit hole so long as you are looking at advertising—or the company can claim you did. The plus for marketers: all that angst begs for release, leading to more online shopping, more time with influencers, and more doomscrolling. For Americans, this averages two and a half hours a day on social media.

This is the environment in which the cult + marketing continuum exists. I developed this framework to help us envision the broad scope of how cult tricks have permeated the consumer and political landscape. This continuum is the scaffolding for *Hoodwinked*, and each of these ideas is examined in depth throughout the book.

The continuum starts with brand cults, which prime us to create personal relationships with a brand. Next are social media influencers, who come to feel like our friends as we spend time with them. This is followed by influencers who game the system by keeping us angry so they can make more money. Finally, there are multilevel marketing companies. These marketers most closely reflect the tactics of traditional cults. Let's examine these one by one.

Brand cults are products for which marketers have worked assiduously over time to make you believe they have to be part of your life. Take Apple. Apple is a computer or a phone or a content provider. That's it. In the past, we would have thought of an Apple product as nothing more than a piece of technology that helps us do our job or make a phone call. Now, Apple users are a tribe whose members believe Mac users are better than PC users. Some users believe the products have almost mystical powers and worship Steve Jobs as godlike, even after his death. Brand cults are not simply about purchasing a product, but about creating an identity and engaging in a community.

I refer to **influencers** as **"cult lite"** because they can be both brand cults and the gateway to more extreme belief systems. Brand cult influencers run the gamut from kidfluencers, like Katie Anderson (@kcstauffer) who promotes her two daughters eating yogurt or using pancake mix to their three million followers on Instagram, to David Dobrik, who you may have never heard of but who has 18 million followers on YouTube and 11.9 million on Instagram and drives around the country giving away new cars and a year's worth of Chipotle. Andrew Tate, on the other hand, falls into the category of "gateway to extremism." This bald, bearded, tattooed kickboxer found fame by spewing hatred for women, and he has been awaiting trial on charges of rape and human trafficking in Romania. He conned more than 127,000 followers into paying $49.99 per month to become members of Hustler's University, "a community for men to earn income via various money-making schemes, including copywriting and investing in crypto."[12]

A bit more under the radar are what are known as nano- or micro-influencers. These are people who have fewer than ten thousand or fifty thousand followers respectively, but marketers love them because they interact with their followers more, creating what seem to be true relationships.

"Cult lite" influencers to social media extremism fall into two camps: those who start out spewing hate and those who begin by selling a luxurious lifestyle or health and wellness and then morph into purveyors of cultlike ideologies. The latter is more subtle and more dangerous.

Spiritual and wellness influencers have come to mix spirituality with conspiracy, what academics Charlotte Ward and David Voas dubbed "conspirituality."[13] This online movement exploded during the pandemic, when political disillusionment converted into conspiracy theories, most prominently the fear of a secret group controlling the social order. Many people came to believe that the best way to manage the looming totalitarian world order was to live by the traditions of a New Age "paradigm shift." Yoga instructors and weight-loss gurus besieged their followers to try juice fasts one minute and then the next told them not to trust pharmaceutical companies, to do their research, and to think for themselves. Influencers, whom their followers had come to know and trust, were claiming 5G caused cancer and vaccines were opportunities to embed us with tracking devices, and those ideas were widely disseminated. I don't know if those influencers believe this nonsense, but I do know it made them lots of money.

Multilevel marketing (MLM) aka cults include direct sales firms whose structure is similar to a pyramid scheme and whose tactics most replicate those used by extremist traditional cults. Prospects are groomed by members looking to bring them into the group. Ex-MLMers I spoke with were approached online. Taylor, a twentysomething from Long Island, said she was recruited by someone who "stalked her" online and then praised her social media posts, claiming she was a natural marketer.

Once onboard, recruits continue to be bombarded with praise, which happens in the many, many multiple group chats to which they've been added. They are told to buy inspirational books or view self-help videos, including content outside the company, like entrepreneurial influencer Ed Mylett, who is as overpumped as you imagine him to be. The longer someone is part of an MLM, the more they take on its belief system, including bringing others into the group and staying away from those who speak negatively about it.

Most people I spoke with did not get this far into a company, but there are plenty of horror stories shared by people who do, and we get to those later in the book. For now, know that those who do become isolated are less likely to question when things don't quite make sense, like the MLM reneging on its return policy or your "upline"—the person who brought you into the group—working way too hard to keep you from leaving. As in other cults, anxiety is constant. The pressure to sell is constant and leaving becomes harder because members have few social relationships outside the group. MLMs are the canaries in the cult + marketing coal mines. Having been around for decades, MLMs are experts in implementing these strategies.

One last thing about the continuum. I am in no way suggesting that there is a natural progression from one category to another. What I am arguing is that techniques used by cults are increasingly being used by marketers—wittingly or not—and that engaging with them can expose you to people and organizations whose intentions are nefarious. Second, the further you are to the right on the spectrum, the more you experience extremism and anxiety. Once in these spaces, it becomes more difficult to extricate yourself. Learning how all this works will help you avoid becoming ensnared in the first place.

ANXIETY IS THE KEY INGREDIENT

The cult + marketing continuum would not exist without our willingness to give our time and attention to marketers—even while we run screaming from obvious advertising. Our attention is a scarce resource that marketers and social media platforms want to mine for all it's worth by manipulating our data and playing with our emotions. Economists have called this the "attention economy." That's far too benign for my thinking, especially when we know that social media platforms gin up our emotions for maximum intensity. Using the same sort of persuasive design that keeps people endlessly hitting the buttons on a Las Vegas slot machine, companies embed systems into the technology to keep us staring at our phones, tablets, and laptops. On Facebook and YouTube, for example, the algorithms are designed to feed us content that we want to see based on what we already looked at, only more extreme so we'll keep coming back. Given this, we can no longer say we are living in an attention economy. We are living in an *anxiety economy*.

I first heard the term "anxiety economy" several years ago when I saw a research report from Wunderman, a major advertising agency.[14] It said that, according to the American Psychiatric Association, America's anxiety level has been ticking up at a pretty fast clip. Quoting a report by Quartz, 30 percent of millennials and Gen Zers are so anxious or depressed that it disrupts their ability to work on a regular basis. We are stressed about the environment. We are stressed about work or the lack thereof due to a "gig economy," where short-term jobs and freelance work are more prevalent than long-term careers. We have to eat right and have the right body image and use the right skincare treatment. The irony of ironies is that a multitrillion dollar industry has been built to help us ease the stress, and all it does is make us stress out more because we haven't become Zen fast enough. Headspace, anyone?

Wunderman got it wrong, though. The anxiety economy is not about reducing our anxiety. It is about creating it.

Think about it: What drives our attention? What is the underlying emotion that leads us to pick up our phone ninety-six times a day? It is not an overwhelming need for information. It is fear—fear of missing out (FOMO), fear our jobs will disappear because of artificial intelligence, fear of government collapse, fear that our friends and family may not be safe, fear of yet another new viral strain. Because we are at a loss to do anything about these events, we are fearful of the future. Fear combined with uncertainty is anxiety.

What do we do when we want to manage that anxiety? We grab the closest cell phone or tablet. We either doomscroll on X or its equivalents to make sure the world hasn't blown up or flip our way through TikTok, trying to lose ourselves in the latest dance moves or find indestructible dog toys that are going viral.

Does that assuage our fears? Of course not! It is the *cause* of our anxiety! But we do it anyway.

This is all to the benefit of marketers. The more time we spend online, the more time they have to gobble up information about us and then use that data to "improve our advertising experience." We have been lulled into believing that the YouTube videos and the TikToks and the Facebook posts and the Google searches are free. They are not. They come with a price, and only now are we coming to grips with what we have had to give up. Yes, we pay with our time and our attention, but we also pay with our mental and emotional well-being.

Part and parcel of this economy is monetizing relationships and turning personal interactions into market transactions. Some of this relates to the gig economy, which is an underlying factor in so much of social media, from influencers to MLMs to legitimate small business owners. But what moves social media is us and our willingness to turn our engagements into "likes" and shares and making "friends." The question you need to ask yourself is this: If the share button was called "pass-along advertising," would you use it?

Advertising has always played on people's anxieties. As I tell my students, there is no ad that will tell you that you are fabulous just the way you are, because if it did, you would never buy the product. But what is going on in social media spaces is different. Algorithms and data are being used surreptitiously to manipulate you into being angry and fearful and anxious, and they do this so you will stay connected—not to your friends and family, but to technology.

Platforms need us to give up our time—our lives—because *we are the product*. We are what is being sold. And we have to be online, or advertisers have nothing to buy.

INFORMATION IS OUR BEST DEFENSE

I know the question on a lot of people's minds is, "Is there any way to get Uncle Bob out of MAGA?" or "Can we get Aunt Susie out of Amway?" For moms, the question is, "Is there a way to help my child manage his or her mental health?" Parents are asking how to navigate the college admissions process without succumbing to overhyped pitches that drown them in debt. And all of us want to know how we can take back our lives from the time suck that is digital technology. Cult practices and cult indoctrination are at the root of all of these issues. So the answer is maybe, even probably. But it won't be easy. Throughout this book, you will read stories about people who have been sucked in by these groups and, importantly, how they got out. You also learn how marketing and technology played a key role in making this all happen. Knowing how the hoodwink works helps prevent you from getting sucked in, in the first place. Forewarned is forearmed!

First, you need to know how cults groom their prospects. From there, you learn how cult-like tactics have been applied to sell consumer products and the stealth modes through which you are led to buy. I use the "cult of higher education" as a case study to show how easy it is to be sucked in, especially when kids and parents are likely to be most vulnerable. Next, we look at how that process translates to MLMs. You meet folks who bought the lie and were able to come out the other side. Influencers are up next. Here, we look at the tools and technology that help ensnare us into following them. Once connected to these pitchmen and -women, we become open to what they sell, whether it is a product or a conspiracy theory.

Anxiety is not a bug; it's the feature. We are purposefully driven to extreme emotions in the expectation that we will turn to marketers to soothe our angst. For those who are sucked in—to an MLM or an extreme weight-loss regimen or Trumpism—the path to recovery is a long one. For the rest of us, our hope to save our sanity, our wallets, and, yes, democracy lies in not getting bamboozled to begin with.

Hoodwinked takes you behind the curtain to show how technology and marketing have converged to create an all-encompassing cult by preying on our need for community. We see how marketing experiments are designed to push us to emotional extremes so we spend more time online. We learn that social media companies could put safeguards in place to protect teenagers from content that negatively impact their mental health, but they don't because that would affect their bottom line. First to last, social media is about goosing your anxiety for profit.

With this understanding, you learn how to avoid being taken in by the hustlers and the hypers, saving you money on everything from education to investments. You can take back your time and, with it, your—and your family's—mental health.

That's what this book is all about.

PART I
THE CULT + MARKETING LANDSCAPE

1

THE CULT TRAP

My first week of college in Boston, I was walking down Boylston Street with my hippie-dippie, guitar-toting friend Catherine when a cute young guy carrying a clipboard approached us.

"Could you answer a few questions?" he asked, shuffling to a new piece of paper.

"Sure," we said. We were eager to immerse ourselves in the college town experience—and he was cute.

Rather than handing over the clipboard to fill out what we thought contained a questionnaire, he started walking down the street. Being young and frankly stupid, we followed him—straight to the Church of Scientology.

Once in the church, he turned around to face us and smiled. "How old are you?"

"I'm seventeen," I admitted.

"Oh, sorry. You can't take the survey." He turned to Catherine and said, "Follow me."

As I waited in the lobby, I started reading some of the literature arrayed on the table. When I got to the part about E-meters—basically two cans attached to a string, which gives the user a spiritual audit—I suddenly realized where we were. I had just finished reading *Let Our Children Go!* by Ted Patrick, *the* 1970s book about cult deprogramming. I walked into the room where Catherine was, grabbed her by the arm, looked at our friend from the street, and said as if we were late for dinner, "I'm sorry but we've really got to go."

Getting sucked into a cult can happen that fast. You are in a new environment (like going to college), you are experiencing a traumatic life event (a death or a divorce), or you are just plain tired or depressed. In this fragile state, we look to do things that will help ease our pain, which includes doing things to bring us further acceptance from a new group, even if we feel something is a bit off. This is important to understand, because I bet one of the first things that came to mind when you heard the word "cult" is "brainwashed." People who join cults aren't brainwashed. They are socialized into a group and follow that group's norms in order to continue to experience the good feelings and support they receive.

Another element at play is the chameleon effect. This is the idea that when we experience a new social situation where we're unsure of how to act, we sit back at first to see what the rules are and follow what other members do. We mimic people around us in order to fit in. The founders of Facebook were well aware of this. They knew people would lurk for a while to see how others interacted on the platform and then the "community" would teach each other how to engage. That's why you'll never see an instruction manual on Facebook, at least not for visitors. The company provides user guides only to advertisers.

Like social media spaces, cults offer a form of relief and communal support. They promise happiness and acceptance in the form of an ideology that answers all of life's questions. Believing such a system exists can be incredibly appealing, particularly when someone is vulnerable. Anna's experience is typical. She joined a cult in her twenties, soon after she started out on her own, at a time when she was feeling lost and out of sorts. "He [cult leader] said he would take care of us. We would forget everything that had happened to us that had caused us pain in our lives and we would now be fine. . . . The way that I think of it now is that I climbed back into Daddy's lap and it seemed very comforting that there was someone who had this spiritual vision about my destiny who was going to be my guide and tell me what to do."[1] Feeling like you have a safe place to fall is compelling—and effective—when the world seems overwhelming.

THE RECRUITMENT PROCESS

The initial come-on is subtle; it is innocuous and nonthreatening. An invitation to answer a few questions, a free meditation class that turns out to be an introduction to ISKCON (formerly the Hare Krishnas), or it could be a bereavement group at a church. Most likely, though, a friend, coworker, or family member invites you to join a great new group that's changed their life.[2] You go because you are looking to change your life too.

When I researched the Kabbalah Centre, I learned about a new spin on this: classes come with a "free" individual session with the course instructor. I was led into the teacher's office by a volunteer. The teacher, a short, plump Israeli guy who I would come to learn had talked a woman into believing she could cure her cancer by drinking Kabbalah water, sat behind a large, intimidating desk. He moved from behind the desk to sit in a chair across from me, in an effort to appear more welcoming. I had high expectations that I would receive personalized attention via one-on-one training. I wanted to better understand the intricacies of Kabbalah and why people were so attracted to it. Boy, was I wrong!

Quickly the conversation turned to a laser-focused, intensely hard sell from someone obviously well versed in finding someone's pain points. For forty-five minutes, he tried to get me to write a check for $415 so I could get the Zohar, a set of twenty-three sacred books, entirely in Aramaic, which are the key to salvation even if you simply scan the letters. He could have them delivered to my house that afternoon. Better still, I should buy two sets so I could have one at my house and one in my office. I was there as a researcher, and I repeated over and over and over that I'd just bought my apartment and I had no money.

Under normal circumstances, that response would not have dissuaded him. Members and former members I interviewed said that resisting because of lack of money was used against them: "If you really want this—if you are really committed—you will find the money. You should borrow it, put it on your credit card, use a friend's credit card. You need to do whatever it takes." Most people sitting in that office are already vulnerable and give in because of feelings of shame or fear or because they have come to believe that Kabbalah is their chance for enlightenment or to save the world.

The one-on-one push is important because making the initial commitment to buy the Zohar—or pay for the class or attend a workshop—opens the door to upselling the recruits still further. Their defenses softened, recruits are bombarded to attend even more classes, attend more services, buy more books, or give lots of money. The more you buy, the more immersed you become in the group's teachings.

THE INDOCTRINATION

Early in the indoctrination period, new members are treated with kid gloves: They are rarely exposed to extreme beliefs and are "love bombed" by being told how wonderful, special, and talented they are. Who wouldn't want that to continue?

After this honeymoon period and once buy-in is achieved, more dramatic steps can be taken to get people to conform to the cult's belief system. Indoctrination practices vary by group, but there are a handful of tools that we see used again and again to break down recruits' defenses. One way is to strip new members of their individuality. Hare Krishnas, for example, require members to dress alike. Restricting food is also a popular strategy. For some cults, it is central to the philosophy, like Gwen Shamblin's Weigh Down Diet, or it is used as a coercive tool, such as Sun Myung Moon's fat-shaming sermons. Sleep deprivation is often used for gaining compliance. David Koresh held marathon Bible sessions. Keith Raniere of NXIVM fame had midnight volleyball games.

We can see some parallels of this practice in fitness programs, consumer brands, and social media. Peloton and other cycling groups both feed a sense of belonging as well as foment competition. You are encouraged to sign on to see your numbers on the leader board, which is boldly displayed at the front of the room. Falling behind encourages participants to work harder, which can be healthy, but not if pushing oneself beyond one's limit is done to avoid shame. Meta (Facebook's parent company) provides a worldview of life being better because everyone is connected, and Apple suggests that technology has the answer to all of life's problems.

As members become more enmeshed, it is imperative that the belief system not be questioned. To protect against second thoughts cropping up, recruits are isolated from friends and family members. Disconnection can happen quite subtly. Renee, a dancer who became part of a meditation cult, explained it this way: "They start giving you so many tasks that so much of your time is consumed in the group that you start distancing yourself from friends, family and activities you loved. Without realising it, my support structure started to disappear and the groupthink started to set in."[3]

People used to call the implementation of these tactics "brainwashing." That's a misnomer. If you ever pulled an all-nighter at college or forgot to eat, you know you don't make the best decisions under those circumstances. If you experienced a trauma in your life or are vulnerable due to daily stresses, overwork, or a major life change, you probably weren't thinking straight. Understanding this is important: while cults have undue influence, they do not have total control.

Finally, to keep people in the cult, a variety of influence tools are put into play. The showering and withholding of affection is used as intermittent reinforcement. Like Las Vegas slot machines, not knowing when you are going to get a reward keeps you locked into the slot machine—and your social media. Groups also use surveillance, guilt, and shame to get members to stay. NXIVM required women to text their leader before they could eat even the smallest morsel of food. MLMs blame their consultants if they don't hit sales goals. Adam Neumann, the cofounder and former CEO of WeWork, guilted his employees into attending annual companywide sales events, and they needed to look ecstatically happy, or else.

At this point, you may be thinking, "Why don't they just leave?" Members stay because they are embarrassed or because they fear retaliation or because they think that if they stay a little bit longer, things will get better. It is also common for cult members to leave one cult for another, believing the issue wasn't with the system but with the individual cult. We see that with MLMs as well.

THE NINE STEPS OF CULT RECRUITMENT

1. **Identify prospective recruits**—Recruiters target people who are vulnerable, such as new college students or those who are bereaved, divorcing, or depressed. Recruiters are trained to have a ready answer for any type of pushback.

2. **Lure recruits with deception**—Initial interactions are nonthreatening and do not reveal what the group is. Ploys can include promoting the group as self-help oriented or as an invitation to a free dinner and a lecture. This can occur online or off.

3. **Upsell**—Once prospects show interest, they are pressured into an escalating number of activities (lectures, retreats, and trainings). Recruits are kept separated and questions are quickly quashed. "Negative" people are weeded out to maintain the appearance of happiness and harmony. Prospects are repeatedly shown all the things that would be theirs—that is, a life surrounded by smart, smiling, happy, successful people.

4. **Love bomb**—Prospects are showered with affection and told how wonderful they are. This moves recruits closer to conversion and reduces their sense of skepticism. In MLMs, downline recruits are told how easy it is to sell and how good they would be at it. In religious cults, love bombing can include sex as a lure, most notably Children of God members evangelized via "flirty fishing," when women were used to seduce men to join.

5. **Tough love**—Once prospects begin to accept what the cult has presented, stronger measures are taken to indoctrinate them by increasing their dependency on the group. A popular tactic is to use activities that elicit confessions. The group taps into past fears and turns that

information against recruits to keep them connected. Feelings of in-adequacy among young people make them a particularly vulnerable target.

6. **Sensory deprivation, hypnosis, meditation**—Recruits are deprived of adequate nutrition and sleep. Cults have also been accused of inducing trance states and using meditation practices to reduce psychological defenses.

7. **Renounce those who question the group**—In most cases, recruits are told to remove themselves from their personal networks—anyone who would question the cult. They may also be asked to give their personal posses-sions to the group. Isolation increases the likelihood that recruits become invested in the cult's beliefs and limits their ability to leave. I have no proof of this, but I would argue that QAnon was able to flourish in no small part because of the COVID lockdown and the isolation it entailed.

8. **Introduce core beliefs**—Cults withhold the essence of the creed until after recruits have had a long indoctrination period, enabling them to milk recruits of labor and money for as long as possible.

9. **Severe repercussions for leaving**—Members must be made aware that they will be cut off if they leave the group and shamed if they do not demonstrate complete acceptance. The examples here are too numer-ous to name, but the Church of Scientology is notorious for stalking members after they leave the organization, and one ex-MLMer told me that the company she worked for sent her a letter saying that it was going to sue her for content she had posted online explaining the com-pany's deceptive practices.[4]

THE CULT LEADER

A charismatic, typically narcissistic leader is a cult hallmark. When we think of religious cult leaders, the most well-known is arguably Jim Jones. Jim Jones by all accounts started out as an entertaining and inspiring preacher who appealed to people across races and age groups. He founded the People's Temple in the 1950s in Indiana and later moved the congregation to California, preaching a combination of Christianity, socialism, and racial equality. The congregation reportedly grew to include several thousand members. Because of bad press and growing paranoia, Jones cajoled or coerced many of his flock to go to Guyana, where members believed they would build an all-accepting paradise called Jonestown. Unfortunately, Eden was not meant to be. Concerned family members in California contacted

Congressman Leo Ryan, who flew to Guyana to investigate. Although most members put on a show of being happy, several slipped messages to the representative, asking that he help them leave. Ryan left Jonestown with a few former Temple members in tow, but Jones had ordered that he be gunned down. Ryan and others were killed on the airstrip before the plane could take off. In a final act of desperation, Jones orchestrated the mass murder-suicide of 909 people who drank Flavor Aid mixed with cyanide. This is where the saying "drinking the Kool-Aid" comes from.

Jones is one iconic example. We look at many others throughout this book. For now, it is important to be aware that cult leaders can be female as well as male, and they, too, can be deadly. And, like cults generally, cult leaders are not limited to religious beliefs. Trump, for example, was not only charismatic but also offered an all-encompassing vision for his followers' lives. This differentiated him from other politicians, and it, in part, accounted for his appeal. We see in chapter 9 that Elizabeth Holmes and Sam Bankman-Fried were successful cult leaders, but they weren't perceived that way because the context wasn't steeped in religion and their followers weren't confined to a remote compound. Whether charismatic spiritualist, politician, or businessperson, as cult leaders they share these characteristics: they are power hungry, narcissistic, controlling, and provide a world vision.

Most cult leaders are both smart and lazy. I note this because it helps to dispel a prevailing myth: that people pulled into cults are crazy or stupid. This could not be further from the truth. Yes, young people are an important target group because of their vulnerability and because they will do a lot of work, which is necessary to keep the organization going. However, cults want smart, successful, and preferably wealthy people, because such individuals tend to be good managers and the best form of marketing. Scientology has John Travolta and Tom Cruise; the Branch Davidians had Douglas Wayne Martin, a graduate of Harvard Law School; NXIVM lured in Mark Vicente, who had just come off the successful New Age-y film *What the Bleep Do We Know?* People want to be with other successful people, who in turn attract others to the group. Key here, too, is that although the leader may be the initial draw, the only way the group grows is through recruitment—just like a pyramid scheme.

A CULT BY ANY OTHER NAME

Say the word "cult" and what comes to mind? Jim Jones and hundreds of bloated, dead bodies in the jungles of Guyana? David Koresh and the fifty-one-day government standoff in Waco, Texas? The Heaven's Gate cult, whose members committed mass suicide while laying on bunk beds wearing identical Nike sneakers?

I debated for a long time about whether to use the word "cult" when discussing this phenomenon. *Cult* is a loaded word. When I teach Media Studies 101, I like to use the idea of cults to help students understand how framing works. I walk into a massive three-hundred-seat lecture hall at a public university in New York and write two words on the whiteboard in huge block letters. First I write "cult" and ask students what thoughts come to mind. They quickly shout what some of you are thinking: "brainwashed" and "crazy" and "Kool-Aid." Then I write "religion" and ask the same question. This time, I get words like "faith" and "church" and "spirituality."

Then I show a documentary about Waco and the Branch Davidians. You may remember the standoff between the FBI and this sect of the Seventh Day Adventists as a fifty-one-day siege that ended in the compound going up in a fiery blaze and a U.S. military tank bulldozing its way in. What the documentary tries to argue is that because the FBI saw the Davidians as a cult (and as an opportunity for positive publicity and funding from Congress), it caused them to make terribly misguided assumptions about the group that led to its demise. This event is shocking to most students, who weren't born when the siege on Waco happened. They are also surprised to learn that this tragedy is often cited as a motivator for Timothy McVeigh to bomb the Alfred P. Murrah Federal Building in Oklahoma City.

We can't help but think of Waco and Jonestown and Heaven's Gate. But as soon as you designate a group as a "cult," you create preconceived notions about who and what that group is, as reporters and the government did in Texas. More importantly, you shut down the possibility that the group is worthy of further analysis or that it might relate to you. After all, cult members never think that they are in a cult.

Religious studies scholars prefer the more benign term new religious movements, or NRM. They argue that at one point even Christianity was an NRM and was looked down upon by the prevailing belief systems at the time. Linguist Amanda Montell coined the term "cultish," suggesting that certain terms and linguistic patterns engender cultish behavior. Specifically, cultish behavior (1) makes people feel special while connecting them with a community, (2) leads to dependence on a leader or group or product, and (3) persuades people to act in ways that conflict with their previous ethics and sense of self. Part of me likes that better, but like sociologist and cult expert Janja Lalich, I believe you need to talk about a topic the way that most people do, and outside of the academy, people call them cults.

Dr. Lalich asserts that cults are fundamentally about control. She lists more than a dozen patterns of behavior to look out for when assessing a group, but there are four key factors that define a cult:

1. The group is led by a charismatic, often narcissistic, leader.
2. The group has a "transcendent belief system"—an all-encompassing ideology that provides answers to all of life's questions.
3. The group uses "systems of control," like telling members what to eat, what to wear, who to marry, and who to have sex with in order to keep them obedient.
4. Finally, "systems of influence"—such as surveillance by other members and reporting transgressions to the leader—ensure that adherents follow orders. Importantly for this discussion, this also includes self-criticism.

Not all cults end tragically, but the pain they leave in their wake can be devastating. We've seen this in dozens of cable TV series, Netflix documentaries, and YouTube videos. There are the cult tactics of Scientology exposed by Leah Remini's *Scientology and the Aftermath* and Alex Gibney's *Going Clear*. There are numerous series about Warren Jeffs and the FLDS (an extreme sect unrelated to the Church of Latter-day Saints, aka Mormons), including *Escaping Polygamy*, which follows the escapades of a group of women who left the cult and their machinations to help other people leave. And if you haven't checked out iilluminaughtii on YouTube, you must! Her avatar is a woman's body in a shlumpy sweater and sweatpants in shades of purple and turquoise, her head a pyramid drawn with a single eye flaunting very long lashes. The pyramid relates to uncovering the disingenuous doings of MLMs, but the content goes far beyond that to include everything from corporate cults to taking down therapist-turned-self-righteous-talk-show-host Dr. Phil.[5]

Cults are not only about religion. There are political cults and self-improvement or personal growth cults peddled by online hucksters selling webinars on how anyone can be an entrepreneur. Our obsession with the perfect body has been dubbed "the cult of thinness." The inability to disengage from something that may or may not be healthy for you can be applied to religious or spiritual leaders or to noxious communities, like QAnon, or brands, like CrossFit or Harvard.

As we have seen, the method for indoctrination is very specific. It is slow and it is purposeful. It plays on people's emotions. And rest assured, it will lighten your wallet.

2

CULT-Y BRANDS AND BRANDED CULTS

I've been fascinated by cults for as long as I can remember. So when COVID led to lockdown, and there was not one but two documentary series about the NXIVM cult, I was all in. As always, I was intrigued to know how smart people were pulled into the quicksand of a group that took so much and yet seemed to give back so little. There was always the thought in the back of my mind: If it could happen to them, couldn't it happen to anyone? Could it happen to me? And, importantly, how did they get out? How did they get past the fear of leaving and the shame of having stayed so long?

I jumped on my elliptical each morning to follow the adventures of the cult that had become infamous for branding—literally burning a logo—into the pelvises of "favored" women. These women had risen to the highest ranks of the organization, and they had done so by denying themselves food, by becoming slaves to those higher up the ranks, and by skipping sleep to attend late-night volleyball games to be in the presence of Keith Raniere, the group's leader and, frankly, no looker. They so debased themselves that they had to text to ask permission to eat the slightest morsel of food, and they had to be at the beck and call of their master, ready to respond to texts at a moment's notice, no matter the time of day or night.

These women weren't stupid. That's one of the prevailing misconceptions about cults—that the people enmeshed in them are ignorant and easily swayed. Really, that couldn't be further from the truth. High-pressure groups target smart, beautiful, and accomplished people because they help attract others to the fold. Think John Travolta and Scientology or Madonna and Kabbalah. NXIVM did the same, recruiting Allison Mack, an actress known for a decade-long stint on *Smallville*, and India Oxenberg, daughter of Catherine Oxenberg, star of the 1980s primetime soap *Dynasty* and second cousin to King Charles.

But it wasn't the tawdry aspects of the group that got me buzzing. I became riveted by the use of scarves as a visual tool to demonstrate one's movement up the ranks of the organization.

If you've ever taken martial arts classes or sat through your kid's classes as I have, you know how this works. First you get a belt (or a scarf). As you gain experience at that level, you get a strip of tape until you have four of them. Then you get the next level belt, and the process starts again. Belts are designated with different colors—white, yellow, green, brown, and so on—until the revered black belt is attained demonstrating excellence in the sport. Unlike in martial arts, however, these scarves were used to keep members grasping for the next dose of approval, the next round of "love bombing," or even an opportunity to get paid by the group instead of teaching classes for free. The scarves showed others how committed each member is to the group while also functioning as a stick with an unreachable carrot. There was always one more scarf to get, one more level to climb.

It was around this time I attended a virtual academic conference about MLMs. I'm a former marketer turned professor who has spent the last twenty years criticizing marketers' dirty doings. Lately you can't throw a brick without someone talking about multilevel marketing, or MLMs, so I had to check it out.

Multilevel marketing companies are direct sales organizations that rely on "independent consultants" to sell their products rather than traditional retail distribution channels. In the old days, this looked like your mom having her friends over for a Tupperware party where she served a Jell-O mold with mini marshmallows or perfectly coiffed Mary Kay ladies pushing cosmetics to earn a spanking new baby-pink Cadillac. Today, it's Herbalife and Amway and Monat and dozens of others, and you don't host parties in your living room, you host Facebook Live events from your in-home showroom.

Live events and overly chipper social media posts ("Hey, Hun!") hide the dirty underbelly: MLMs are legally sanctioned pyramid schemes: organizations that generate profits by continually recruiting people who are obliged to pay a fee to be part of the organization. Selling the product or service is secondary at best. By design, these companies make tons of cash for the few folks at the top (who get a percentage of sales from everyone below them on the pyramid), while those at the bottom—99 percent of members—earn nothing or even lose money. And what's truly shocking is that according to the Direct Selling Association, an innocuous-sounding name for the lobbying group that protects this industry, "one in six American households is involved in the industry."[1]

Throughout the conference, the brand that kept coming up again and again was LuLaRoe. LuLaRoe? I'd never heard of it before, which is not surprising, since I'm a bit older than their target demographic, and I spend limited time on Instagram. Like NXIVM, there are more than a few documentaries about this unscrupulous organization, as well as a hilarious Samantha Bee takedown, and boy did I get an eyeful.

LuLaRoe became famous for selling bright and comfortable leggings. Initially, women legitimately bought them and liked them. Consultants eagerly sold the product, and their lives became enmeshed with their customers and fellow salespeople. But the company grew too quickly. It began producing an inferior product. It made disastrous management decisions like hiring family members to do jobs they weren't qualified for. It held lavish conferences with major pop stars like Katy Perry to erect a facade that the company was incredibly successful. It wasn't.

Higher-ups became desperate to shift consultants from selling product to selling the potential for a better life through being your own boss, promoted with the now infamous hashtag #BossBabe widely used by a variety of MLMs. They applied manipulative techniques to keep current salespeople from fleeing—pushing on pressure points, like reminding these women how much they wanted to make a better life for their family and how staying was the path to success. Ultimately, the company went too far. The State of Washington sued LuLaRoe for wildly exaggerating how much money a consultant could make, and the state won, forcing the company to pay millions in restitution to its former employees.

You may be asking yourself, "Don't all MLMs do this? Why aren't they all getting sued?" They do, but they don't do it in Washington, which has strict pyramid scheme regulations. Sadly, the U.S. federal government does not.

Watching these docuseries in tandem, it suddenly hit me: NXIVM was a cult *and* an MLM. LuLaRoe was an MLM *and* a cult. I began to wonder if there were other organizations that functioned this way, and if so, what were they? I've been studying the intersection of marketing and religion for more than a decade. I've seen churches use database marketing and consumer brands use religious symbolism. This was different. Cults and marketing have blurred in a way we have never seen before. But why? And why now?

BRAND CULTS AND BRAND COMMUNITIES

The cult + marketing nexus is not a one-shot phenomenon connected to MLMs. LuLaRoe and NXIVM aren't isolated cases—they are the bellwether for what's next. MLMs have had decades to perfect how they groom members to their number. Other marketers are only a decade into this process, but they have been slowly cultivating consumers under the guise of brand cults, an idea that began as benign coalescing around a product.

Brand cults—or, said nonthreateningly, brand communities—arose in the early 2000s out of the need to serve a new kind of consumer. One who was looking for interconnectedness through the market and who expected the brands they consumed to be aligned with their values rather than a simple exchange of product for money.

As Laurence Vincent of strategic branding company Siegel + Gale noted, "We use brands to validate our lives. A lot of our consumption activities are becoming more sacred because we attach meaning to them."

This is why products by companies like eyewear maker Warby Parker, which uses a buy-one-give-one strategy, have been so successful. Same with Ben & Jerry's, which supports voting rights issues, the Black Lives Matter movement, and the LGBTQ community, even going so far as to temporarily change the name of one of their ice cream flavors from Chubby Hubby to Hubby Hubby when gay marriage became legal in their home state of Vermont. Lush supports numerous causes, including transgender rights and environmental issues, through the sale of its soaps and bath bombs and shut down all its social media platforms after reports surfaced about how toxic Instagram is for the health of teen girls. Brands like these with compelling narratives inspire people to buy their products while enabling millennials and Gen Z to express who they are or want to be. The brands tap into the need to find community and values and meaning for these younger demographics, much as their parents might have done through a church or synagogue or mosque.

When groups come together around shared interests—religious beliefs, sports teams, a social cause, or, yes, even a brand, sociologists call it "neotribalism." Today, the ability to come together is facilitated by social media and other digital platforms.

Marketers tap into our fundamental desire to connect, to commune, to fill a void no longer occupied by traditional churches or other faith groups. Robert Putnam's now-famous *Bowling Alone* thesis demonstrated that old types of community like bowling leagues are no longer robust, but that newer ones, like the environmental group Sierra Club and women's groups, are growing and have replaced traditional communities. Brand communities are yet another newer method of coming together.

Brand communities, unlike traditional communities, are not located in a physical space. The social relationships that form occur in connection to a brand.[2] The stronger the brand—its image and its mythology—the more likely a community will form around it. Nutella fans are a great example here. People love this gooey chocolate-hazelnut spread. Columbia University students were reportedly "stealing" it from the cafeteria at such a ridiculous rate it became a story in the New York Times, The Atlantic, and BuzzFeed. Fans created "World Nutella Day," a date in February to share stories and recipes about the product, an idea the company co-opted because it was such a huge success. More typical, however, is when a company prods and promotes to bring people together (think Nike Run Club or streaks on Snapchat). These are not disparate people liking a product, but true communities because they exhibit three key elements: "shared consciousness, rituals and traditions, and a sense of moral responsibility."[3]

Members feel connected to the brand and each other and shun nonusers. The obvious example here is Mac users who disdain anyone who would touch a PC. Rituals and traditions maintain community culture. Saab owners wave or honk at one another. Comic-Con fans cosplay, wearing costumes they spend months creating that turn them into physical replicas of their favorite comic book and manga characters. There are oodles of websites created by Disney devotees that provide "insider" information about how to have your best day at Disney theme parks. Knowing these rituals and traditions defines the true believers, and they carry the moral responsibility of integrating new members, notably by explaining the proper ways to use or interact with the brand, like the best strategies for using Genie+ at Disney World.

Importantly, online interactions are bolstered by offline connections. Experiential marketing—events where people can interact in the physical world with brands—enables a visceral connection to the brand. This can be in the form of pop-up stores or at festivals like SXSW, where brands are given space to create experiences for attendees, like filming their own sashay down the catwalk to promote Project Runway or five-minute dates on a miniature golf course offered by dating app Bumble, or through brand-sponsored events, like Camp Jeep, where Jeep owners learn to drive off-road to feel firsthand the key value of the vehicle.

The most committed of brand communities are called brand cults, and this has become the gold standard for success. Douglas Atkin, a strategic marketer and the creator of the cult brand concept, found that *"[T]he same dynamics are at play behind the attraction to brands and cults.* They may vary in degree of strength (although not always), but not in type. . . . When research subjects recounted their reasons for joining and committing, they described the profound urges to belong, make meaning, feel secure, have order within chaos, and create identity. . . . The sacred and profane are being bound by the essential desires of human nature, which seeks satisfaction wherever it can."[4]

Thus, products become a form of religion, providing rituals, traditions, and a shared worldview for members who worship at the altar of Apple, Harley-Davidson, the Volkswagen Beetle, Jimmy Buffett, and Oprah.[5]

YOU HAVE AN INTERNAL CULT LEADER

For most of us, the cult leader is not an external ruler but an internal tyrant embedded by marketers and media messages.

Let's take the example of how women are "supposed" to look and dress. For decades, the market has defined the size of our waistline, portraying one that is unrealistic and far smaller than the average person. To conform to what the market decides, we have been trained what to eat, how much to eat, and when to eat, based on advertising and external cues.

A University of North Carolina survey found that "**75 percent of women reported disordered eating behaviors or symptoms consistent with eating disorders.**"[6] Like a cult, the vast majority of American women restrict their food intake, turning what should be a natural process into one beleaguered with rules and regulations.

The market "helps" with low-calorie product options and protein shakes as meal replacements. As Sharlene Nagy Hesse-Biber writes, "**What we lose is not weight, but control over our lives.** We are increasingly dependent on a force concerned not with our bodies, minds, and hearts, but with the dollars in our wallets."[7]

LOTS OF BRANDS ARE GETTING CULT-Y

The Gathering, whose website is https://cultgathering.com, is an annual marketing conference celebrating leading brand cults. The conference was launched in 2014 with a video shot in dark sepia tones and shadowed lighting of a silhouetted man walking through what looks like a medieval castle full of dark hallways and oversized chandeliers.

A male voiceover with a British accent explains, "This is a story about a meeting of minds. This is The Gathering, a gathering for those who have cult-like followers, not just friends. A gathering for those who are slavishly adored, not just liked . . . this is to finally celebrate those who quietly go about their business, the cult brands and those that lead them, who know how to make their followers hang on their every word."[8]

The conference logo is an eye with rays of light emanating from it encased in a pyramid, much like "the all-seeing eye of God" on the back of a dollar bill. The conference is hosted by . . . wait for it . . . CULT, a marketing agency "that specializes in turning everyday customers into brand advocates . . . [by helping brands achieve] cult-like adoration."

I attended this conference virtually in 2021 for the first time. Netflix, Peloton, Budweiser, and Shopify were among the brands being feted as achieving cult status. TikTok, Zappos, the NFL, and Chobani are some of the many brands that made the list in previous years.

The brand I was surprised to see included was Barbie.[9] Sure, the anatomically unrealistic doll has been around for decades, but after *The Lego Movie*, Mattel, the doll's producer, lost its first-place standing to the plastic building blocks. Leave it to Barbie to take advantage of a global pandemic and systemic racism to pull a brand back into cult status by embodying social change.

Barbie has become an authority on social issues from racism to anxiety and depression to the "sorry reflex," when girls overly apologize. Her best friend Nikki is Black and their conversation on race and privilege went viral with more than two million views.[10] Barbie had her best year ever in 2020, becoming the number one doll brand on YouTube and selling a slew of Barbie Dreamhouses, which were made available outside the usual holiday sales window to take advantage of millennial families' desperate need to keep the little ones occupied during the pandemic lockdown.

That The Gathering exists tells us about the need for marketers to make a brand not merely something you buy, but something that you wholeheartedly engage with. Barbie isn't just a doll; she's an animated character and a film star and the leader of an online community and . . .

Cult status used to be limited to a few well-established brands with a strong identity. Companies like Apple and Harley-Davidson and maybe Coca-Cola, though this last has little to offer in terms of community building. Now, every brand wants to be a cult, or at least claims to be one. Trader Joe's shoppers have inside tips for finding new products or how to eat keto. Men swear by Dollar Shave Club with its f★★king great blades for a dollar a month. I've seen Glossier fans stand in 90 degree heat for hours waiting to get into the New York City location just so they can experience the store. Do I even need to mention Tesla?

As I write this, I can imagine someone saying, "Well, isn't this just lifestyle branding?" In many ways, yes. Lifestyle brands articulate for consumers how a brand fits their lifestyle and their values beyond simply using the product. Red Bull, for example, is not just a high-energy beverage; it's a high-energy lifestyle that includes extreme sports, or at least watching them. REI is not just a store; it's a place to interact with people who love the outdoors and care about the environment.

Fundamental to lifestyle branding is the idea that experiences (not physical goods) drive happiness.[11] The more a marketer can attach feel-good, heartfelt emotions to their product, the better. The difference is the level of devotion that is expected from the consumer. The industry is starting to see this too. Now, a new term is increasingly being used by marketers: lifestyle *cult* brand.

THE BRAND/RELIGION NEXUS

To understand why marketing and cult-like views are colliding, you have to realize that religion and marketing do similar sociological and personal work for us. You're probably saying, "Aw, come on!" but stay with me. Religious or spiritual practice, first and foremost, helps us make sense of the world through rituals and texts. We attend weekly services so that we can separate ourselves from our mundane routines and reset our internal lives. We meditate or pray to connect to a higher power. We read scripture or other religious texts filled with parables and myths that help us bring meaning to our daily experiences and put our lives into a broader context. Marketing makes meaning too. We saw a little bit of how that works already with brands like Lush and Barbie, but we dig into it more here.

In her book *No Logo*, Naomi Klein's key insight from investigating the manufacturing of major brands around the world is that marketers are not producing a product so much as they are producing meaning. They do this through branding, which is a combination of a logo, a tagline, and a mythology or story.

Nike is the swoosh and "Just Do It" and the best of athleticism. Apple is the logo and "think different" and stories of the genius of Steve Jobs. Disney is Mickey Mouse or Cinderella's castle and "magic." The most invasive brands are not merely an image on a product or in an ad, but also some kind of representation in physical space, like stores or theme parks or experiences like sporting events. If Mark Zuckerberg has his way, we will be living in branded virtual realities in the Metaverse.

Of themselves, products have no meaning. They are coffee or shoes or a way to listen to music. David Ogilvy, the famous ad man, once claimed that he could have sold Dove as a man's soap or a woman's soap. He simply chose to market it to women. When you think of Marlboro cigarettes, you most likely think of it as a men's brand because of decades of seeing the image of the Marlboro Man cowboy riding the lonely range. When first introduced, the cigarettes were promoted to women, the brown wrapper intended to hide lipstick stains. It is the story of these brands that we are purchasing rather than the products themselves.

This is *the* concept to grasp: our interactions with brands are not about physical products. They are about what we think and feel about the products beyond their physical attributes. They are about what hopes and dreams and voids we want products to fulfill.[12]

They are about what using them says about who we are or who we think we are. Are you Starbucks or Dunkin'? Do you drink Starbucks because you envision how they ethically source their coffee? Because of their cool Seattle heritage? Because you know you will consistently get the same kind of coffee at any of their stores? Because you love that burnt coffee smell? Although you may not ponder these things when you walk into your local coffee shop, everything you know about the brand, including your past experiences with it, unconsciously comes into play at the time of purchase.

If you don't believe me, know that one of the biggest things in marketing right now is sensory marketing.[13] This is when brands use all five senses—sight, sound, taste, touch, and smell—to bypass our critical thinking. Some of this is not new. Logos, of course, are visual cues. Jingles are audio cues, and you might be old enough to remember the Maxwell House coffee percolator sound. Today, though, this type of marketing is more sophisticated and insidious.

Companies are relying on "embodied cognition—the idea that without our conscious awareness, our bodily sensations help determine the decisions we make."[14] Think of it as aromatherapy, only for shopping. Leather and wood make you think "rich" and "wealthy," which is great for a bank or high-end car. Cinnamon and sugar and the next thing you know you've wolfed down almost 900 calories of Cinnabon without thinking. Disney uses a patented device called a Smellitzer to diffuse various aromas through their theme parks to increase the visceral experience.[15]

Sonic branding—audio cues connected to a product—happen when you swipe a MasterCard or they are embedded in the latest pop tune you are listening to. What makes this kind of marketing so deceptive is that these sense-based messages aren't perceived as marketing—if we are aware of them at all—so we don't put up the kind of resistance we would to traditional advertising messages. What they engender—consciously or not—are good feelings about the brand and, in so doing, they create stronger connections.

Through these machinations, brands produce meaning and emotion and community, much like religions do. I am not the only one who thinks this. Jim Twitchell, in *Branded Nation*, suggests that religion and marketing are virtually one and the same thing. He claims that we are looking for redemption, and it doesn't much matter where it comes from, though it increasingly comes from the marketplace.

Every ad ever written is a story about making us better. Since the turn of the twentieth century, ads have been created to engender feelings of anxiety and the belief that purchasing a product would "magically" lead to self-improvement.[16] That's why problem/solution advertising continues to be the most popular sales approach. You have a problem—dirty laundry, uncomfortable bras, existential angst—and our product can fix it. Just as prayer can be magical thinking, so is marketing (how many times have you bought a product and not ended up as happy as the people in the commercial?).

Both prayer and marketing sell us a belief in the chance for salvation through storytelling and a willingness to believe in what is intellectually unbelievable. Whether we are talking about spiritual practice or brands, what we are searching for is a sense of hope, a sense of happiness, and fulfillment. Today that sense is as likely to be generated by a product as it is by a preacher.

The marriage of marketing to immersive experience answers the question "why?" Left with limited avenues to find connection and community, brands now create spaces for us to come together around consumer experiences. Most of these interactions will not rise to the level of MLMs, but some come pretty darn close.

Fitness brands like SoulCycle and CrossFit engender unfailing devotion from their members. Influencers (who are absolutely brands), from the Kardashians to Silicon Valley CEOs like Adam Neumann of WeWork or Elizabeth Holmes of Theranos, hoodwink their followers to do things against their best interests. QAnon members hang on every "Q drop," and parents work frantically, even risking jail time, to get their offspring into the "right college."

In short, advertisers have upped their game when it comes to telling us they can solve our many woes. They fill the void left by the disintegration of religious and civic institutions. Think about it: did you call your clergyperson or employer or even your friend the last time you felt overwrought, or did you jump online to ease your anxiety? It is this addition of technology, particularly the almost ubiquitous use of social media, that has put cult marketing over the top.

WHY NOW?

In 2018, we first learned about a political consulting firm named Cambridge Analytica. This British-based consultancy was instrumental in affecting the outcome of elections around the world, famously Brexit and the U.S. presidential election. It was able to change the expected election results using data it had amassed through Facebook.[17] By analyzing behavioral data (likes and shares), the company developed "sentiment profiles." These emotional profiles enabled them to parse people in groups based on who would vote, who could be kept from voting, and what messages to post to manipulate the outcome.

According to reporting in the *Washington Post*, Black voters were specifically targeted in the 2016 election in sixteen states including Michigan, Georgia, and Wisconsin with messages that were intended to deter them from voting, notably footage of Hillary Clinton talking about a crime bill in the 1990s and using the term "super predator," a term widely perceived as racist, especially among the African American community.[18] What was shocking about the Cambridge Analytica revelations was that targeting and persuasion techniques widely used by social media marketers were now being applied to politics. That data wasn't being used to find out about our sex lives or our finances so much as it was about figuring out our psychic vulnerabilities to change our behavior.

Marketing research like this happens online twenty-four hours a day, seven days a week. Data is being collected about what you look at, what videos you watch on YouTube or Netflix and how much of it you watched, whether you check out photos of your exes, and what food you post in your pictures. Much of it is innocuous, like A/B testing in which a marketer will see if a blue background in an ad gets more clicks than a yellow background. Or information is used to retarget you: if you left a pair of shoes in an online cart, advertising will be programmed to follow you around the web with the hopes that you will finally cave and buy them. But not all data collection is quite so harmless.

In a now-famous experiment, Facebook manipulated visitors' emotions by changing the algorithm to show negative content to one group of people and positive content to others. Those shown negative content posted more negative content and vice versa. This "emotional contagion" experiment played with the feelings of close to seven hundred thousand people—all without their knowledge.[19] It doesn't get more personal than that.

Why try to make us feel bad? Because the truth is, engaging with social media is all about inducing terror. Fear of missing out (FOMO) is not a social term; it is a marketing tool, and it is especially potent when targeting younger demographics.

Frances Haugen, the Facebook whistleblower, helped the whole world understand that the company is fully aware that it is increasing anxiety levels in teen girls on Instagram and that those young people feel powerless to stop because they feel they have to be there or face the dreaded FOMO, a term coined by a strategic marketer.[20] Well before that, researchers knew that negative emotions were the driving force behind social media. Jonah Berger, a marketing professor at the Wharton Business School, explains in his 2013 book *Contagious* that we are drawn to share what is in our feeds because of heightened emotions, particularly anger. More anger means more sharing, which means marketers get free advertising because we promote their products for them. Win-win for marketers and social media platforms; lose-lose for us. But just as sensory marketing taps into areas of our subconscious to circumvent our logical thought process, so too do online marketers play on our emotions—especially fear and anger—so as to bypass our critical thinking.[21]

These online marketing experiments and algorithms that push you to emotional extremes are all in the service of seeing how much of our lives can be swallowed up. As Tim Kendall, former president of Pinterest and former ad director for Facebook, said, "How much time can we get you to spend? How much of your life can we get you to give to us?"

In 2022, it was estimated that Meta (formerly Facebook), Google, and Amazon would control 50 percent of all advertising dollars. These three digital companies were on target to control not just the majority of online advertising, but 50 percent of *all advertising spending*[22]—close to $150 billion. Although they were not able to maintain that level into 2023, they remain the dominant players in the market. Most disturbing, those companies have already shown themselves to be highly effective in changing your behavior and perceptions.

We live with a handheld piece of technology within reach twenty-four hours a day. That technology is designed to keep us connected to it through persuasive design. "Persuasive design describes the process by which a designer exploits cognitive biases to guide and influence user behavior."[23]

So what characteristics influence our behavior? What gets us dependent on technology? Nir Eyal, a former tech entrepreneur turned consultant, explains how tech companies do this in his book, *Hooked: How to Build Habit Forming Products.*[24]

Eyal claims that there are four steps to getting people hooked.

Step 1: The trigger, which can be external or internal. You see external triggers every day. A push notification from Instagram is an example of an external trigger. Internal triggers are personally motivated due to memories, typically due to emotions, specifically negative emotions. So when we feel bored or stressed or anxious, it leads us to take an action like pulling out our cell phone without giving it much thought. Get in an elevator and pull out your cell phone. Want to avoid working on a project? Play a game of Wordle. Eyal says we do this because we are looking to modulate our mood, which he argues is the only reason anyone buys a product.

Step 2: The action phase. The action phase is when someone does something in anticipation of a reward. There are unending examples of this online, but the most obvious one is the newsfeed. You don't know what you are going to get when you go on TikTok or Facebook, but the hope is that it will be entertaining or informational.

Step 3: The reward phase, but it's a reward with a twist. The product will "scratch the itch" but leave you wanting more (just like NXIVM's scarves). That's because the technology is designed to provide a variable reward. This is based on the work of behaviorist B. F. Skinner. Through conditioning, he discovered that if sometimes you get a reward and sometimes you don't, you will click on a button more often than if you know you are going to get a reward every single time. That's called variable rewards or intermittent positive reinforcement, and it's the same philosophy used with slot machines in Las Vegas.

Step 4: The investment phase. The investment phase is when you put something in, anticipating a return in the future. This is the very essence of social media posting. You post online in hopes that others will see and like it, giving you positive reinforcement to do it again and again. This last step sets up the never-ending habit that connects you to the technology. It's what keeps you hooked. How Eyal ended a talk he gave tells you how intentional this hook is: "Here's the message I want to leave you with: when these habit-forming products get us to invest in them, it doesn't matter if a better product or service comes along. This is a really important point. Why? Because it shatters the myth that the best product wins. That is a lie. . . . It's not the best product that wins. It's the product that captures *the monopoly of the mind*. The thing that we turn to first with little or no conscious thought."[25]

Getting people hooked, then, has a lot to do with being manipulated to engage with technology without thoughtful consideration. Persuasive technology taps into our basest psychological needs to keep us attached to our phones and tablets. Married with this are marketers (or political consultants) who use your emotions to not only make us want a product or connection but to desire it with cult-like fervor. We see this in everything from megachurches like Hillsong, which worked with Facebook on developing its online streaming services, to Weight Watchers, which uses data to "customize" your diet program, to dating apps that purport to help us find Mr. or Ms. Right, but in truth do not want you to succeed because if you do, you would no longer need their services.

We are living in a state of being almost constantly online while being pushed to not just anger, but downright rage. At the same time—again, unthinkingly—your personal relationships are turned into commercial transactions with each share or like. Given all this, is there any wonder that we are facing a mental health crisis in this country?[26] Or that a website exists that eggs people on to suicide?

But, this *is* where we are. A world where technology and social media companies have ginned up our emotions to the point of inducing heart palpitations. It has enabled a space for cults and marketing to converge, a place where the slow, steady, seductive tactics used by spiritual charlatans to groom their flock are finessed to sell everything from toothpaste to Trump to fitting into a size 2.

3

THE COLLEGE CULT
A Case Study

Hannah (a pseudonym) is a high school senior and a BWRK, a term college admissions directors use to describe a bright well-rounded kid. She attended one of the country's top public high schools, and she scored a 34 on the ACT. That was the "sacred number" her guidance counselor said she needed and one that put her in the ninety-ninth percentile. In addition to academics, this overachieving high schooler was a varsity athlete, the president of the art club, a member of multiple school government bodies, and a volunteer for a voting rights organization.

She was groomed from the time she was in junior high to know that she had to package and promote herself to college admissions officers if she wanted to get into a top college. She's not alone. American adolescence has become an exercise in racking up the best grades via the hardest AP classes while demonstrating talents and abilities far beyond one's years. This compulsion toward perfection is all part of the college indoctrination process.

Like her classmates, she received endless pieces of snail mail. Thick, glossy viewbooks arrived from Barnard and Vassar and the University of Chicago. A die-cut deck of cards appeared from Johns Hopkins, intended to be interconnected to create elaborate structures with pictures and posted on social media with the hashtag #EmbraceTheS (it's *Johns* Hopkins). Oversized postcards arrived from Mount Holyoke and Penn State and Brown.

The common thread through all of this was the exhortation to visit a website or come for a campus visit or email the admissions office with any questions. These calls to action are all about getting the student into what is called the "comm flow"—the process of getting students to opt in so colleges can digitally track them and gently nudge them toward the goal line of filling out the application.

The most prolific tactic in the higher ed marketing tool kit, however, is email. These incessant missives are primed to be sent to hundreds of thousands of eager high-school students the minute standardized test scores are posted. The number on the test score will determine the number of emails. For top students, that can reach well into the thousands—and not one or two thousand, but five or six thousand.

The emails follow a promotional pattern familiar to any marketer trying to promote their product under a limited, or contrived-to-be-limited, time frame: find the pain point and push on it—*hard*. For this target market, that means appeals to fragile adolescent egos. Come-ons include praise lines like:

> You're an impressive college prospect.
> Congratulations! We hear you're a great student.
> You are extraordinary!!! Why not attend a university that recognizes that?

Next is to become the prospect's friend, an important step when dealing with Gen Z. Admissions offices send silly poems, dumb jokes, and, yes, even kitten photos to "awwwww" over. Personalized e-cards are sent for birthdays, Thanksgiving, Christmas, and Halloween. They commiserate with students about the stress of applying to college (never owning up to how they have ratcheted up that stress) and offer sympathy in the form of kind words as well as distractions like games and puzzles, and the emails are signed, "From your friends in the Office of Admissions."

Friendship, of course, has nothing to do with this. It's all about luring prospects to increase their level of engagement. Students are pushed to go to a customized website (SusieSmith.XYZuniversity.edu), to follow the school on social media, particularly X (formerly Twitter) and Instagram, and to attend live online events where they can chat with current students or admissions and financial aid personnel. Campus visits are an unspoken requirement, especially for top institutions.

Students are presented with a highly produced information session by admissions and financial aid personnel. Some may even spend a night on campus being regaled with fine food and upscale amenities, these last two being tactics not unlike selling exotic time-shares. Going through the time and expense to visit the campus and spending time on social media or on the university website is mandatory because it allows schools to track whether a student is truly interested.

If all of this begins to sound cult-like, it's because it is. The road to college is a slow steady indoctrination process that is promoted by the colleges, fueled by corporations looking to squeeze every dime out of the system, and reinforced by the entire U.S. education system.

With complex, high-tech tools and hard-sell tactics, colleges (and consultants) play on parents' concerns about getting their kid into "the best school," knowing full well that students and their parents are making these decisions within a limited time frame and with little access to unbiased information. Marketers are also acutely aware that under this scenario people are more likely to pay for a higher-priced product believing that the expensive price tag means it is inherently better.

The target audience they are marketing to—our children—is ripe for this consumer-focused message. Today's college student has grown up immersed in consumer culture and digital communication. They expect brands to cater to them, to make them feel special, and they expect brands to embody their beliefs. Brands like Rare makeup from Selena Gomez appeal to these demos because they embody support for those suffering with mental health issues, or ThredUp, the online thrift store, taps into this generation's concern about the environment.

Think about this, then, as it relates to college applications: prospective students are charmed and pursued and befriended—one might even say love bombed. But what happens when they don't get into the schools they wanted? In every other category, the consumer transaction ends in a simple purchase and a continuing customer-marketer relationship. In this case, the choice to purchase is out of control of the consumer. The eager teens have been led to passionately desire the school. To be accepted, they have done everything they are supposed to do: engage with current students and financial aid and admissions officers, spend time browsing on their website, post praise on various social media, and then when they want to spend their money, the seller says, "Nope. Sorry." And although there are myriad reasons why this happens, what the teenager hears is "I'm not good enough."

That's what happened to Hannah. No Ivy Leagues or elite schools offered her a spot—not even with early decision or early action. Highly selective schools extended no offers—not for admissions, but a few put her on the waitlist. The one and only school she got into was a selective school, a designation that simply means the school does not accept everyone.

U.S. COLLEGE TERMS DEFINED

Ivy League—Eight northeastern colleges that belong to the Ivy League Athletic Conference. These include Brown, Columbia, Cornell, Dartmouth, Harvard, Princeton, University of Pennsylvania, and Yale.

Elite—Colleges that are similar to the Ivies in that they are very selective and have prestigious professors and large endowments. This includes schools like the University of Chicago, MIT, Johns Hopkins, Amherst, and Stanford, among dozens of others.

Highly selective—These schools accept less than 35 percent of applicants and include colleges like Boston University, Colgate, Middlebury, and Carnegie Mellon.

Selective—The college doesn't accept everyone—but they accept a lot.

Early decision—Students submit their applications for admission on November 1 with decisions made by mid-December. This means that students can know they are accepted into a college before the regular applications are in (most are due January 1). They could be one and done. However, if the student goes this route, the offer is binding. They must go to the early decision school if they get in—if they renege to attend another institution, the second institution's acceptance is likely to be revoked.

Early action—Students submit their applications on November 1, like early decision, but students do not have to accept the offer and they can make a final decision on May 1, when most schools require students to make a final decision about what college they will attend. This can take pressure off students because they know early in their senior year that they have been accepted to college.

The truth is this wasn't a hiccup or a blip. It was systemic. Schools are playing psychological tricks with vulnerable teenagers who spend their high school years creating a personal brand to present to admissions personnel instead of just being kids. Parents have become obsessed worrying about where their child will go to college and how they are going to pay for it. But for what? There is no good reason why applying to college—never mind going there—should be so overwhelming and expensive. There is no good reason why applying to college has to be the "Cult of the Ivy League" (or University of Chicago or USC), but we know that it is when Aunt Becky risks jail time to ensure her daughter's admission. But, a more sophisticated, more targeted, more over-the-top marketing philosophy has changed college searches from getting into college to getting into *the* college.

A deep dive into the U.S. college admissions process provides a helpful illustration of the cult + marketing tactics at work. The parallels of the recruitment-deception-indoctrination process are both strikingly similar and subtly effective.

Marketing has created the cult, and we look at that first. But we also need to look at what propels colleges to promote so aggressively: a shrinking number of prospective students, increasing costs, and rapidly changing technology. Combined, they have created the perfect storm for the over-the-top competitive college marketplace we see today.

A MORE SOPHISTICATED HIGHER ED MARKETER

A multi-tentacled college promotional industry has grown over the last decade. I know how massive this has become because I spent five years attending numerous conferences specifically dedicated to marketing higher education. At these confabs, I met marketing consultants for everything from college branding to enrollment management to improving alumni giving. There were dozens of edtech (education technology) companies including Google and LinkedIn providing everything from admissions management to curriculum. Speaking from the stages were newly minted chief marketing officers (CMOs), many of whom tout corporate pedigrees from marketing powerhouses like Pottery Barn and General Mills.

Corporate marketing refugees have been hired because they understand the importance of branding. How successful these folks have become is nowhere more painfully obvious than "Ivy Day," the day when all the Ivy League schools announce whom they have admitted. If you visit a social media site on that day, you will see a deluge of tweets and posts and videos of admitted students screaming and crying, all posted with the appropriate hashtag (i.e., #Harvard2028, #Brown2028, etc.). You know those teens will be walking down the halls of their high schools the next day wearing the swag they got from an on-campus visit or overnight event. It is marketing at its best—it's word of mouth, it's peer to peer, and it's all free.

To be sure, branding universities isn't new. Harvard and Yale and Princeton, to name a few, have existed with well-established identities for years, and thanks to very strong alumni, those brands will not change anytime soon. These big brands can get by with very little marketing directed at the incoming undergraduate class. Like Nordstrom or Tiffany, consumers flock to their doors, willing to pay top dollar for a top-of-the-line product. Students compete with each other for the limited number of slots, and—when necessary—the top-notch universities roll out the red carpet for the country's most stellar high schoolers.

What is new is the application of marketing techniques to sell universities like you would sell a car or a can of tuna, something that would have been denounced not long ago—"reputation" is okay, branding not so much. Colleges now try to use one-word descriptions, just like corporate brands: Reed College, home of alum Steve Jobs, is "unconventional"; the University of Chicago is "intellectual"; and Brown is "independent." A solid brand increases the school's appeal, which in turn improves its sales numbers and makes it stand out in the ever-important rankings. Butler University, a highly ranking regional school, took this to the extreme. No fat envelope for them. Admissions personnel showed up at admitted students' homes with the school mascot—a picturesque bulldog, social media–ready, with a banner with the hashtag #Butlerbound.[1]

Colleges like Butler push the connection to the pooch and the hashtag to establish an "identity" or a "reputation," that is branding. No matter what you call it—brand or identity or reputation—students need an immediate reference in order to differentiate one college from another. There is a large swath of these schools that fall in the middle, especially small liberal arts colleges that command $30,000 to $40,000 a year in tuition, which desperately need to define themselves or go bankrupt—an increasingly more frequent event.

Branding is important, but you can't talk about higher ed marketing without talking about *U.S. News & World Report* rankings. Look at almost any piece of college marketing, from ads to websites, and that number will be prominently displayed.[2]

The ranking began humbly in 1983, when *U.S. News* was a ho-hum newsmagazine that ran a distant third to competitors *Time* and *Newsweek*. To compete with these giants at the newsstand, it created a special issue about colleges, much the way *Sports Illustrated* created the special swimsuit edition. By the 1980s, a college degree was no longer seen as a luxury—as it had been for centuries—and enrollments had increased by almost 50 percent during a single decade. A degree was now perceived as a mass market good and a steppingstone to the middle class. Large numbers of new, inexperienced college "consumers" were rapidly entering the marketplace. To help those families evaluate schools (and to bring in new advertisers), *U.S. News* produced a ranking by sending a survey to 1,308 university presidents to see how they would position schools around the country and publishing the result in its pages.

Fast forward forty years, and that ranking has taken on a life of its own. Instead of being based on surveys, it is based on quantitative measures more easily compiled by computer.[3] *U.S. News* counts things like graduation rates, how well the school retains students, faculty resources, which includes small class size, and the one most influenced by marketing—student selectivity. This last gets a lot of attention because it is so easily manipulated by ginning up the number of applications in order to reduce the acceptance rate. To get or keep that number low, colleges need more applicants—thousands and thousands of them—so they can accept a smaller percentage of students and appear to be more selective. Being able to claim an acceptance rate of less than 10 percent is essential to the top schools in today's exceptionally competitive marketplace. To do this, marketers and admissions officers cater to the bottom 99 percent, because those students have to be made to feel like they can go to these schools, too, even if they have a snowball's chance in hell of getting in.

The more these rankings have become entrenched, the more schools have worked to game the system. Baylor University paid freshmen to retake their SATs.[4] Five schools—including Tulane, George Washington, and Emory—were caught misreporting data to *U.S. News*.[5] Clemson's president admitted to downgrading other schools on the survey. One last way to "game" the system: build a great sports program. Sports are not included in the ranking, but they are the number one way to market a school. Get a successful sports team, appear in the Rose Bowl, and boom—your applications soar the following year. More students mean the school increases its entrance requirements for GPA and test scores, which in turn boosts the ranking.

College rankings have become like doping in the Tour de France. School administrators know everyone is cheating, but you can't possibly win if you don't cheat, so cheating levels the playing field. Schools do this by investing more money in facilities, like fancy student centers and climbing walls and up-to-date dorms or dumbing down requirements to increase graduation rates and, of course, marketing the heck out of the school in order to get lots and lots and lots of students to apply. This is why we can't discuss rankings without also discussing the Common App.

CAN WE TALK ABOUT THE COMMON APP?

When I went to college, I applied to five schools, which was considered high at the time: two target schools, two safety schools, and one reach school. I needed to cover my bases more than other applicants, because I was applying as an acting major and acceptances to my top choices depended on an audition. It was not uncommon back then, though, for high schoolers to apply to just one school, and that school was likely close to home. There was good reason for that; applying was a major pain and spending lots of money on application fees seemed like an unnecessary expense. We filled out paper applications that could be received only by snail mail. Essays were drafted by hand and then typed out—and you can be sure we had Wite-Out at the ready.

Today, that process and that number of applications is an anomaly. Applications, of course, are done online, and that has fundamentally changed the equation in terms of the number of applications submitted. In 1995, 61 percent of prospective college students applied to three or more schools, while a scant 10 percent of first-time freshmen applied to seven or more schools. By 2016, fully 81 percent of students applied to three or more schools, while a whopping 35 percent applied to seven or more.[6] I've seen averages quoted as anywhere from seven to ten and fifteen to eighteen schools.

This is driven by the fact that the Common App, an online one-stop shop for submitting applications to more than one thousand colleges, allows for twenty applications per student. One click and another application is sent through the ether. Okay, it's not quite that easy because the top schools ask for additional essays, but there are plenty of schools that don't. It's no wonder that students apply to the maximum. Really, what can it hurt?

But it does hurt. That's because schools can't tell if you *really* want to go to their institution or if you filled out the application because all it took was a mouse click. This is where we need to talk about yield. Yield is the percentage of accepted students who step on the campus in the fall. Admissions directors care about this first, last, and always. When students applied to one or three or even five schools and most of those were close to home, colleges had a pretty good idea if they were target schools or safety schools. That is no longer the case when students apply to a dozen schools or more. Combine this with schools working to increase selectivity by getting oodles of students to apply and what you have is a system overwhelmed with applications. As Cathy O'Neil explains in her book *Weapons of Math Destruction*, this all but eliminated the safety school. "A traditional safety school, for example, can look at historical data and see that only a small fraction of the top applicants end up going there. . . . With the objective of boosting its selectivity score, the safety school can now reject the excellent candidates that, according to its algorithm, are most likely not to matriculate."[7]

Because the school is concerned about yield—getting butts in seats in the fall—great students who really did want to attend a particular institution are getting rejected from mediocre schools, because those institutions are making decisions based on computer data and market pressures to increase their ranking.

This is exacerbated by the inability of admissions personnel to give these applications any more than the briefest of evaluations, because while the number of applications has grown exponentially, the size of admissions staffs has not. Students are led to believe that admissions personnel are assiduously poring over everything from letters of recommendation to extracurriculars to the essay to understand the whole student, not simply glancing at GPAs and test scores. And don't get too sanguine about test scores not being required; in just one example, 93 percent of MIT students submitted scores even though it is no longer a requirement.[8] Though not required, test scores can "bolster" you application. Either way, the lack of required SAT scores is leading to students applying to more schools—leading to what is being called application inflation, when colleges get more applications than they could possibly consider. Admissions directors hide the once-over approach behind the latest marketing buzzwords: "holistic review." They claim to look at the whole student, but there is no evidence that this is happening. There is even evidence that the 650-word essay that students torture themselves over isn't being read. "Window dressing" was how one former admissions director described it. Are the top students' pieces being read? Sure. But for students who don't have the slightest chance of getting into a top-tier school, that chance to write a stellar essay provides a thin ray of hope that they can overcome bad test scores—and so they apply, and the school's ranking improves, all while playing on adolescents' emotions at a time when they are already vulnerable.

According to the *Wall Street Journal*, elite schools are reviewing applications in eight minutes or less. Worse still, the application review is divided so that test scores and transcripts are reviewed by one person while essays and extracurriculars are reviewed by another.[9] When admissions directors say they look at an application holistically, it is merely marketing.

WHERE HAVE ALL THE STUDENTS GONE?

For the last two decades, millennials—those born between 1980 and 1995, who now outnumber baby boomers—have provided an unending supply of college customers. Because there were just so many of them and they were all clamoring to get in the door, it was easy to hide any flaws in the college product. Who needs to market when the product sells itself?

Here are some of the statistics: Enrollments between 1980 and 1990 rose by a mere 2 percent. Between 2000 and 2010, enrollments were up by 30 percent.[10] Much of that growth was fueled by the rise of the millennials, though some of that number includes students returning to the classroom during the Great Recession of 2008.[11]

Another social change that influenced those numbers is that students were willing to go to school farther and farther away. This pull to look beyond the local college was driven by standardized testing companies who began selling student information to universities. Colleges targeted the best and brightest—no matter where they lived. This greatly expanded the pool of prospective students beyond those living within a few hundred miles, which had been standard. Although this started in the 1970s, selling student mailing lists to colleges is now a major revenue source for these "nonprofit" companies. According to the *New York Times*, a decade ago the College Board sold eighty million names to approximately twelve hundred colleges.[12] Jeffrey Selingo, a longtime researcher and writer about higher ed, notes that deans assume that number is higher today.[13] Today, the College Board charges 47 cents per student. So let's assume it's one hundred million names at 47 cents apiece: $47 million is a lot of money to accrue through very little work!

Because students would now look past their own backyards, schools like New York University and Boston University transformed themselves from commuter schools to national universities in the 1980s and 1990s, making themselves truly competitive by the 2000s. Public institutions promoted themselves beyond local markets to bring in higher-paying out-of-state and international students. At the same time, while the high school population continued to grow, home prices were up, allowing for access to equity lines of credit, and the internet provided new ways to communicate with students in far-flung markets. With all this, schools were able to take advantage of this demographic gold rush.

But . . . millennials have now aged out of their undergraduate years, and colleges are starting to get desperate (and this is before the pandemic took its toll). For the top schools, the pressure to attract the best, the brightest, and the (don't kid yourself) wealthiest is intensifying as the number of prospects declines. Even with all the rhetoric about diversity and opening up the Ivies and other highly selective schools to those of lesser means, these campuses remain primarily populated by the well-to-do. According to the *New York Times*, there is a growing number of schools that accept more students from the top 1 percent than they do from the bottom 60 percent, including New York University, University of Southern California,

Vanderbilt, Baylor, and Boston University, several of which no one would have considered worth the price tag just a decade ago.[14]

So the elite schools have to compete for the very best, while every other school is simply trying to "get butts in seats." The schools must strike a delicate balancing act between getting students who can pay top dollar versus increasing the student population in order to increase overall tuition. This means schools need to sell, *sell,* **sell.**

FROM PUBLIC GOOD TO PRIVATE BENEFIT

Traditionally, universities didn't have to worry about the ups and downs of a consumer marketplace. Partly this was due to guaranteed government funding, but it was also due to a worldview wherein schools were producing citizens for a democracy and not worker bees for corporate employers or the next social media entrepreneur. Reduced government funding means more out-of-pocket spending by students and their parents. Switching who pays for college from the government to the backs of students and their parents had a fundamental impact on what colleges offer, as I show here.

Reduced Government Spending → Higher Tuition → Graduates Need to Make More Money to Pay Off Debt → Colleges Offer More Job-Related Majors and Amenities

The impact of saddling you or your children with the increasingly excessive costs of higher education cannot be overemphasized. Government spending—which heavily subsidized college in the United States through the mid-1980s and which still funds universities in most industrialized countries around the world—has all but dried up in America. In the 1970s, government funding covered upward of 65 percent of costs, whereas forty years later, the percentage is closer to 30.[15] Know, too, that this is occurring at the same time when middle-class wages have remained virtually flat. Combined, this means that a college education consumes a much larger percentage of a household budget than it did when you went to school. This is all thanks to Ronald Reagan.

Most Americans are unaware of the defunding of higher education. According to a 2019 American Public Media study, "34% of U.S. adults think government funding for public colleges and universities has stayed the same over the past decade, while 27% think it has increased." The truth is, state funding decreased by $9 billion.[16] So what happens without government support? Tuition—the money that you pay—goes up and up and up.

When tuition or endowments or grants don't cover costs, universities turn to financial markets. This is a bit in the weeds, but stay with me because it impacts how colleges spend money considerably. Positive bond ratings and the ability to borrow money have become crucial as funding from other sources declines and the "amenities arms race" increases. The Roosevelt Institute's report, *The Financialization of Higher Education*,[17] outlines the growing dependence of colleges and universities on financial markets and the consequences of this market-based funding. As capital markets moved from being loan facilitators to profit extractors, they offered new, complex, and often risky financial products—think credit default swaps. As public and private schools compete to attract students by offering new dorms and expansive student centers with everything from career advisement to multifloor food courts to fitness centers, many entered into risky financial instruments and are now paying the price for having done so. In several cases, this is happening to the tune of hundreds of millions of dollars, money going to Wall Street instead of student educational advancement, and it is an underlying contributor to increased tuition costs.

These changes in financing have turned higher ed on its head. With government support, schools operated like film studios or publishing companies, producing the blockbuster in order to support the small "important" film or literary work. Media Studies 101 with an enrollment of two or three hundred students supports the handful of students who study ancient Greek, for example. Not anymore. Being "marketing focused" means giving consumers what they want, and today students want high-end jobs that will help them pay off out-of-control student loans. That's why you'll see lots of ads for cybersecurity majors and engineering programs and Insta posts about how fabulous the career and internship office is. This is not the students' fault. It is the consequence of government reframing education as unimportant to a functioning democracy.

Fewer available students and the rising cost of education are two of the reasons why colleges are so heavily promoted. Over-the-top promotion has created the all-encompassing theory that higher education means Ivy League or nothing. That cult tactic combined with whipping up fear that not getting into the most expensive school means that your life is somehow doomed is the stuff that cults are made of. But it's not only these factors that push the cult of higher ed. The rise of digital technology has enabled marketing to be more ubiquitous and less expensive than ever before.

DATA TRACKING AND DIGITAL MARKETING

Before I explain more explicitly how universities are using online marketing, let's review some basics about how digital and social media marketing work.

Digital marketing—any marketing that happens on your cell phone, your tablet, or even through your TV screen if it is connected to the internet—is dependent on data tracking. When you go online, you leave a trail of information—from what you clicked on, to what term you searched, to how long you spent on a page. This information isn't specifically connected to you, but rather to your IP (internet protocol) address, a string of numbers that individually identifies a device connected to the internet. Marketers use that data to understand who you are, how you shop, and what pushes your emotional buttons. Data is also collected through social monitoring, meaning that marketers "listen" online to see if people talk about their products and analyze the photos you post on, say, Instagram. Did you take a picture in front of the college sign during the campus visit and post it online? That's information the school wants to know about, and the savvier ones are going online to find it.

Social listening is the act of tracking conversations about brands, competitors, topics, and keywords related to a company or industry. Some of this is simple monitoring of mentions on X (formerly Twitter), comments made on Facebook, or pictures posted to Instagram. Sophisticated marketers use it to find out what their audience is talking about so they can develop engaging content for them or establish a "personal" relationship.[18] Delta Air Lines, for example, monitors its social feeds so it can assist travelers in real time. Purina regularly interacted with individuals on Twitter, embellishing pet photos by drawing hats and jackets on animals and tweeting the modified photo back to the pet owner, thus initiating a one-on-one connection.[19] In my discussions with higher ed marketers and consultants, no one could or would confirm that this more aggressive form of listening is being done at the college level—though they admitted that if it is, it would be only schools with larger budgets. More typical is for an admissions officer to check an individual student's social media accounts to try to garner additional information about an applicant.

Remember, keeping us connected is all done in the name of amassing data so that "relevant" advertising can be sent to your computer or mobile device. Companies have been using online advertising for years, and now colleges make it a key component of their marketing plans as well. Advertising on Facebook and other social media sites is typical, as is a paid search campaign on Google, Bing, and Yahoo. Paid search is a form of advertising in which companies pay search engines to place their websites at the top of the results page when particular terms are input. Colleges target students who search for certain keywords, say "University of Michigan" or "Notre Dame" or "political science majors."

In addition to search ads, colleges use a menu of marketing tools that scoop up students' data in order to deliver advertising. One company boasts its ability to combine mobile location-based targeting with IP targeting. The company draws a virtual "geofence" around a location—say, a high school—which allows marketers to "capture" mobile devices within that space. High schoolers can then be contacted via text, email, or app notification while within the geofence. When they later connect to their home Wi-Fi, the marketer gains access to the entire household through IP targeting, enabling schools to message parents as well. This is something that is allowed by regulators in the United States, by the way, that is utterly verboten in the European Union or the United Kingdom.

Colleges are able to text students because there is now a box on the Common App in which applicants can opt in to receive these communications. Research shows that students who are interested in a school will opt in to receive text messages, but more tellingly, those who ultimately enroll engage in two-way interactions with the school. This, then, becomes part of the calculus when deciding which students will be extended offers, and for students, it becomes one more means to market themselves to the university.

TRACKING THE COLLEGE APPLICANT

The admissions process is all about lead generation—creating lots of viable prospects who will turn into sales. The more sophisticated schools are "lead scoring," assigning points to prospects based on information provided (gender, age, what major they are interested in) combined with online behaviors. Add all those things up and give the kid a number. Like corporations, colleges do this using customer relationship marketing (CRM) software. The college tracks student browsing behavior on the college website, such as monitoring page visits, time spent on the site, and whether a brochure has been downloaded. Key indicators that a student is interested in a school is whether they have signed up for a visiting day, a college fair, or an information session or webinar. More robust CRM software packages can connect the school-based information profile with social media interactions, enabling schools to score follows, comments, and shares. The higher the score, the better the prospect.

Research shows that 76 percent of students use social media during their college search.[20] If the school is not tracking students automatically through a CRM system, the college admissions officers review students' social media pages. Kaplan, the test prep company, surveyed admissions officers and found that 35 percent participate in this practice. Ithaca College, for example, tracks uploaded photos and the number of friends a prospect has, whereas University of Denver tracks who joins its online community because those who do are 3.6 times more likely to put down a deposit.[21]

But so what? U.S. colleges are tracking students, just like every other marketer on the planet. The difference here is that the stakes are much higher. Prospective students don't simply receive eerily accurate ads for shoes or trips for spring break; they are evaluated on their educational potential and emotional connection to certain colleges and ultimately rewarded or punished based on their online behaviors.

MARKETING MISDIRECTION

Colleges aren't marketing education. Just like MLMs, they are marketing the American dream, the belief in a narrative that an equal playing field exists for any rugged individual willing to pull themselves up by their bootstraps.[22] We see this play out every day on social media, where influencers create one of the thousands of businesses on Instagram. Or you hear people talk about their "side hustle." This entrepreneurial mentality is embedded in the notion of the Silicon Valley startup that turns one brilliant idea into a multibillion-dollar empire. Think Mark Zuckerberg or Sergey Brin or Elon Musk. These fantasies are drummed into us through a myriad of media from shows like *American Idol* and *Shark Tank* to every advertisement ever made telling you that you can be better, smarter, or more beautiful to real-life rags-to-riches stories like Oprah.

But not everyone can sing, and Herbal Essences can't give you perfect hair, and working really, really hard doesn't always make a difference. That's why education—and, in particular, access to higher education—is held out as a fundamental steppingstone on the road to success.

So why believe it? Because we've been fed a growing list of assumptions about a college education—assumptions that are to the benefit of the government, the banks,[23] and a whole slew of high-tech/edtech companies like Google and Facebook, Amazon and LinkedIn, but not to the benefit of our kids. Here are just a few misdirections: everyone goes to college, everyone that gets into college finishes in four years, and everyone in college is starting right out of high school. No, no, and no. All myths, all misdirections.

Higher education is a perennial platform for politicians from Barack Obama to AOC, eager to appeal to young voters. Every spring we see articles with headlines that read "Homeless to Harvard," or "I Got into All Eight Ivy League Schools" (inevitably with a picture of an African American male), and my favorite "North Carolina Teen Accepted to 113 Colleges and Awarded $4.5 Million in Scholarships Accepts Full Ride to HBCU." Adjacent to these soft news stories are articles demonstrating that college graduates make more than their high school counterparts or, worse, branded content (advertising disguised as articles) saying, "College Is Still Worth It, Despite Rising Costs," brought to you by Discover Card, a company all too happy to provide credit to students whose financial aid doesn't cover their tuition and other expenses.

But the truth is that given the current economic environment, colleges are strongly motivated not to open the doors to everyone, but to find students who can pay the $90,000-plus sticker price. However, *they have to chase after cash but not look like they are.*

A key way that schools suss out wealthy students is through an increasing reliance on early decision, a trend that started within the last five years and shows no sign of abating, as evidenced by how often schools tout the growth of these numbers combined with their need to guarantee enrollments. With early decision (ED), students submit an application that includes an agreement stating that they commit to attending the school if they are accepted. Because students must attend if accepted, they also must accept the financial package that the school offers. These offers tend to be far less generous than those offered to students who apply general admission. Early decision has another benefit for the school: guaranteed yield numbers. Under regular admission, for example, if Yale accepts ten students and only four step foot on campus in the fall, that's a 40 percent yield. With early decision, if five students are accepted, five attend, resulting in a 100 percent yield. It's easy, then, to see why schools are turning to this option with a vengeance. But schools report these numbers deceptively. UPenn promoted its acceptance of 18 percent of the ED applicant pool; what UPenn did not say was that more than half of the class of 2023 was determined by early applications. This doesn't just happen in the Ivies. Boston University, for example, which ten years ago took 350 students early, last year accepted approximately 1,100 early decision students, or close to a third of the freshman class.

If all this fails and students get into schools they don't like, they can transfer. But that's a pricey proposition, too. Most schools have little, if any, funding for transfer admits because it is all used to entice incoming freshmen. Schools that are "need blind" for freshmen have their eyes wide open for transfers.

THE IMPACT OF THIS OBSESSION ON OUR KIDS

Generation Z are true digital natives. Sure, millennials are tech savvy, but Gen Z is the first generation to be born into a digital world. They have never known a world without smartphones or free WiFi. They find their celebrities on TikTok and YouTube, and fully 92 percent have a digital footprint that continues to grow unabated.[24]

Gen Z is more connected to technology and more comfortable moving from one task to another. Connections to tech help erase the delineation between home and work; tasks might start at the school, move to a cell phone, and continue while watching TV. While Gen Z uses Slack (and email if they absolutely have to), most prefer face-to-face interactions, at least relative to their predecessors.

Professor of psychology Jean Twenge calls this group iGen, as they have grown up with iPhones, iPads, iPods, and other cellular technology. That connection has come with a price. In her *Atlantic* article *Have Smartphones Destroyed a Generation?* she argues that although more physically safe, this generation is at a mental health crisis point, and she correlates rises in depression and suicide among twelve- to seventeen-year-olds to the increased use of cell phones starting in 2012, the year that usage topped 50 percent.[25]

But technology alone is not the culprit. Social media and the drive to not only create the perfect online persona, but also to compete with one's peers is what has led to this mental health crisis. A survey of college students found that the more they use Facebook, the unhappier they felt. Why? Because it becomes a space for measuring yourself against your peers. In the past, if someone wasn't invited to a party, it was a private matter. Not today. Teens post their parties and shopping trips and dining experiences online. Facebook, Instagram, and Snapchat become spaces to find that you've been left out. Or these become sites for bullying—which affects girls far more than boys. Other researchers admit, however, that there is a bit of chicken-and-egg going on here: are teens going online because they are anxious or vice versa?[26] Either way, the statistics are overwhelming in establishing a connection between social media usage and teen emotional states.[27]

This constant ranking of abilities on social media with the anvil of college looming overhead has led to increases in anxiety and depression at rates never seen before—an issue more acute for girls. The Higher Education Research Institute at UCLA found that 41 percent of college freshmen in 2016 feel overwhelmed, up from 29 percent in 2010. This crosses economic lines, with more privileged youth showing the most anxiety, according to a report in the *New York Times*.[28] The numbers are staggering: three million teens suffered with depression in 2015 according to the Department of Health and Human Services; 6.3 million suffer with an anxiety disorder, 30 percent of which are teenage girls and 20 percent boys per the National Institute of Mental Health. If your child feels like they are on a hamster wheel, like they can never do enough or be enough, they are not alone. As getting into the top schools becomes more like a game of chance, the psychological fallout is exacerbated because hard work and achievement don't translate to the perceived ultimate brass ring.

High schools are complicit in this as well. Requiring students to use apps like Pupilpath, which notifies students every time a grade gets posted, keeps them in a hypervigilant state about their GPA. Research shows that these push notifications release dopamine into the brain to give a little jolt of pleasure. They pick up their phones with the expectation that they'll receive good news—sometimes they do and sometimes they don't.

Knowing that you spend your time on social spaces and that there is fear about grades and fitting in and paying for college become pressure points to get you on campus. What do I mean by pressure points? Those are the topics that marketers bring up over and over and over because they know they will have the biggest impact emotionally. It's the same tactic used by cults and MLMs.

REALITY CHECK

If you want to get a sense of how out of proportion the marketing of higher education is, go to the *U.S. News* ranking page. On the left, a tool allows you to list schools by name, tuition, location, enrollment, and acceptance rate. When I looked in 2023, there were 1,859 colleges listed. If you look at schools with an acceptance rate of 30 percent or more, the number is

1,484 schools; at 40 percent or more, there are 1,431 schools, including a number of schools in the top one hundred that were less expensive state colleges. In total, there are 4,294 four-year colleges in the United States. Most of those schools accept most of their applicants.

Students and parents are led to believe that there aren't enough seats because of what happens at the top of the market. Elite schools limit their enrollments. To game the acceptance rate and increase their asking price, the next tier schools are now doing the same. Commensurate with this is that as supply seems to get smaller and smaller, people become more willing to pay those exorbitant price tags—whether they can afford them or not.

There is no reason to buy into this obsession. Students can get a per-fectly good—if not a stellar—education outside the top fifty schools. Lesser institutions often provide more access to tenured faculty. And for the best and brightest, the opportunities to be a big fish in a small pond can far outweigh the supposed benefits of buying the brand. I've talked to many Harvard undergrads who were unhappy with their college experiences. That's because major research institutions put their efforts into graduate students. Another reason to rethink these institutions.

IVY LEAGUE—YES OR NO?

If you go to college, you will make more money than if you didn't. That is known as the wage premium. Graduates will make about 65 percent more than people who do not go to college.[29]

However, you must consider the college wealth premium[30]—your personal wealth based on your assets and liabilities. Take on too much college debt and you erase the wage advantage.

You only enjoy the benefits of a wage premium if you go to college within your means. Does that mean you shouldn't try for an Ivy League school? No. They may come up with cash for you, and if they do, terrific.

Does it mean you have to major in STEM because it is the only way to pay off your degree? No. But if your major is social work or teaching or in the arts, don't go to a high-cost college unless you can afford it going in.

There are so many emotions around higher education that people seem to forget about living within their means. I don't blame this on stu-dents or parents. I blame it on the system. I blame it on counselors who do not provide the reality check that they should. And I blame it on the marketing.

You will get the highest value out of a college education when you go into it knowing what you can afford—and sticking to it.

Finally, as the price of higher education continues to rise, the market for alternatives grows. Disruptors in this sector are computer boot camps, short courses from companies like General Assembly, an explosion in online options post-pandemic, and apprenticeship programs from companies like Praxis. In an educational environment where a common catchphrase is "Cs get degrees," where costs are prohibitive, and where workers are expected to continually upgrade their skill set, students are questioning whether a traditional degree is worth the time and the expense. If a six-month class for a fraction of the cost of college leads to a six-figure salary, there really is no competition. As one college administrator admitted to me, "They [short course providers] don't have time for shrimp cocktail and climbing walls."

Hannah's story had a happy ending, not because of an improvement in the system but because of a fluke of circumstance. She went to her safety school, because she had no choice. You might be thinking, "Why didn't she just take a gap year?" The answer is simple: she couldn't. A gap year is a marketed concept, not a viable option. As currently structured, taking a year off before starting college works if you get into a school you want to go to, like Malia Obama taking a gap year before going to Harvard. Hannah would be taking a year off to avoid the inevitable. Or, if she did take the year off without deferring admission, she would be reapplying against graduating high school seniors, and she would come up short in comparison.

Instead, she started college and, like thousands of other students (37 percent of students nationally), she put in applications to transfer during her freshman year. When she applied the second time, she got into ten out of twelve schools, including top institutions that had denied admissions or waitlisted her the first time. Truly, no kid changes that much in a year. She was just as smart, just as talented, just as ambitious. The difference was that her parents didn't ask for money. This became proof positive to me that everything I thought I knew about college admissions was wrong. It wasn't about education. It was about marketing, especially to people at their most vulnerable. When you are vulnerable is when cults swoop in. They sell you with a theory of the world, in this case the world of higher ed. The admissions officers and guidance counselors are the charismatic leaders that sell the pitch—year after year after year. The digital technologies become systems of influence that lead parents and students alike towards fear. The U.S. higher education system is set up like a cult, plain and simple.

PART II

MULTILEVEL MARKETING

The Canary in the Cult
+ Marketing Coal Mine

4

MLMS ARE PYRAMID SCHEMES, AKA CULTS

Facebook Live became widely available in 2016, and suddenly multilevel marketing (MLM) consultants started popping up like late-night ads for psychics. Instead of posting a static picture on Instagram (the preferred site for influencers and their wares) followed by copy containing lots of exclamation points (!!!!!!), these independent contractors conveniently hawked their leggings and essentials oils and weight-loss powders from their homes. Being able to interact with potential buyers in real time creates the kind of "personal, authentic relationships" that lead to online sales. Camera-ready consultants who had a flair for the medium did pretty well, at least for a while.

Their efforts may have been thwarted in part by none other than John Oliver. Not long after this Facebook feature streamlined online selling, John Oliver did a scathing—and hilariously accurate—report on multi-level marketing, aka direct selling, aka network marketing aka a whole lot of other names. Included in the piece was footage from an MLM sales event that shows a blonde, thin, expensively dressed spokesperson making outrageous income claims and in a slip of the tongue calling the company a pyramid scheme—oops! An undercover news report showed a man explaining how the sales levels work to a woman he is attempting to recruit into Vemma, an MLM dietary supplement company that no longer exists. When a reporter confronts him and asks him if it is a pyramid scheme, his response is, "it's not an illegal pyramid scheme, it's direct selling." And Oliver responds with a quip, "so it's not a pyramid, it's just pyramid shaped like a Dorito or an Angry Bird or just a pile of. . . ." The bulk of the piece focuses on Herbalife, an MLM that has existed for decades. The company sells shakes and vitamins and weight-loss products, and it has gotten into trouble for making false health claims—professing to cure everything from heart disease to infertility. Of course, consultants are motivated to exaggerate the products' benefits in order to sell, sell, sell. But even those exaggerations don't help. Most end up with a lot of inventory in their garage and a whole lot of debt.[1]

Herbalife was also the focus of *Betting on Zero*, a 2017 documentary that follows Bill Ackman's multiyear crusade to stop this company. Ackman is a young, salt-and-pepper haired Wall Street hedge fund manager who became famous for shorting stocks. Simply, shorting stocks is when you bet that a stock is going to fall. Ackman bet a billion dollars that Herbalife stock would drop to zero after word got out about the company's deceptive tactics, how it preyed on people desperate to make money, and its deliberate targeting of minorities and the undocumented.[2] It didn't. It rose due to the combination of a nasty feud between two Wall Street big shots and the promotional and press savvy of Herbalife. Although this was a huge disappointment, Ackman's crusade led to increased attention in the mainstream press and a Federal Trade Commission (FTC) investigation of Herbalife. Sadly, that didn't matter either. MLMs continued unabated, and in 2017, retail sales totaled $34.9 billion.[3]

The tide began to turn on these deceptive marketers with the 2021 release of *LuLaRich*, one of the most watched shows on Amazon Prime. The docuseries recounts the rise and fall of LuLaRoe, a California-based company made famous through the sales of brightly colored and wildly patterned leggings. Heartbreakingly, this exposé shows the shocking lengths to which consultants felt compelled to go in order to reach their sales goals: time away from their families and stockpiling inventory they couldn't afford, but far worse was the demand that top salespeople have cosmetic surgery because appearance was so important to maintaining sales.

What made LuLaRoe different from other MLMs, however, is that the State of Washington successfully sued the company, gaining restitution for some of the company's former salespeople. But, like Herbalife, the punishment was a slap on the wrist and the company continues its destructive business practices. I came to learn that trying to eliminate an MLM is like playing a lightning round of Whac-a-Mole.

I began studying multilevel marketing companies (MLMs) in earnest shortly after the pandemic started. Surprisingly, there wasn't a whole lot written on the subject, particularly in the academic literature. Some legal articles, a lot of books about how to get rich quick, and a few business school articles, most of which extolled the benefits of MLMs and direct selling. In one case, I came to learn that an article written by a professor at a top business school was bought and paid for by—wait for it—Herbalife.[4]

Not only did I want to understand what MLMs are and the deceptive marketing tactics they use, I also wanted to know the political and economic conditions that allowed these businesses to thrive. Some readers may know about the relationship between the DeVos family and Amway, one of the oldest MLMs around. They are an important political and legal part of this story, and I talk about that later in the chapter. Economically, I discovered a key player in this world is the Direct Selling Association (DSA), a trade group for companies that sell products and services using an independent sales force.

According to the DSA website, the organization "serves to promote, protect and police the direct selling industry while helping direct selling companies and their independent salesforce become more successful." It claims to do this by requiring members to uphold a stringent code of ethics that prohibits overpromising or misleading consumers and sets guidelines for things like earnings statements, product claims, and sales and marketing tactics.[5] In truth, it acts as a shield for MLMs, which make up more than 94 percent of the DSA.[6]

Nonprofit organization Truth in Advertising (truthinadvertising.org) has documented thousands of violations of the DSA code of ethics by its members. Truly, its work is stunning. In 2017, it evaluated every member on the DSA list and found that "more than 97 percent have made or are making—either directly or through their distributors—false and unsubstantiated income claims to promote the companies' business opportunity."[7] These infractions are perpetrated by MLM stalwarts like Herbalife and Mary Kay as well as lesser known entities, like Modere, which claimed to treat menopause and PMS, and Essential Bodywear, which made false income claims. As Bonnie Patten, executive director of Truth in Advertising, noted, "The DSA Code of Ethics has been used to give the appearance of self-policing, while the trade association has instead served the private interests of its members at the public's expense."[8]

But that's not all. The DSA also has a questionable relationship with colleges and universities via the Direct Selling Education Foundation (DSEF), the organization's charitable arm. In September 2022, *The Chronicle of Higher Education* published a blistering article about the DSEF. The piece outlined the many ways in which the MLM industry "has been making quiet inroads into academe" through providing fellowships and grants to professors, making industry leaders available for classroom visits, teaching MLM case studies, and creating course materials that present MLMs and direct selling as simply another legitimate form of promotion.

Connecting the DSA to the academy isn't new. It has been working to establish inroads since the foundation's inception in 1973, but it seems to have gained momentum in 2016 with the creation of DSEF fellows. This program enables professors to work with the DSA for a three-year period, giving them access to data and executives and providing internship opportunities for students. But the DSA gets the better part of the deal. Professors become (minimally) paid spokespeople for the organization by using its materials in their classrooms. This is a powerful tool for giving this industry legitimacy. It works like sharing content online—you might look at a post if it is from an advertiser, but you give it more credibility if it's sent from your best friend or your boss.

The heart of the *Chronicle* article was an examination of the fellowship program. In December 2021, the website listed 239 fellows, most of whom were U.S. faculty. The *Chronicle* talked to more than a dozen of them, and their evaluations ranged from lukewarm (MLMs are not so bad, and all business models have challenges) to ebullient (the DSEF is a great resource, and the DSA doesn't deal with pyramid schemes). Some faculty members contacted by the *Chronicle* didn't even know that they were still fellows or that their names were on the website. Having a long list of faculty from a variety of institutions behooves the foundation by giving it credibility. But it's also misleading. It should not surprise anyone that by the time the article appeared, the DSEF had taken down the list of fellows. If you go to the website today, there is still a link to access the list, but it reroutes you back to the fellowship page.[9]

I was all set to attend the DSEF conference in 2022 (unironically titled "Building Trust in the Marketplace") to learn firsthand about its relationship to universities. I had the perfect cover as a professor who teaches advertising and marketing. That I teach media *criticism* is not anything the organization needed to know. But then, just a few weeks before we were supposed to meet in Atlanta, the conference was cancelled. Boom. Done.

Except for COVID, I'd never heard of this happening. This was a sizable event. You don't just cancel something like this. So I contacted the DSEF to find out what happened and was told that the cancellation was due to the death of the daughter of one of the organizers a few months earlier. This is incredibly sad news, devastating really, and a good reason for that person not to attend. DSEF did not, however, provide a legitimate explanation for canceling the conference. Why would it crumble because one person was unavailable? A more likely reason was that the *Chronicle*'s DSEF exposé would publish a few weeks before the conference. I knew the exposé was coming out because Bill Keep, professor of marketing at the College of New Jersey's school of business and an MLM policy advocate, brought it to my attention.

I had met Professor Keep a few years before when he began hosting the first academic conferences on multilevel marketing. He is a critic of MLMs who has worked for decades to shut these companies down. The conference brought together some of the biggest names in MLM—current and former FTC commissioners, lawyers who had worked on defining MLM cases, researchers from around the world (this is not just a U.S. problem by any means), ex-MLMers, and even the producer of *LuLaRich*, the phenomenally successful docuseries.

Presentation after presentation, I wondered why these companies still exist. They perpetuate blatant fraud and are so obviously detrimental to those who get sucked into them. No different, in fact, from those who find themselves enmeshed in a cult. This led me to ask a question of an ex-MLMer as well as a cult expert: if you draw a Venn diagram of MLMs and cults, what part of the circles would intersect? Without hesitation, they both said, "All of it. It would just be a circle."

I see MLMs as the proverbial canary in the coal mine. The same bait-and-switch tactics used by these companies are used by packaged goods marketers, political pundits, and Silicon Valley salesmen every day, especially on social media. Online digital platforms are designed to make us unwitting salespeople. We share and like content, often without even knowing there's a sponsor behind it, all while turning our personal relationships into commercial transactions.

Economically and socially, there is another reason why these companies prosper today. During the last fifteen years, we have been lured by the myth of the gig economy—the idea that anyone can be an entrepreneur through digital piecework: part-time jobs, consultancies, and so forth. The goal in all of this is to create a successful company and plan your exit strategy or to create a product that leads to passive income. Think about Candy Crush. The developers produced the game, put it online, and all but forgot about it, except for the billions of dollars it generated. This idea has been trumpeted by Silicon Valley and bolstered by companies like Uber and Airbnb and every social media site with an integrated sales link.

The "gig economy" and the "side hustle" hide the harsh reality that companies are slashing jobs, or when jobs do exist, they are not paying a living wage. Gig work is valorized for giving workers flexibility and creativity and entrepreneurship and extra income.[10] In truth, it is hard work with no health benefits, and as anyone who has worked freelance knows, income is rarely stable or steady. Whether Uber or TikTok's Creator Fund, this structure has put the risk on the backs of the workers while making those at the top of the organization disgustingly wealthy. MLMs are yet another example—and a particularly pernicious one—of companies taking advantage of workers desperate for jobs, particularly during the pandemic. All while Jeff Bezos launched a spaceflight to nowhere and inordinately increased his personal wealth.

Before we get into explaining the structures that allow MLMs to continue to exist, let's start by examining what they are and some examples of who they are. In the next chapter, I dig into the marketing tactics that are used to draw people in and their similarities to cults.

WHAT IS AN MLM?

You've more than likely heard the term multilevel marketing, or MLM, especially with the rise in books, documentaries, podcasts, and YouTube posts on the topic. Or you may have seen posts on social media touting one of the thousands of companies like doTERRA or Monat or Rodan + Fields. These direct sellers are still rampant online, and they continue to promote an upscale lifestyle to people—usually poor, usually disadvantaged, usually female—suggesting they can make oodles of extra cash in their free time. Nothing could be further from the truth, and it's illegal for them to say so.

But what constitutes a multilevel marketing company, aka an MLM? According to the FTC, an MLM company "distributes products or services through a network of salespeople who are not employees of the company and do not receive a salary or wage. Instead, members of the company's salesforce usually are treated as independent contractors, who may earn income depending on their own revenues and expenses."[11]

That definition—like most things related to MLM—is as clear as mud. Let's unpack it a bit. First, MLM companies sell through individuals who are not employees. As independent contractors, they do not receive salaries and are not entitled to benefits like health insurance or paid time off. Rather, these "consultants" or "distributors" or "independent business owners" (online, the infamous #BossBabes) work for themselves. This structure alone is a form of deception that helps the company and hurts the salesperson. Besides saving the Herbalifes and Mary Kays of the world a ton of money on the cost of benefits, it provides those companies with plausible deniability when they get sued for trade and marketing infractions, such as illegitimate product claims.

I spoke about how companies monitor what consultants say with a number of current and former MLM corporate marketers who asked not to be identified. They explained that MLMs have compliance departments that are responsible for monitoring reps' social media content. Compliance departments run the gamut in terms of their level of scrutiny. A company like Melaleuca, for example, monitors its reps assiduously so they don't say anything they shouldn't. Other companies, the scams and the fly-by-nights, are completely hands-off, allowing reps to do things like recklessly post miracle cures. Most companies fall in the middle. They monitor social media and send warning letters when necessary.

But compliance is hard. There are millions of reps and only so many people to oversee their work, similar to the FTC trying to ensure that influencers properly label their sponsored content. When compliance can't keep up with the surveillance on their own, they create an atmosphere in the corporation in which the reps police each other and report their fellow reps to compliance. This is solidified at the annual convention where compliance officers stand on stage and say, "Protect your business. Don't let your other fellow reps destroy your business." This kind of internal policing is the hallmark of a high-control group.

Next, these salespeople "*may* earn income." In theory, they earn money from selling a product or service, which is key. Having a product or service to sell and not simply recruiting new salespeople differentiates these companies from pyramid schemes (see textbox on page 58). Skim the surface of any MLM, though, and you'll discover that the products are beside the point. Whether clothing, diet aids, jewelry, or essential oils, the MLM products are qualitatively not as good, not as convenient, and inevitably more expensive than anything you could order online or buy at retail.

Most people don't make money from MLMs. I'll say that again: *people don't make money from MLMs*. Like a chain letter, it is mathematically impossible for most of the distributors in this game to achieve even modest earnings.[12] Rather, most people lose money because, as independent contractors, they have to invest in all the upfront costs, including marketing, inventory, and whatever they do to keep up appearances.

I am emphatic about this because whenever I post this notion on social media, I am swarmed with people saying they made money or their sister made money or their third cousin once removed made money. Sure, *some* people make money from MLM, but they make up 1 percent of the sales force. In an MLM one researcher studied, 84 percent of commissions went to the top 1 percent.[13] This small percentage of successful salespeople perpetuates the myth that everyone can make money . . . and if you can't, there is something wrong with you.

What's crazy about all of this is that MLM financial information is not hard to find, if you know where to look for it. The FTC, in an article entitled "Multi-Level Marketing Businesses and Pyramid Schemes," states "Most people who join legitimate MLMs make little or no money. Some of them lose money."[14] Okay, maybe that's too subtle, and it's not like people are rushing to the FTC site. Receiving broader exposure was a study fielded by the American Association of Retired Persons (AARP), the most widely distributed publication in the United States. It found that 47 percent of consultants lost money while another 27 percent broke even.[15] Why AARP? Because although more millennials and Gen Zers get wrapped up in MLM, older folks are likely to lose a whole lot more money.

But finding MLM financial information can be even easier than that, when you know where to look for it. MLMs post income disclosure statements. They don't make it easy to find, but the information is usually somewhere in the bowels of their website. This is not required by the FTC, but it is strongly encouraged. Although this information is not required to be posted on the website, it must be made available to prospective reps. I picked a few sites at random:

> **Forever Living** (wellness and beauty products): "In an average month 88.6% of purchasers globally did not receive any meaningful compensation or earnings from Forever."[16]
>
> **Monat** (haircare products): More than 93 percent of its U.S. "Marketing Partners" made an average of $144 in 2021. (That's not for a month. That's the entire year.)[17]
>
> **Young Living** (essential oils): In 2023, associates (64.1 percent of the company) averaged $22 in earnings for the year. The most money made by someone at that entry-level rank was $599. The bottom two sales rungs (associate and star), which represent 90 percent of the sales force, have average earnings of less than $300 for the year.[18]
>
> **Herbalife** (protein shakes, supplements, etc.): This company provides a chart that seems straightforward but actually requires a bit of deciphering. The key information follows:
> - 50 percent of distributors make less than $247 per month.
> - Among first-year distributors, only 130 (out of 13,000—the top 1 percent) made $7,880 or more per month; the top 10 percent make $1,780 or more.

- Among all other distributors (most of whom had been with the company between five to twelve years), the top 1 percent ("about 550" out of 55,000) made more than $18,598 in a month; the top 10 percent made more than $4,419 in a month.

So, in the case of Herbalife, even if you have worked for the company for a while and are among the top 10 percent, you are not making the average salary in the United States. Know too that the numbers in the chart reflect revenue, not profit, because the data does not account for the cost of doing business. The only people making any money are those in the top 1 percent, and for new distributors, that was a whopping 130 people out of 13,000!

I could have looked at a whole lot more of these sites, but there's really no point. They all say the same thing—if you are part of the 1 percent, then you can make a living, and you have to be in the .01 percent to rake in the big bucks. Otherwise, you are chasing after a dream of riches that's just not mathematically possible. It is important to note, too, what is not highlighted on these sites: the numbers presented are *gross* income figures. Once you account for marketing (which the company can't do because it doesn't lay out that money) and any other expenses (like out-of-town travel to seminars, motivational books and tapes, and buying product to keep your standing), those numbers drop significantly.

Like all gig workers, MLM purveyors take on the risk and costs, while the people at the top of the company reap the rewards. And, like influencers, they work ridiculous hours presenting a romanticized world of a glamorous lifestyle online, which reality in no way reflects.

By now, you're probably asking yourself, why would anyone work insane hours selling "meh" products for no money? They do it because they have been promised a large payment further down the road . . . as long as they work hard enough.

Keeping salespeople on a hamster wheel is built into the multilevel marketing structure. Here's how: Each person who joins is expected to recruit others to sell the product, typically three to six people. Those you recruit become your "downline," and you get a percentage of everything they sell. The expectation is that each of the people you recruit will recruit six more, and you get a percentage of those sales as well. Then those people will recruit six more, and so on, and so on, and so on. The higher up in the food chain you are, the more money you make because you get a percentage of all the sales below your level. Most MLMs expect that each salesperson will buy a monthly amount of product, whether it will be sold or not. The monthly minimum of $100 or more guarantees that those in the upline will make money every month. If this sounds like a pyramid structure, it is.

PYRAMID SCHEME VERSUS MULTILEVEL MARKETING

A **pyramid scheme** is defined as "a fraudulent system of making money based on recruiting an ever-increasing number of 'investors.'"[19] The creator of this scheme—the one at the top of the pyramid—makes money by recruiting other investors. Those investors, in turn, recruit more investors under them, and so on and so on until you have an organizational structure like the one shown here.

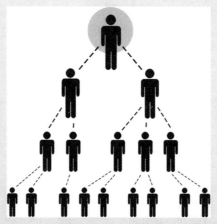

Pyramid Scheme. *Source*: Pixabay; public domain

Pyramid schemes are usually thought of in terms of financial investment opportunities. The people at the top of the pyramid get paid only if new recruits bring more money into the system. People join the pyramid because they have been scammed into believing that they will receive extraordinary returns on their investments.

Some of you may be thinking this sounds like the Bernie Madoff scandal, and it is close. Madoff's con was a Ponzi scheme. The difference between a pyramid scheme and a Ponzi scheme is that a single person, in this case Madoff, manages the entire recruitment process.

Multilevel marketing has the same structure as a pyramid scheme, though the particulars are slightly different. In general, an MLM company distributes products and services through independent contractors who are not employees of the company and do not receive salaries. They may earn

income depending on sales revenue and expenses for running the business. In most cases, the MLM is not directly involved in recruiting the sales
force. Rather, existing salespeople recruit other salespeople who recruit
other salespeople below them. This creates multiple levels of distributors
who become each recruiter's downline. In theory, the way MLMers make
money is by selling the product and by recruiting more people who also
sell the product, thereby receiving commissions on recruits' sales as well
as their own. I say "in theory" because most consultants make money—if
they make money at all—by recruiting others who are required to make an
initial investment in the company's product. The only difference between
a pyramid scheme and an MLM is that the latter entails selling products.
That alone makes this a legal enterprise.

This dream of sitting back and reaping the big bucks has two fatal
flaws. First, by the time you get to the thirteenth level of the pyramid,
you have effectively enrolled every person on the planet. And, well, that's
never going to happen. Second, since most people will not be successful at
selling, they drop out, which was true of people I spoke with. That means
consultants have to constantly pitch new people to add to their downline.
Just writing this feels exhausting.

A SHORT HISTORY ABOUT HOW MLMS TRANSITION FROM SOCIALS TO SCAMS

Multilevel marketing companies have been around for decades. Tupperware, for example, started in the 1940s offering a product that people
couldn't buy anywhere else. Those plastic containers closed tight, and the
"burp" let you know that you had gotten all the air out, helping your food
last longer. Demonstrating the product in the comfort of someone's living
room puts potential buyers at ease while enabling them to interact with the
product.[20] It's the very essence of sensory marketing. Women sold directly
to their friends at a time when there was no internet, no Amazon, and no
Instacart. That wholesome, Americana image of Tupperware continues
today, fueled by product placement on *The Marvelous Mrs. Maisel* and tie-
ins with the latest Minions movie. The problem is there is no longer any
value added to buying direct, and there are dozens of substitutes—from
Rubbermaid to Pyrex, and the latter doesn't have any nasty BPAs. Even
if consultants can sell product (and unlike other MLMs this company has

some good ones), Tupperware's branding is all about being virtually indestructible. If products don't need to be replaced, you either need more
new customers or you need to keep expanding your product line. That's
why Tupperware's website is chock full of superfluous products like potato
bins and Minion canister sets—all of which are in opposition to their stated
support for sustainability and waste reduction.

Fast forward thirty years, and multilevel marketing companies begin to
grab the attention of the FTC, the government body responsible for protecting consumers and for ensuring companies comply with federally regulated trade practices. Three cases brought by the commission in the 1970s
would come to define the MLM regulatory marketplace as we know it.

In re Holiday Magic Securities and Antitrust Litigation (1974) was the first
case the FTC brought to rein in these companies. This MLM had all the
earmarks of a pyramid scheme that we recognize today: a company that
"fudges" its product claims, wildly overpromises income potential through
its marketing materials, and, at the top of the company, a charismatic CEO
who not only sells the product but pitches the salesforce on his "Leadership
Dynamics" motivation course (for an additional fee, obviously). This company was a disaster waiting to happen. It was led by William Penn Patrick,
a pre–social media version of Elon Musk. Patrick was so brazen, it was as if
he wore a neon sign saying "try and sue me—go ahead!" The first authority
to take him up on that was the U.S. Securities and Exchange Commission
(SEC), which sued Holiday Magic in 1973 for swindling $250 million from
eighty thousand distributors. The SEC claimed recruits had entered into an
investment contract, not a sales contract. The same year, an FTC investigation leveled three charges against the company: (1) it misrepresented income
potential, (2) it fixed prices, and (3) it misled prospective recruits about the
realities of market saturation. This last issue seems complex but isn't. The
ability to recruit a downline, and therefore to make money, is impossible
when there are too many distributors in the market. The administrative
judge found in the FTC's favor, and the company agreed to settle the case
without appeal. Civil lawsuits against Leadership Dynamics followed. Participants said they were beaten and coerced during training, made to eat rot-
ten food, and even forced to get into a coffin and to be strapped to a cross.
This was the 1970s version of LuLaRoe coercing its consultants to undergo
facelifts.[21] Under the weight of these lawsuits and the untimely death of
Patrick in a plane crash, the company folded in 1974.[22]

Another important case is *SEC v. Koscot Interplanetary* (1975). The
company claimed to sell cosmetics. In reality, it mostly sold the possibility of selling cosmetics. Participants made money by recruiting others, and

these wages are garnered "unrelated to the sale of product to ultimate users." The disconnect between product sales and how a distributor makes an income (through recruiting) is fundamental to how the FTC defined an illegal pyramid. This is known as the "Koscot Test."[23] To comply with federal regulations, companies must prove that sales are taking place and that those sales are the mechanism driving the compensation plan. What gets fuzzy here is the issue of whom the ultimate user is. Many MLMs claim that distributors join the company to get product discounts, in theory making them the end users, not desperate distributors trying to maintain their status in the company by inventory loading.

The last and most important MLM case is *FTC v. Amway* (1979). When it comes to MLMs, Amway is the largest. The company sells more than 350 products, mostly in the areas of beauty, personal care, and home care, like laundry detergent. In 2022, Amway reported global annual revenue of $8.1 billion.

Like other MLMs, Amway has a long and sordid corporate history.[24] Here's a bit of background to help understand the company, the case, and its implications. Amway was founded in 1959 by Jay Van Andel and Richard DeVos, who met at Christian High School in Michigan. Richard DeVos is the father-in-law of Betsy DeVos, former education secretary under Trump. She, her brother, Erik Prince (the founder of Blackwater), and sundry other members of the DeVos family are longstanding contributors to the Republican Party and, through their foundation, have supported conservative causes like the Heritage Foundation and Focus on the Family.[25] I mention this here because the connection between Republican politics and MLMs is salient still today.

In 1975, the same year as *Koscot*, the FTC accused Amway of being an illegal pyramid scheme. According to Robert L. FitzPatrick, a longtime opponent of MLMs and the author of *Ponzinomics*, "FTC attorneys argued the Amway pyramid scheme prosecution on essentially the same bases [*sic*] as the cases it had brought against at least two other MLM schemes, Holiday Magic and Koscot, which were both successfully shut down. Only Amway was allowed to stay in business."[26] The commission even used the same attorney that had won the Holiday Magic case.

Unlike the Holiday Magic case, the administrative judge ruled against the FTC on almost every count. The judge claimed there was no market saturation, relying on testimony given by witnesses called by Amway. He dismissed the commission's claims of saturation, ignoring both its witnesses and the enormous amount of data that had been amassed for the Holiday Magic case. The data was considered superfluous because it demonstrated saturation, but not in the markets Amway used as defense in its case. The judge did agree with the FTC when it came to price fixing, but only because the company had been caught dead to rights. The FTC had a recording of Richard DeVos, the president of Amway, saying that distributors had to use the prices designated by the company, but they shouldn't put this in writing because they would be in trouble if the commission found out about it.[27] The two sides appealed the judge's decision. On appeal, the commission agreed with the judge about the saturation charge, allowing the company to avoid being shuttered for being a pyramid scheme.

But why was Amway successful when the other companies were forced to pay large fines and even shut down their operations?

A lot of this has to do with perception—that is marketing. Amway was not like other MLMs. The name is short for "American Way." The company wrapped itself in the American flag and Christian values. So much so that comedian Bob Hope, who was most famous in his later years for entertaining U.S. troops overseas, was the company's spokesperson. You don't get squeakier clean than that.

To bolster the idea that it was different from those other disreputable companies, it created rules—during the trial—that were meant to give the appearance that it was taking proactive steps to avoid being a pyramid scheme. These were not guidelines used within the company; they were PR that was invented specifically for defending the case. Known as the "Amway Safeguard Rules," the company claimed that

1. Distributors were required to make ten sales to ten different retail customers in order to be eligible for commissions and bonuses in their downline.
2. Reps had to sell a minimum of 70 percent of their purchase before they could place new orders.
3. The company has a "buy-back policy."

These rules are ridiculous on their face. The company does not keep records of sales executed by independent contractors. "Personal use" qualified for inclusion in the 70 percent rule. As for the buy-back policy, the restrictions are so complicated as to be almost impossible to implement.

Yet the judge claimed these "safeguards" enabled him to claim the company was not a pyramid scheme. As if by magic, these rules became the standard and the shield that companies use to avoid being investigated. All they have to do is claim that they have rules . . . just like Amway.

Was this just a bad decision by a judge? Some awful mistake in the court system? People in the know don't think so.

That's because of the relationship among the FTC, the White House, and the DeVos family. The FTC has five commissioners and a three-to-two political party split. The party in the White House determines who the chair of the commission is and thus the balance of power. At the time of the case, the country was recovering from Watergate, and Gerald Ford became president. Ford had been the leader of the Republican Party in the House of Representatives from 1965 to 1973. He was a representative from Michigan, specifically Grand Rapids, home to Amway and its founders. According to FitzPatrick, President Ford was friends with the company's founders and "major funders of his campaign." In 1975, Van Andel and DeVos had a forty-three-minute meeting with Ford in the White House while the company was being investigated. A month after that event, "Van Andel was quoted in a Michigan newspaper as saying that Ford was aware of Amway's troubles with the FTC."[28]

Many believe that had Amway lost, the MLM industry would have been dead in its tracks.

At one time, direct selling was a legitimate way to distribute products. Some of you might even have memories of encyclopedias or vacuum cleaners being sold door to door or even of the "Fuller Brush man." Reading *Death of a Salesman* in high school burnished this idea in our psyches.

The question is, does that make any sense in an age of Amazon, overnight shipping, and readily available substitutes? Not really, but marketers can make it look that way. One tactic they use to do this is false scarcity. False scarcity is when marketing leads you to believe that you have to buy the product *now* or you risk losing out on ever being able to acquire the product. With LuLaRoe, it was a particular pattern of leggings that was available only for a limited time. For tech companies, it is selling a limited number of X-Boxes or Nintendos leading into the holiday season. For Trader Joe's, it's limiting pumpkin spice and ube flavored foods. Creating this perceived lack foments fear of missing out, enables the company to charge a higher price, and gives MLMs the appearance of having something valuable to offer.

It's one thing to enjoy pumpkin spice; it's another to lose your moral compass trying to feed your family.

5

AUNT SUSIE GOT SUCKED IN BY THE MARKETING . . . AND THE "HEY HUN"

Roberta Blevins was a wife and a busy mom looking for a way to make a few extra bucks. A friend suggested LuLaRoe, and after some hesitation, Roberta plunked down $9,000 to become a consultant. She was great at sales, creating videos and alerting friends to the latest leggings.

Then LuLaRoe started producing inferior products. Worse, Roberta realized she was causing people to go into debt and even possibly lose their homes. She wanted out. It took months to drum up the courage to leave. This wasn't just leaving a job—it meant losing her support group, her "friends," and the LuLaRoe lifestyle. But she did.

You may know Roberta from watching her in *LuLaRich* or the *Vice* documentary called "Why Women Are Leaving MLMs." I met Roberta via Zoom, first at a multilevel marketing (MLM) conference, and then through an email exchange. She, like many women drawn into MLMs, simply wanted to do right by her family. She didn't realize that she was going to get sucked into the LuLaRoe vortex that utterly overwhelmed her life. At one point, she even considered converting to Mormonism because she thought it would give her a leg up in the company. In an email she told me, "I was NOT raised in a religious home, and often felt that pressure in MLM and even VERY BRIEFLY considered possibly joining the LDS community because of LuLaRoe. I've never told anyone that before! It was about a month's worth of hemming and hawing back and forth, but ultimately I decided against it because it started to feel very culty."

Since leaving the company, she has become one of the most outspoken leaders in the anti-MLM movement. I talk a lot more about the rise and impact of that movement in the next chapter. Here, I dig into how people are lured into MLMs and how marketing, digital technologies, religion, and toxic positivity work together in perpetuating these scams.

GETTING SUCKED INTO AN MLM

No one who joins an MLM believes he or she is joining a nefarious company any more than someone joining a cult believes he or she is joining a cult. Scarily, the onboarding process is strikingly similar.

Imagine you are at home, scrolling through your socials. You've been laid off, you've recently gotten divorced, or you've had a baby and can no longer leave the house to go to work. Someone—your long-lost high school friend, say—approaches you claiming there's a way for you to feel better about yourself. You can make money from the comfort of your home, all while making friends and being part of a community. Your friend praises your social media skills, saying he or she has been following you for a while and loves your content. Your friend *knows* you have what it takes!

Or you are at church and someone invites you over to try some essential oils or have a hair-washing party. I specifically mention church, because the phenomenal growth of MLMs is disproportionately led by Christian women, and the connection between MLMs and the Mormon church has been well documented.[1] In the United States, MLMs are more numerous in the South and the Midwest, where Christianity exerts a larger social presence. Economist Stacie Bosley explains that local churches engender "a strong expectation of reciprocity and willingness to support one another, whatever those endeavors might be."[2] In marketing, we call that a virtuous circle, where one action leads to a positive outcome that reinforces a continuous loop of success. So, for example, Nike invests in top athletes to promote its products, leading to increased consumer loyalty and increased sales, which gives the company more funds to continue to invest in athletes and other influencers. Religious communities are by definition meant to be virtuous circles, and MLMs have piggybacked on this "strategy." Numerous MLMs having been started by Christians or with Christian values embedded in them, including Mary Kay, Young Living, Pampered Chef, and of course LuLaRoe.

COVID was a boon for MLMs, fitness, and faith. The pandemic led to a mass shutdown of local gyms (and many churches) at the same time that women were forced to leave the workplace. MLMs saw exponential growth, including Beachbody, which added more than 140,000 new coaches and half a million subscribers during the first three months of the pandemic lockdown.[3] As scholars Kai Prins and Mariah Wellman explain, the company creates what they call "muscular postfeminist evangelism" that provides "a convenient network and self-contained program where one can go to encounter the Divine through their upline and build their flock through their downline."[4] The virtuous circle does double duty—it creates fitness missionaries while spreading the word of God. Through a case study of Beachbody, these scholars encapsulate the tensions that exist in MLMs for so many women: the ability to create a "fitness ministry" (or to sell cosmetics or supplements) and become healthier mothers and wives allows them to push past the shame of their own bodies as well as their shame related to wanting to be an entrepreneur.

The connection between MLMs and religion permeates the industry in the ethos of the prosperity gospel. If you have ever watched Joel Osteen or T. D. Jakes or Joyce Meyer, you have seen the prosperity gospel in action.

The prosperity gospel—also known as the health and wealth gospel, "name it and claim it," and a whole lot of others—preaches abundance in all things. This is very different from preachers of old who bellowed about fire and brimstone. Today, negativity doesn't cut it. People don't want to hear that they are going to hell. They want to hear that their lives will be happier, more prosperous, more fulfilling.

Within this context, if you bow to the will of God or the market (tithing the church, paying for your monthly MLM inventory), then you will receive all the riches of the world. Within MLMs, the most faithful (seemingly) are those at the top of the pyramid. Those vying for prosperity are encouraged to demonstrate their faith by purchasing inventory upfront, an act of "fake it till you make it."

The prosperity gospel morphs into toxic positivity more broadly. Toxic positivity posits that one should maintain a positive attitude and express positive emotions to the exclusion of how one really feels, particularly when life is not going well. We see this play out online with the endless "Hey Huns" and #BossBabes, which are meant to present a positive front and a light, unaggressive mood. We see it in the admonitions to "just keep going" and "have you done your I am's?" Or in even more religious self-talk like, "I believe if you serve more, you sell more."

A whole happiness industry now exists, and not just for MLMs. Mindfulness and yoga classes are offered on the job to make you calmer, sure, but also to make you more productive.[5] As people turn away from traditional religion and spend more time at work, they increasingly find faith and community in the workplace, as Carolyn Chen discovered in her case study of the tech industry in her book *Work, Pray, Code*. The founders of SoulCycle created a company called Peoplehood (www.peoplehood.com), in which people can pay to connect with one another in order to increase their happiness. They are not the only ones who have turned relationships into a space for capitalism. Soul Chicks (www.soulchicks.com) offers coaching and retreats for women, and Nearness (www.nearness.coop) matches groups of five or six people for ten weeks of discussion based on psychology and spirituality, leading to personal connections.

To fuel positivity and to keep people selling, MLMs provide training, or in today's parlance, "coaching." These teachings are more about wishful thinking than anything having to do with sales and marketing. Amway, for example, has Worldwide Group (wwghq.com), which according to its website is "an accredited and approved provider for Amway Training and Education." What isn't explained is who provides the accreditation or, for that matter, that Worldwide Group only works with Amway. Page after page of the website talks about "values" and "impact" and "vision" and building good habits.

Other MLMs use in-person trainings led by company founders. We saw that with Holiday Magic and William Penn Patrick. A more recent example is Nick Sarnicola, the cofounder of ViSalus, a fitness MLM. Nick has the swagger of a bro as he walks on the stage. He is young and fit, wearing tight jeans, a casual shirt, and an unstructured blazer. He embodies Tony Robbins in a much smaller package; he is charismatic and yet seemingly approachable. Here is some of what he teaches in his master MLM recruiting training:

> Let me tell you about a great MLM lie. Act "as if." Act as if, act as if you're that; act as if you're this. . . . It's a lie. "Act as if" is a lie, right? That's called acting. Right? . . . No. Tell the truth. Act "as are" . . . "So Nick, you want me to run around and tell everyone I'm broke?" No, that's not what I'm saying. "So Nick, you want me to run around telling everybody, 'Hey, you should join me because my car is gonna be repossessed.'" No, that's not what I'm saying. I'm saying I want you to act as you are going to be.[6]

Nick follows this up with call-and-response from the audience. "Are you going to be a champion?" Yes! "Are you going to be a winner?" Yes! Of course, no one is saying that he is talking out both sides of his mouth. And no one will doubt what he says, because he has science to back this up.

> These are the components of influence, influences why somebody does or does not listen to you. . . . Fifty-five percent is your physiology, your body language, your conviction, which if you haven't put this together yet, is 100 percent tied to your belief. . . . Here's the second thing, 30 percent is your voice qualities. . . . Meaning 85 percent of why some-

body says yes or no has nothing to do with what you say and everything to do with who you are and how you say it. . . . And then when you say the words that you've been taught throughout this weekend with these other two things, it's game over. It's game over, because they go: check mark, check mark, check mark, all three add up. This, ladies and gentlemen, is the science of influence.

This isn't the science of influence. It is the science of nonverbal communication, known as the 55-38-7 rule. This theory holds that the majority of our communication is not transmitted through words alone. In that, he is correct. However, in this context, he uses this theory as a scientific framework that hangs the blame on salespeople when they don't close the deal. Making a sale has nothing to do with the product, price point, or market saturation; it has to do with you slouching while you were making the sales call.

Nick is an expert salesman. He turned ViSalus into a multimillion-dollar company. Today, however, the company is holding on by a thread. In 2019, a class action suit, which included eight hundred thousand people and was spearheaded by a former distributor, led to a $925 million judgment against the company for making fraudulent robocalls. This would have ended the company if an appellate court hadn't stayed the monetary damages (this is still working its way through the courts) and the company hadn't hitched itself to Pruvit, a dietary MLM. The full nature of that relationship is unclear, but for now they work as separate entities.[7]

If the company does not provide its own coach, the people with whom I spoke said that their uplines recommended watching videos by big-name motivational speakers, like Ed Mylett, on YouTube. If you are at the top of the pyramid, you get top-of-the-line coaching from the likes of Tony Robbins, who might even headline the annual convention.

Positivity in service of the market is all about ensnaring women, who are the primary target for MLMs. They make up 75 percent of MLM participants, and among female-targeted companies that sell beauty products or jewelry, that number can go up to 95 percent.[8] They recruit women using fake feminism—claiming they support women, when they are doing just the opposite. MLMs know that they are being obtuse because they never call these women "salespeople." They are "consultants," "stylists," "wellness advocates," or "coaches." They are not enabling women to be entrepreneurs; they are turning them into desperate housewives selling the latest snake oil. Having been indoctrinated into positive thinking, many women join one MLM after another, believing their lack of sales results from their lack of skill and not the MLM. And, just like cults, few are immune.

Meet Angelique, a woman with large hair, large glasses, and a large laugh. She's not someone you would think would join an MLM. Angelique is no pushover, to put it mildly. She has a big personality and uses phrases like "Lord have mercy on my soul!" and "that's not my jam." She had worked for several years in the retail cosmetic space and her personal mission has always been to make women feel good about themselves. Angelique was recruited when someone she had known her entire life messaged her. She thought, "This isn't a scam because so-and-so is doing it. They would never do something that was like a scam." But she was wrong. This is how she explained her introduction to hair and skincare company, Monat. "There's four pillars that they say, like, [to use] to talk to people . . . to hit their spot. So number one, you want to talk about how they can make money. You know, make money from home . . . okay, well, girl you can go on trips; there's trips you can go to the Bahamas . . . number three: girl, you can get a car like there you can get a Cadillac . . . and she's like 'okay, girl, you can make friends.' That was my button, the making friends thing . . . that's what made me say yes."[9]

In sales, this is known as finding the prospect's pain point. Chat the person up, discover the place where they are most emotionally defenseless, and push on that issue . . . hard. It's used at varying degrees of insistence, but at its worst it is incredibly skeevy and manipulative. For-profit colleges, like Trump University or Corinthian Colleges, which no longer exist, were notorious for using this hardcore practice. "You want an education to be a role model for your kids, right?" or "Don't you want to make more money?" "Want to be your own boss?" It's also rampant in the online space. Influencers selling online courses use this method with come-ons like: "Create an online course and you can quit your day job," or "You can write a book in thirty days!" Yeah, no you can't.

Another tactic is the long grooming process that takes place. Often this happens online, where an upline trolls for new recruits on social media. Over time the upline and recruits begin to interact, the upline often using flattery and then praising the recruits' social skills. Or the upline might have thrown enough incentives that the prospect finally cries uncle and decides, "what the heck!"

That's what happened with a former MLMer who is known online as the MLM Police.[10] Her real name is Courtney, and I was introduced to her by Bill Keep, the business school professor and MLM adversary you met in the previous chapter. When we talked via Zoom, she was casually sitting in her living room in what looked to be a beanbag chair. She was relaxed and dressed like most of us did during and post-pandemic lockdown—loose pants and sweatshirts. Hers was for a heavy metal band.

Courtney became part of Younique, a makeup company, through someone who had approached her via Facebook. She wasn't initially interested, and she was particularly turned off by anything that asked her to spend money to make money. The recruiter offered to pay for the starter kit, so Courtney thought, "why not?" Although she didn't get particularly immersed in the company, she was interested in its charitable foundation, which claimed to support women and children affected by sexual abuse. When she learned the foundation was a scam, it was like someone had thrown cold water in her face. The spell was broken, and she extricated herself from the group chats. However, she took it one step further, posting online about the company's deceitful practices. It wasn't long before she received a FedEx letter from Younique stating that it was going to sue her.[11]

Sadly, there are thousands of examples of people being drawn into MLMs. That's because the companies have their recruitment playbooks down to a science: Be positive and nonthreatening. Once the prospect signs on the dotted line, get them so excited that they focus on the product discounts they are going to get and the list of people they can sell to. Keep them distracted so they don't stop to check the company's income disclosure statements or research how much time, effort, and money it will take to make it work. All of this—from recruiting to training to nonprofit foundations—is marketing.

MARKETING MLMS IS ALL ABOUT DECEPTION

Marketing, specifically deceptive marketing, is what pulls anyone into an MLM (or a cult). When most people think of marketing, they think of an ad they've seen on TikTok or a sale sign in a store window. Marketing is much more than that. If you've taken a basic marketing course you know about the four Ps—product, price, place, and promotion. What are you selling and how do you brand it? What do you charge for it? Where do you distribute your product? And how do you promote it to prospective customers?

For MLMs, this is not so straightforward. First, the products—the potions and notions—are not the product. The product is the lifestyle. Since the physical products are superfluous, price and distribution are secondary. Promotion is extremely important in this category, and it happens at multiple levels. First, it occurs at the distributor level—the "Hey, Huns" and direct messages on social media and connections made on dating apps and apps like Bumble BFF, which ban MLMs on the app but can't control what happens in conversations offline.[12] Remember, these are independent contractors, so whatever they do is kept arm's length from the company. This is to the benefit of the MLM: (1) marketing costs are foisted onto someone else, and (2) it allows the company to have plausible deniability. Second, at the corporate level, marketing isn't as extensive as you would expect from large companies. MLMs rely extensively on social media and the coveted annual conference to push their message to distributors who will in turn perform marketing's heavy lifting.

At both levels, promoting the upscale, carefree lifestyle is paramount. That's why they use words like "freedom"—freedom from money troubles, the opportunity to have more free time, and the freedom to be your own boss. One company called Damsel in Defense sells stun guns and pepper spray using language on social media like "Our independent Damsel Pros are not only arming women and experiencing financial freedom, but also offering empowerment." Or there's popular Instagram influencer the_karen_louise, wearing a blue tank top and reflective aviator sunglasses, claiming that she works from "magical Bali." Her Instagram post goes on to say, "I had always dreamed of working online but had no idea where to start. A friend approached me about working online and creating a freedom lifestyle for ourselves." This unrealistic, glorified lifestyle is being pitched to people—usually poor, usually disadvantaged, usually female—who believe, or want to believe, that they can make oodles of extra cash in their free time.

The myth that endless riches are open to anyone permeates society. Oprah is a rags-to-riches story. *Shark Tank* is about everyday Marys and Joes hoping to hit it rich. Amazon.com is flooded with book titles like *Think and Grow Rich* and *Rich Dad, Poor Dad*. Online influencers depicting a glamorous lifestyle (although most can barely make ends meet) and life coaches claiming to be able to help you to achieve your full potential sprout like daffodils at Easter. These stories and TV shows and books perpetuate the American Dream and the notion that we live in a meritocracy. Tapping into these aspirations is why MLM salespeople (and scam artists generally) can be so successful: They piggyback on widely held, fundamental beliefs.

So when your Aunt Betty or your BFF tells you about a great new opportunity that can help you to make money, she isn't doing it to mislead you. She's doing it because she believes it.

Social media plays an important role in facilitating this deception. Yes, because of its simplicity and the convenience, but more importantly, because of personal connections. During the last few decades, we have been trained to use our relationships to service the marketplace. We read, post, share, and "like" content without giving it a second thought. That content gets shared and liked by other people, all to the benefit of marketing companies and the social media platforms. Unwittingly, *we* promote brands and influencers, *we* endorse a product or a post, and because we are the purveyor of the content, our friends and family more readily watch and share it. As content creator, content promoter, or both, our very beings have become fodder for the market and with it our relationships. Our connections—personal and not so personal—have become commodities, no different than selling soft drinks or shoes.

Day by day, this shifts our perceptions as we reframe our relationships as opportunities for market interactions. Turning personal interactions into tools for capitalism is not great in general, but it's worse for those involved in an MLM. According to the Talented Ladies Club website, which provides career advice for women, "one of the biggest complaints we've heard about MLMs is that once someone joins one, they see every social interaction as an opportunity to make their sales, or add to their downline."[13] And, of course, this doesn't bode well for those relationships when the person leaves the MLM. That person has lost not just money, time, and hope, but friendships and family.

The speed of social media also works to facilitate marketing deception, because we have little time to think. The line from awareness of a product to purchase is much faster now than it ever has been. This has to do with a framework known as the marketing funnel, the process by which marketers move someone from potential customer to loyal user. The top of the funnel is wide and draws in anyone who might be interested in the product being sold. At this step, marketers create awareness for the product through promotion and word of mouth, like when people approach a prospect online. When the prospect starts to consider the product, the marketing becomes more intense—more emails, more texts, more imploring to join group chats, and so on. The hope is that through all of this, the person will convert (they really use that term) to a purchaser, then become a loyal user, and ultimately an advocate for the product. Today, advocates are often called marketing evangelists.

Before the internet, this process took time. Say you were looking for a new pair of hiking boots. You might see a commercial for Timberline or an ad for Merrell in a magazine. Maybe you asked friends what boots they like. Then you'd go to REI and try a few pairs on, chat with the salesperson, and ask his or her opinion. You might stand in the store staring at the wall of shoes and boots and decide you can't afford to spend the money right now. In short, there was time and space to ponder. Online, the funnel is collapsed. There is no time between awareness and purchase. Without time to think, you are more inclined to click the "buy" button. Daniel Kahneman's bestselling *Thinking Fast and Slow* encapsulates how this works psychologically. Fast thinking is about emotion; slow thinking is about being deliberate and logical. We are more likely to make errors of judgment with fast thinking. Social media thrives on fast, emotional, error-prone thinking.

Social media is the tip of the iceberg. Behind the independent consultants is a marketing machine that shows you what they want you to see and hides the ugly underbelly. This starts with an organization we met in the previous chapter, the Direct Selling Association.

DIRECT SELLING ASSOCIATION

The Directing Selling Association promotes direct selling as being as time-honored as apple pie. In some ways, it is. Direct selling, or one-on-one marketing, has a long tradition. Even when people learned about products from commercials on TV, advertisers understood they were talking to a group of people who, they hoped, would try the product, love it, and then tell their friends to go out and buy it. This is word-of-mouth marketing, and it is still recognized as *the* most effective way to sell. Online it works the same way. Think of your favorite influencer or the last time your best friend forwarded a post to you about the best new foundation she saw on TikTok. It's all the same idea. In most cases, MLM distributors aren't effective as authentic word-of-mouth promoters; unless and until they have created a platform, they are doomed to fail, because direct selling is based on relationships established over time, which have engendered trust and credibility.

When I teach about direct selling, I use the example of pharmaceutical marketers selling directly to physicians. Maybe you've been in a doctor's office and seen a well-dressed woman stroll in pulling a heavy rolling case behind her. She discreetly goes to the desk and asks to see the doctor, and the receptionist invariably tells her she needs to wait. Once allowed through the door, she introduces the doctor to the latest drugs, making sure to leave a cache of samples behind that can be given to patients. Whatever your thoughts about selling drugs in this way, it is one of the few places where one-on-one selling makes sense. It is a specialized product requiring expertise on the part of the salesperson who can answer complex questions on the spot.

Direct selling is not to be confused with direct-to-consumer (DTC) products, a category that expanded exponentially during the pandemic. DTC brands include Dollar Shave Club, Billie (a body positive personal care brand for women), and sustainable shoe company Allbirds. These brands eliminate the middleman, period—no retail, no independent contractors. Since sales occur online, promotion relies heavily on digital marketing and cultivating an online community.

To summarize, then, there is direct to consumer, which is aboveboard, and there is direct selling, which is sort-of, sometimes legit. To complicate things just a bit more, direct selling goes by several aliases, including network marketing, social selling, and multilevel marketing.

This confusion is purposeful. Direct selling sounds innocuous. The Direct Selling Association (DSA) presents itself as a watchdog of the industry, but as we saw in the last chapter, they do little to protect independent contractors or consumers. Working under the assumption that most people don't understand that and won't do the research, MLMs readily put the DSA seal on their websites as if it was the *Good Housekeeping* Seal of Approval.

The DSA further hides its deception in the fine print of its promotional materials. At the top of a DSA "fact sheet" is a infographic showing a map of the United States with the number "7.3 million" in bold letters followed by an asterisk. At the bottom, in teeny, tiny "rat type" it says, "16.2 million people in the United States had signed independent contractor sales agreements with direct selling companies in 2021. Of these 16.2 million, 7.3 million were direct sellers who worked to build businesses and 8.9 million were discount buyers who purchased products for their own use but chose not to build a business."[14] Meaning that less than half of the people who signed up to become independent contractors sold anything. This is very different from an AARP survey that used a representative sample of Americans who were participating or had participated in multilevel marketing programs; more than 90 percent expected to make some money from their efforts.[15] It also differs from recent research that found that 75.7 percent of 601 participants "joined with intent to make money in MLM" as their primary or secondary reason for joining.

This same research also found that 26 percent participated for less than six months, 48 percent for less than a year, and 70 percent less than two years. Only a small minority said they would join the MLM knowing what they know now. Although they felt misled by how much time it took, that was not the only reason. Other reasons include that it felt awkward to pitch friends and relatives (39%), that they did not make as much money as they expected (36%), that they did not like selling all the time (35%), and

29 percent said "that the commission structure mostly benefitted those at the top."[16] Tellingly, 65.2 percent were recruited by a friend, relative, or coworker—just like cults.

IS [FILL IN THE BLANK] COMPANY AN MLM?

One of the reasons why it is so easy to get caught up in MLMs is because there are just so damn many of them—literally thousands of them. MLMs further the confusion by changing their names or rebranding their companies. Beachbody became Bodi, for example. And, new companies pop up all the time.

Hugh & Grace is a newer company that has attracted the attention of MLM watchdogs. By now you will recognize the MLM clues by what it says on its website: "The Hugh & Grace Advocate community is a fun, caring circle of brand advocates on a mission to transform lives by leading a global wellness movement." Rachel Zoe appears on the site as a promoter and an investor (see textbox). The product is embedded with its impact goal: reducing chemical exposure to improve health, all while providing an opportunity to live cleaner and start your home business selling skincare products with a $180 price point!

Other more established companies are more adept at hiding their multilevel status. Take Rodin + Fields. This beauty company was tapped by Anastasia of Beverly Hills (ABH)—a well-known and reputable company that's regularly promoted on *RuPaul's Drag Race*—for a promotional tie-in. The company was flooded with social media posts from consumers asking why Anastasia would muddy its name by working with an MLM: "Time to dump your Brow-wiz and Dip Brow for supporting pyramid schemes" and "if it's true that anastasia beverly hills is collabing with rodan and fields, i'm done using ABH forever. #pyramidscheme"

According to BuzzFeed, the company did not know that Rodin + Fields was an MLM. They put out a statement saying, "We have not previously participated in MLM marketing. . . . We do not have any plans to do so in the future." Rodin + Fields was forced to pull the offering, saying that it was due to "misconceptions on the business model."[17]

If savvy marketing companies like ABH can be fooled, it is not surprising that regular folks can be hoodwinked. Daily, you can see people asking if one company or another is an MLM. The growing number of anti-MLM sites and the anti-MLM Reddit forum are helpful sources in sussing these companies out.[18]

CELEBRITIES SELLING MLMS

Companies use celebrities to promote their products because of borrowed interest. Borrowed interest is simply the tactic of connecting your brand with a celebrity in order to draw more attention to your product. Think here of Snoop Dogg and Martha Stewart teaming up with Sketchers for a Super Bowl ad.

Today, celebrities are not just famous, they are influencers. As that term suggests, they persuade those who follow them.

Here are a few famous names that have been connected to MLMs.

Tyra Banks created her own MLM called Tyra Beauty in 2015. The company was pitched as a Mary Kay for millennials and included a product line that made sense for the former model and TV host of *America's Next Top Model*. However, the company failed miserably and was shuttered in 2017.[19]

Former president Donald Trump was involved in two MLMs. ACN, a video phone company, paid him $8.7 million to promote this MLM through DVDs and on his popular TV show, *The Apprentice*. The company had been deemed a pyramid scheme internationally, and the technology was considered obsolete by the time it was hawked on the reality TV series. Mr. Trump also lent his name to an MLM that sold vitamins, "The Trump Network," which ultimately declared bankruptcy.[20]

Other celebrity endorsers include Madeleine Albright (Herbalife), Warren Buffett (Pampered Chef), Dr. Mehmet Oz (Vemma),[21] Alexa Vega (Young Living), and Kayla Caputo (Monat).

The danger for consumers is twofold. First, we trust celebrities, particularly ones we have come to "know" online. We feel like they are our friends because we hold them in our hand almost daily. Second, we trust their success. If these ultra-successful people believe in this product, it must be good.

These endorsements are not usually presented in the form of a commercial, but rather as some type of product placement, paid interview, or conference speaker (à la Tony Robbins with Monat). Don't be fooled. This is paid propaganda with serious consequences. We see just how serious in the following chapters about influencers.

CORPORATE MARKETING

Corporate marketing at MLMs focuses on two main components: social media and the annual sales meeting. The sales meeting is an interesting duck because it is both a place to promote the new annual product line and a means to make money from the independent contractors. As a marketer, I've been to a lot of sales meetings in my day, and I never had to pay to attend. Really, that they have to pay is sincerely odd.

MLM corporate sites contain the requisite social media icons, mostly Facebook, Instagram, Pinterest, Twitter, and some have TikTok. I was surprised that more weren't on that platform given its appeal to Gen Z, but I think that has to do with an affinity for and legacy with Instagram. I looked at bigger companies like Monat, Young Living, doTERRA, and Arbonne. On YouTube, the videos on the home pages are at least two years old, with some as much as five years, except for videos connected to the annual meeting. Newer content appears deeper on their channel video pages, but even that is not as robust as you'd expect. Companies on Pinterest have lots of pins, but little to no engagement, which is the whole point of social media.[22] On TikTok, Monat posts get six hundred or seven hundred views. For reference, a mediocre post gets two hundred views. Here, too, engagement is limited. The company has seventeen thousand followers and posts get one or two comments and a couple dozen likes. What that says is that a lot of people have signed on to follow the company, but most couldn't care less about the content.

Hands down, Instagram is the social media of choice for these companies. By keeping the content focused on a single platform, consultants can boost each other's content (and they do) as well as leverage user-generated content. Just like having a family or friend share your content, the best way to sell a product is to have your customers say they love it. It gives the salesperson instant credibility. Instagram is particularly good for this, because most people aren't comfortable creating videos, which is necessary for TikTok. It's also a lot easier to ask people to follow you or to boost your content in text than it is on camera. That said, the most successful salespeople use product demos and tutorials to promote their products, particularly makeup and haircare (see @thatcurlygirlmonica). These videos help position the salespeople as experts while giving their followers useful information. Other content that is regularly promoted are contests and giveaways (which motivate followers to create their own content showing what they won), business success stories ("six months ago, I was in debt but Monat changed my life!"), and, of course, the lifestyle. There are varying levels of production value on these posts but the people who are successful spend some serious cash to create their content. Finally, as they say in the business, "social media is about being social." The most successful share stories about their lives (not just their lifestyles) and engage regularly with their followers (see @kay_caputo).

I asked corporate marketers what kind of assistance they provide to their independent contractors. They explained that the large corporations provide fact sheets containing what you can and cannot say, such as: What are the ingredients? What do they do? How do you take it? How long does it last? Are there any contraindications? Companies also provide social "shareables," such as Instagram posts that say: "Want to learn about vitamin C? Ask me," or they provide short videos that can be shared. On the Younique page (@younique_corporate), you can see examples of this, such as professional product shots, contests, or videos of the convention bag and the goodies it contains. doTERRA (@doTerra) focuses on product shots, and Bodi (@bodi, formerly Beachbody) provides a breadth of content across fitness, nutrition, and mindset. But not all companies do this. Elomir reps were obviously given little to no guidance about what they could say. They made wild health claims about the company's dissolvable strip, which when put on your tongue was supposed to cure everything from ADHD to autism. These statements are not only patently false, but it is forbidden by law to say this.[23]

Traditionally, the whole point of social media was to get people to go to a website and buy your product. Today, you can buy a product directly from a post, but you may still want people to explore your entire product line. Driving people to your content has to do with paid, owned, and earned media. Paid media are things like advertising. You want to limit this as much as possible because free promotion is better. Owned media is your website and any social media pages you have. Like with advertising, you control the content. Unlike paid, you can produce as much promotion as you want to. Earned media includes any free press or publicity you might get: for example, when someone shares your content or tells people to go to your website. Given this, concentrating marketing efforts on a single platform makes sense. Also having an "army" of workers to drive your content and boost visibility is important for this work. The Mormon church was famous for this during the early days of the internet. It could get church members to drive traffic by having thousands of people visit a site simultaneously or it created multiple sites and connected them to one another, driving their content to the top of the Google search. They are so good at this that if you type "church" into Google, the Church of Jesus Christ of Latter-day Saints (aka Mormons) is second only to the Encyclopedia Britannica entry for church. To put this into context, there are about 17 million Mormons in the world versus 2.6 billion Catholics. Corporations turned to the Mormons to learn their strategies. Although companies could find out about the church's search engine optimization (SEO), most companies could not replicate the mass requests to visit sites or create them.[24] But MLMs can.

A quick note about the websites: overall, they are bare-bones, functional, and formulaic, like a good SquareSpace site. Images of young women who look to be in their late teens and early twenties were plentiful. They were always smiling, definitively multicultural, and generic enough for stock photography. Below this is several rows of product and a final panel with corporate information.

What I found fascinating was that almost every company aligned with social or charitable causes. I shouldn't have been surprised because this has become de rigueur when marketing to millennials and Gen Z. As mentioned in chapter 2, these generational cohorts expect companies to tie brands to causes, and it has been effective. The connections between company and cause, though, were often dubious—what is known in the marketing industry as "purpose washing."[25] Courtney was drawn to Younique's connection to sexual abuse victims/survivors. There's not an obvious connection between makeup and abuse, until one discovers that one of the founders is a survivor. Herbalife also created its own charity called Nutrition for Zero Hunger, which donates Herbalife product to communities around the world.[26] That hit me as being a way to offload a nutritionally questionable product rather than feeding the needy. The oddest one was Tupperware. This maker of indestructible plastic products had a sustainability initiative with the National Park Foundation from 2020 to 2022, which appeared prominently on the website under "do good." I don't know if this is related to coming close to bankruptcy, but the company doesn't seem to be doing good anymore.[27]

ANNUAL CONFERENCE

Talk to those who have been in MLMs, and they will tell you about the annual conference and how they had to pay their own way. Missing this event is steeped in fear of missing out, suggesting that those who don't attend will miss the "tips and tricks" that will help them to build business success. Thousands of women crowd into large convention centers. There's pyrotechnics and top-of-the-line entertainment. Speaker after speaker is met with thunderous applause, with the founder getting the loudest of all. As soon as one convention wraps, promotion for the following year's convention starts.

Videos abound touting the value of attending the annual conference. Smiling women posing in groups and the swag bags that are handed out are standard images, which are backed by upbeat music. Corporate leaders, almost exclusively men, work to ramp up the troops. This exchange is from a Monat video:

> Man 1: As the next three days unfold the forces of nature in your business, you will see that it's your energy that powers every phase of growth in your business.

> Man 2: Today is the day that your success shows up. It's showing up today but it's only showing up today because you stored it up yesterday.

> Man 3: At Monat, we're always striving to get better in every area of our business.

> Man 4: Selling is not an act; selling is a relationship. You can make a living pursuing transactions but you can make a fortune pursuing relationships.[28]

Rachel Monroe, a reporter for the *New Yorker*, wrote about essential oils and MLMs, focusing on Young Living. This is what she said about attending the annual convention. "One thing that was really striking to me was that what was for sale was not just essential oils, but this whole idea of an essential oil culture and essential oil lifestyle. The way women describe themselves was not just 'I'm a person who sells oils' but 'I am an oil person.'"[29] The idea of selling the lifestyle is embedded in the marketing, as is the stress on relationships. Remember, engendering relationships is what makes it hard to leave a company or a cult.

Researching MLM corporate marketers, I came across the LinkedIn page of Brian Gill, the chief marketing officer for Younique. He now works for another MLM called 4Life Research, which sells "nutritional" products. Brian's page included a video of his presentation from Younique's 2015 convention.[30] When I viewed it, I was surprised he included it. His presentation is, for the lack of a better term, cringeworthy. He uses self-deprecating language, but everything about him suggests that he thinks very highly of himself. There is overly effusive enthusiasm: "[Melody] is so cool. She is so cool that she's my boss. How cool is that?" He talks about doing his "I am" statements and asks if anyone else has. Watching him, you just know he hasn't done one in his life. He calls out looking for those with "Black" status: "I want to feel your energy."

Plenty of this is the rah-rah content you'd expect at an annual sales meeting. He went on to talk about how the company works "to provide you with the tools that you need to be successful in your business." That's all fine. It was the condescension, the fake enthusiasm, and the fake self-deprecation that was irksome. Let me give you an example.

Brian introduces the new catalog with a sizzle reel showing a slew of models/"presenters" from the sales force. He then goes on to describe them one by one, using language that would make any self-respecting woman—never mind feminist—nauseous. "Krystal from Tennessee . . . has a southern accent. Right? It's awesome. She loves to wear colorful head-bands and bright dresses." "Tiffany was shy at first and when she became comfortable on set, she was so fun to work with. . . . And she is a beauti-ful person inside and out." "Melissa is very animated when she talks. She is very genuine, very transparent about who she is. She rocks her business on social media, but she values people over making money and business." "Jessica . . . look at those eyes. They're so big. She's like a Disney princess. Yeah, she's beautiful. She's humble and she loves the Younique mission."

This video said the quiet part out loud: These companies think women are objects. Pretty objects or objects for psychological, emotional, and financial abuse, but objects nonetheless.

WHAT ARE MLMS HIDING?

Marketers are always drawing attention to the shiny thing in one hand so you won't look at the terrible things in the other. Coke creates a recyclable bottle but is remiss about explaining that less than 10 percent of bottles ever get recycled. Ivy League colleges pretend that students who are smart enough—no matter how much money they have—have an equal shot of being admitted. And diets tell you that you can lose weight . . . and keep it off!

MLMs hide a laundry list of things they don't want you to know. They don't want you to know that you won't really make any money unless you are already an enthusiastic salesperson. They don't want you to know that your house will be filled to the brim with inventory you will never be able to sell. They don't want you to know that it is not an easy or inexpensive way to make a living.

Instead, what they show you are the very few people who do make money. These MLM faithful become the faces of these companies, speaking at annual conferences and claiming coveted rewards, like the famous Mary Kay pink Cadillac.

But those cars come with strings attached. In the Netflix series *How to Get Rich*, financial adviser Ramit Sethi gives a little glimpse into the specifics of MLMs when he works with a woman who is in an MLM. At one point, she had almost five hundred people in her downline and was making $12,000 a month. She admits that at most she made $2,000 from her own sales, and the rest was from sales from her downline. At the time of the taping, her downline had dropped to 150 people, and her compensation along with it. At the height of her MLM career, she qualified for the car. But the car wasn't a gift; it was a lease that she would be responsible for. As long as she maintained her rank, the MLM would send her a check for $500 a month—which didn't even cover the $660 per month leasing cost. As Ramit so smartly notes, "It's not a gift. It's a trap." Instead of golden handcuffs, what you get is a golden Mercedes.

Even if you do become successful, you never stop selling. If your downline drops from 500 to 150, you have work to do! Remember, earlier I noted that 70 percent of people drop out after two years. According to John M. Taylor, in his ebook *The Case (for and) against Multi-Level Marketing*, that number increases to 90 percent after five years. We don't hear about these people because documentaries focus on extreme stories for dramatic effect. But add up all the millions of people who lost money in three months or six months and you have a sea of personal and financial scrum left in the wake of MLMs.

Top MLMers are a particular personality type—charismatic, exuberant, gregarious storytellers. They would be successful whether they were working for doTERRA or Donna Karan. But most people don't have that drive or inclination. They don't like cold calling, and public speaking scares them to death. That's why there is so much churn in the salesforce. MLM companies aren't stupid. They've seen the numbers and they are fully aware that most people don't have a chance in hell of being successful in an MLM. These people are doomed to fail and suffer the shame of losing money, alienating friends and family, and fear of retaliation from the MLM community that they have built their lives around.

When it hurts more to be in than it does to be out—it's time to get out.

6

HOW TO BECOME AN EX-MLMER

I'm embarrassed that I fell for this. It made me feel kind of stupid. I lost money. And then I also have numerous family and friends that are still using the products. I mean, how do you tell them you don't want to use them anymore when you've pulled them in?

—former Young Living consultant[1]

What draws people into multilevel marketing (MLM) is the marketing and the need—the often exceedingly desperate need—to make money. What keeps people caught in the emotional web of the MLM is the community, the missionary-like zeal, the humiliation of having so publicly promoted this lifestyle, and the shame of having abused personal relationships. Financial mechanisms, too, act like invisible handcuffs. Car leases require maintaining a significant sales quota or the risk of being saddled with $600 a month payments; other "reward" strategies work like the proverbial brass ring: if you just reach a little bit further. . . .

The parallel to cults is striking. Draw people in when they are vulnerable. Check. Love bombing. Check. Withhold information about the company's true mission. Check. Make it difficult for people to leave. Check. Charismatic leaders. Check.

But just like with cults, most people do leave. What pulls people out is a series of events, typically over an extended period of time. Bit by piece, they begin to see MLMs for what they are. They are not the yellow brick road to financial freedom. They are profit-driven companies that spout female empowerment while taking a battering ram to women's self-esteem and ethics. Hearing stories, and perhaps seeing yourself in those stories, is an important tool that helps enable people to leave high-control groups. This

85

is why the anti-MLM movement is both important and impactful. The movement replicates the strategy of #MeToo: when thousands of people tell thousands of stories about how they were abused, the abuse becomes harder and harder to ignore. I share a few stories here about MLM survivors and provide resources where you can find other MLM escape stories as well as resources for leaving a high-control group and how to know if you are in an MLM. At the end of the chapter, I explain why I believe MLMs may be facing their demise, giving us hope that fewer people will be lured into the MLM web in the first place.

We know that most people—70 percent, at least—don't stay in an MLM past two years. That was Taylor's experience. She was at a point in her life where she felt stuck. She was twenty-four, working more than sixty hours a week at a car rental office, and living with her mother after having previously lived on her own. Taylor admitted that she was in a mentally vulnerable state. "My mental health was starting to suffer from not having an adequate work/life balance, and I was only able to find solace in posting on social media." That's when she was approached with an "opportunity" to join Monat.

She found there were products she liked and pitching those items was easy. She used apps like Canva to create static content, she posted "get ready with me" videos on Instagram, and she virtually reached out to those she thought would be a fit with the company.

But then there was the dark side; "the team calls were the worst." Her upline was overly aggressive and combative, saying things like "either you are with us or against us," or "if you are not doing everything we say, you are wasting our time." She also felt like she was left to sink or swim, provided with little in the way of guidance either from her upline or others in her group. "There were those girls that try to pretend like they are there for you and want you to succeed, but all they've really done is spam your Facebook with groups to join and videos to watch." Of course, if she complained to a teammate about not getting enough guidance, she would be texted immediately by her upline blaming her for not doing enough. It was the perfect formula for being set up to fail. And this was all happening while Taylor was still working twelve- to thirteen-hour days at her job, waking up at 5:00 a.m. to avoid traffic so she could open the car rental office on time.

After two years, she'd had enough. She stayed that long only because she connected with a number of the other women, whom she called "good people." But she also realized they were good people caught in a bad system she could no longer be a part of. The berating and the backstabbing and the endless posting all started taking its toll. One day she decided she wanted out. She stopped answering the group chats. It was just that simple.[2]

For those who become fully enmeshed over many years, however, getting out is not so straightforward. These women typically don't have outside jobs, or if they did, they left them as they became more successful. Not having a fallback source of income makes it harder to leave, especially if the woman "retired her husband"; that is, became the solo or primary breadwinner.

After viewing dozens of stories about women who left MLMs on YouTube and listening to an untold number of podcasts, I came to realize something that I don't think gets enough attention: People near the top of the pyramid are kept ignorant to what is happening to their downline. Not the top-top people—they know exactly what they are doing. It's the successful mid-top who have blinders on. I don't blame them for this. It is part of the design of the MLM, just as it is part of the design of a cult not to let members know what is really going on.

For many successful MLMers, once their eyes are opened to the truth, it becomes harder and harder to look away, harder and harder to deny. The reality creates cognitive dissonance, the psychological tension between what they have been doing (putting people into debt) and what they thought they were doing (helping to make women successful). When that tension reaches a crescendo, they are forced to change in order to bring their actions and beliefs back into alignment.

Let me say, too, that these women aren't stupid, any more than cult members are. They were recruited when they were vulnerable and were offered an opportunity to change, to have a better life.

Kelly Noelle was a serial MLMer and she was pretty good at it. She worked for Beach Body for more than three years, but over time she felt that the health and fitness sector wasn't for her, so she switched to Usborne Books & More (now Paper Pie). This book distributor sells toys and books for kids, catering to Christian homeschoolers. The evangelical aspect is not immediately evident on the website. It looks more like a Scholastic wannabe. But read the comments and you can see exactly who is being targeted.

Kelly created "Kelly's Reading Corner" on YouTube to promote her business. This video channel worked well for promoting Usborne because she could display stacks of books, talk about her favorites, and explain why certain texts appealed to different age groups. Being a mom helped her relate to her audience and their needs.

She was drawn to the business in 2018 when her son was nine months old. She liked that she could sell from personal experience, telling stories of reading various books with her child. Kelly also liked that the company was "family focused" and "family friendly," and she "felt like it had a better Compensation Plan and business structure."[3]

Two years later, however, her son was diagnosed with autism. Suddenly, she didn't have the same amount of time that she'd had in the past to devote to her business. That wasn't enough to stop her, though, because her MLM trainings had taught her otherwise: "You're an entrepreneur and you have to overcome obstacles and push through and find new ways." But not having enough time in a day was only part of the problem. Now, she could no longer recommend books based on personal experience because her son's autism resulted in focusing on a limited number of familiar books he would read over and over again. To compensate for the lack of having her own stories to tell, she bought books she knew her son would never read and watched hours of content from other consultants so she could have something to say about why kids loved the books she was trying to sell.

Kelly felt utterly overwhelmed. Who wouldn't be? She was caring for her son, trying to maintain a healthy relationship with her husband, churning out YouTube videos, watching other people's content for material, and trying to run a business. And then a funny thing happened. Anti-MLM content kept popping up on her YouTube recs. "I was watching a lot of that. . . . I think you can call it cognitive dissonance where you know I'm watching this content that's saying things against network marketing and I agree with it, but in the meantime I'm in an MLM and I'm making money and I just continue to try to work with integrity and change how I do things." That was the first chink in the MLM armor.

Still not ready to give up, Kelly enrolled in two trainings—one connected to MLMs and one that wasn't. The unrelated course was a digital marketing class. This class exposed her to tools and tricks she could have easily been using during the years she was building her business. She could not for the life of her understand why these basic skills were never part of what MLMs teach consultants. Didn't they want their consultants to be successful running their businesses? Kelly also signed up for membership in a direct sales academy that gave her access to a life coach. The coach claimed that all network marketers should be making six figures, which by this point only stressed Kelly out more. She soldiered on until she couldn't.

"I had spent six months working with this life coach and I had made so many changes to what I was doing, and I wasn't building income at all. It got to a point where I just needed to focus so much more on my home and my family. . . . I just was over it."[4]

Josie, aka Not the Good Girl on YouTube, was a one percenter. She did everything a good MLMer is supposed to. She was on the team calls, she worked her business 24/7, she read the self-help books, she took self-ies, she used the lingo ("sisterhood," "dream," "business opportunity"), and "when my upline said jump I asked how high."[5] That work paid off in retreats and trips and prizes and speaking opportunities. "I never missed a monthly sales quota for over five years. I built a team and had dinners and special retreats and photoshoots, and I believed I was the ultimate #GirlBoss and was going to help other women lead the way and build a bridge to financial freedom."

Josie had the "perfect" profile for recruitment by an MLM. She had been raised in the church but had left several years prior and missed the sense of community. Plus, she was divorced and in debt. One day, she saw a video of someone who was living the good life and thought that might be for her. The woman wasn't pushy, which she liked, and as soon as she joined this woman's group, she was loved bombed: "We're so happy you're here!" "You're going to do great!" Everyone was so nice. It was exactly what she had been missing since she left her church. She would come to find out, however, that kindness was conditional: As long as you are build-ing the team, you are one of us. As soon as you start to question, you are told not to.

Beyond the upscale lifestyle, what Josie said kept her in MLMs for so long was the framing; that is, the marketing. The companies frame their businesses as about helping people, not about selling products. You aren't selling lowly shampoo; you are working for a higher purpose! But that positioning was only part of it. Any sales shortfalls are framed as a problem with the consultant, never as having anything to do with the product or the price point. "Combine [the sense of working for a higher purpose] with the toxic positivity and you have the perfect formula for someone who will never question, not push back. You will come to assume that you are the one with the problem because you are being 'too negative,' when all the while they are telling you that you aren't good enough."

Josie worked in network marketing for six years. Her change of heart came when she "got to peek behind the curtain of the 1 percent in three different companies and I realized, 'wait, it's not the company. The system is designed to fail.'"

Her first eye-opener was at a retreat with her upline and a few others who were making a million dollars a year. Although Josie was excited to be there at this beautiful mansion with all these successful women, all they wanted to do was rest. They were exhausted! They spent their lives being told that they always had to do more, more, more, and no matter how fast they ran on that hamster wheel, they were still told, "you are never enough." None of these women were happy. Financial freedom and happiness? Yeah, not so much.

Josie thought that burnout must be related to that one company, so she switched to another. But she found that the problem persisted. The top 1 percent were so stressed out that they were being hospitalized. "I started to look around and think, 'Wait, why are we preaching this lifestyle that it's going to get better and better once you get up to this ring?' because obviously it doesn't. Obviously, it's just harder and harder and harder."

Josie worked at these companies because she truly thought she was helping other women. Her main MLM was Beachbody. She loved talking about health and fitness and believed she was improving people's lives. She wasn't. "I didn't realize that 99 percent of the people were losing money. I didn't realize that . . . MLMs . . . do not have the distributor's best interest at heart." Like Kelly, cognitive dissonance showed up when her ethics ran headlong into the reality that the industry is set up to take advantage of people while crushing their self-esteem. "I had to get out because I was tired of recruiting to fail. . . . I want to be clear that I don't believe the people in these companies are evil. I believe them to be victims. . . . It is no different than those indoctrinated into a cult."[6]

HOW TO GET HELP

I am not a therapist so I would never presume to tell someone how to leave a high-control group like an MLM. What I can do is provide resources that others have found helpful and forums to help deepen your understanding of MLMs and how they function.

For information about the risks of MLMs and to find out if a company is an MLM:

Behind MLM (behindmlm.com) covers information about lawsuits and MLMs being taken to court. The site doesn't specifically say who runs it, but I have been told it is an attorney.

Anti-MLM Coalition (mlmtruth.org) has an exhaustive list of current and defunct MLMs. The site also includes resources like documentaries, articles, and a list of YouTubers far longer than I can provide here.

Scam Risk (www.scamrisk.com) assesses scams broadly, including some MLMs.

AntiMLM subreddit (www.reddit.com/r/antiMLM/) is a forum where readers can learn about other people's experiences with MLMs and ask questions.

Resources for getting out of MLMs:

The antiMLM movement is large and growing. Podcasts, YouTubers, and Instagrammers provide invaluable information for people looking to leave an MLM or for those trying to help extricate a loved one. This list contains a few of the most popular creators I have been following.

Podcasts:

The Dream

The Deeper Pulse

YouTubers:

Life after MLM Podcast (www.youtube.com@RobertaBlevinsLAMLM/podcasts); there is additional information on podcast host Roberta Blevins's website (https://robertablevins.com/)

The Antibot (www.youtube.com/@theantibot)

The Recovering Hunbot (www.youtube.com/c/TheRecoveringHunbot)

Hannah Alonzo (www.youtube.com/c/hannahalonzo)

Erin Bies (www.youtube.com/c/ErinBies)

Instagrammers:

Antimlm Nicole (www.instagram.com/antimlmnicole/)

Anti-MLM Movement (www.instagram.com/antimlmmovement/)

MLM Lies is a private Facebook page with more than thirty-two thousand members who share (mis)information about these companies. Many of the posts include screenshots showing how consultants try to bamboozle people. Sadly, people also talk about their marriages unraveling because their partners have been swept up in an MLM.

Online Community:

#igotout (www.igotout.org) is a resource for those seeking to leave high-control groups. It focuses on cults broadly but contains information useful for those in MLMs. Importantly, the website is geared toward sharing stories about how people got out of such groups. Storytelling is a powerful tool in helping people to see that they are not alone and that they need not sit in their shame. The website also provides resources for those in immediate danger.

IS IT THE END OF MLMS?

Even better than becoming an ex-MLMer is living in a world where MLMs don't exist at all. That might be closer to reality than you think.

Based on a confluence of economic, regulatory, and social changes, I have reason to speculate that MLMs could disappear or at the very least be fundamentally restructured. First, although the gig economy was a boom to the industry, now the competition for labor is fierce, and other companies like Uber and Lyft provide better opportunities. Second, during the last few years, the Federal Trade Commission (FTC) has taken on MLMs in a way it had not in decades. Finally, the anti-MLM movement is having a considerable impact. The relentless anti-MLM social media content has been instrumental in creating awareness for those in (and out of) MLM companies, and endless articles in the mainstream media have given the movement legitimacy.

Economically, "gig work" has become the new norm as companies provide fewer opportunities to make a living from a single paycheck. There are Uber and Airbnb. There are freelance labor websites like Taskrabbit and Fivver, and there's the increasing availability of affiliate marketing programs, which allow people to passively make money through online sales. The best known of these is Amazon Affiliates. Here's how it works: you sign up with Amazon, the company gives you a link, and you put that link on your website and social media platforms. If a buyer purchases the product on Amazon.com through that distinct link, then you get a commission. Know, too, that affiliates are not limited to a single item. Many create a "store" of curated products based on their specialties. Recipe bloggers, for example, can link to the products needed to make a fall pumpkin spice apple cake; makeup influencers can recommend products for a variety of seasonal looks; moms recommend favorite books and toys; and so on.

Any product company can create an affiliate model and many MLMs now are. Just like Amazon's program, people add a link on their various web pages and receive commissions without the need to recruit a team. However, some companies—MLM or not—use a two-tier affiliate model. The affiliates earn commissions from their own links plus smaller commissions on sales from anyone they refer to the program. The difference between this and a pyramid is that you can have only one tier below you. That said, you can recruit multiple people to be your second tier. Some MLMs seem to be using this as a training system. Implementing a hybrid model, a new salesperson can start as an affiliate and then be upgraded to distributor as they recruit others to help sell the product.

MLMs know that affiliate marketing is the wave of the future, and "affiliate" has become the new industry buzzword. Some MLMs call themselves affiliate marketers whether they have that system in place or not. It is scammy, creates confusion, and, well, that's the point.

The other economic factor affecting the fortunes of MLMs is changed consumer habits due to the pandemic. E-commerce was well established before COVID, but after many months of lockdown, people got used to ordering from the convenience of their couches. That practice hasn't changed even after the restrictions were lifted.[7] Where this hit MLMs hard is in the vitamin and mineral category; Amazon is now the leading purveyor of vitamins and minerals by a large margin.[8] As a whole, this has led to declining sales in the industry.[9]

The sales decline also coincides with the FTC taking aggressive action against MLMs. Starting in 2014, the FTC brought a series of larger cases against MLMs for being pyramid schemes and for false income and product claims. Remember Bill Ackman and Herbalife? Although that hedge fund manager wasn't able to bring down Herbalife, his crusade led to an FTC investigation in 2014. The commission sued Herbalife for deceptive income claims and the company settled, agreeing to pay $200 million and to restructure its business model. The following year, the FTC brought a lawsuit against Vemma, a nutritional supplement and vitamin company known for targeting college students. The FTC suit claimed Vemma was an illegal pyramid scheme, and the company was ultimately shut down after paying a fine of $238 million. In a highly publicized case, the FTC sued supplement company Advocare for exaggerated income claims. Well-known athletes were hired as spokespeople who promised that Advocare would provide "financial freedom and [the ability to] eliminate the constraint of traditional employment" even though that wasn't true. Sports jargon permeated its marketing. New distributors, for example, were given "rookie bonuses" if they could bring in three new recruits who generated sales—an obvious and improper emphasis on recruiting over retail sales. In an appropriately sports-like fashion, an ESPN exposé put a scathing light on Advocare's deceptions.[10] By 2019, the company was required to restructure its business model and to hand $149 million over to the FTC.

The last major case the FTC brought during this time period was against Neora (formerly Nerium), a supplement and skincare company. The suit asserted that the company not only made inappropriate health and income claims, but also that it was a pyramid scheme. A federal judge found against the FTC in late 2023, however, saying it had not provided enough evidence for its claims. Most people were surprised by this decision because "in 30 of the last 32 cases that the FTC has brought against an MLM alleging it was a pyramid scheme, it has either won on summary judgment or at trial, or otherwise obtained a favorable settlement."[11]

Does this mean that the FTC will move away from litigation? Perhaps for now, but not just because of this loss. Hampering the commission's ability to go after deceptive companies was the Supreme Court ruling in 2021 in *AMG Capital Management, LLC v. FTC*. Because of this, the FTC can no longer obtain large cash settlements for consumers. It does not, however, mean that it can't go after civil penalties, and the commission started moving in that direction.

In 2021, the commission took a major step in response to widespread false and misleading product claims related to the pandemic. According to its press release:

> As the pandemic has left many people in dire financial straits, money-making pitches have proliferated and gained special attention. From multilevel marketing companies offering the dream of owning a business, to investment "coaches" with promises of secrets on how to beat the odds, to ubiquitous "gigs" that pitch a steady second income, Americans are bombarded by offers that often prove to be less than advertised.[12]

The commission sent letters (Notice of Penalty Offenses) to more than 1,100 businesses that pitch moneymaking opportunities, putting them on notice "that if they deceive or mislead consumers about potential earnings, the FTC won't hesitate to use its authority to target them with large civil penalties." Unlike previous sanctions the commission might have leveled at these companies, these letters officially put the businesses on notice that if they or their representatives exaggerate earnings potential to prospects, they faced civil penalties—up to $43,792 *per violation*. These letters inform the companies that what they are doing violates the law (as if they didn't know before). Having put MLMs on notice, however, allows the commission to charge the companies, which can't shrug and claim they didn't know. Of those 1,100 letters, approximately 700 were sent to MLMs.[13]

Of course, it would be great if the FTC could do more, but the truth is that trying to rein in MLMs is like wrangling wet kittens. There are too many MLMs and not enough FTC lawyers. If we were relying only on litigation, I would not be so sanguine about the possibility of MLMs continuing to decline. But we aren't. Broad awareness of these companies and their practices are increasingly known. They can no longer get away with flying under the radar.

Multilevel marketing began to enter public awareness after the Bill Ackman documentary *Betting on Zero*, then John Oliver's exposé, and later *LuLaRich*. At the same time as these nonfiction pieces were coming out, MLMs were making (unflattering) appearances in popular TV series like *Crazy Ex-Girlfriend*, *King of Queens*, *Family Guy*, and *South Park*, among others. There was even an entire show, *On Becoming a God in Central Florida*, devoted to the perils of MLMs. Not to mention oodles of negative press in everything from *The New Yorker* to *Teen Vogue* to *Good Housekeeping*.

Growing along with MLMs' visibility was the boom in the anti-MLM movement. The anti-MLM movement does not exist under a single umbrella, but rather as a group of individuals who have decided to take on the industry. Their goals are twofold: to help survivors and those still in MLMs and to fight for stronger regulations to protect consumers.

One of the most well-known anti-MLMers is a breakout "star" from *LuLaRich*, Roberta Blevins. Using the visibility she got from that film, she has become a major advocate for the movement, creating outlets for survivors to tell their stories on her *Life after MLM* podcast and *Life after MLM* show on YouTube. She has created a community on TikTok of more than three hundred thousand followers and a support group on Facebook.

Instagram is a popular social media platform for anti-MLMers, which makes sense given that consultants spend a lot of their time there. A great example here is Nicole Ziege, a reporter and anti-MLM advocate who goes by @antimlmnicole on Instagram. She posts about the FTC, defines terms such as gaslighting, and catalogs information about individual MLMs. She, too, tells stories of victims who submit their stories to her, often anonymously. These include tales of inventory loading and fake cancer cures.

And, if you spend any time on YouTube, eventually you may find yourself going down the anti-MLM rabbit hole just like Kelly did. Yes, you will find content from people like Josie talking about their experiences. But there is also a plethora of video essays explaining pyramid schemes and individual MLMs. On a recent search of MLMs on YouTube, the following were the top three videos that came up: "The Real Truth about Multilevel Marketing: Scams, Lies & Pyramid Schemes," which had 138,000 views in ten days; "MLM Huns Are Becoming More Delusional" (11,000 views in ten days); and "MLM Top Fails #69: Monat Lies about Their Product Study Results, Unboxing Beachbody-opoly" (39,000 views in three days). Of course, my algorithm is going to be affected by researching the topic. No matter how you look at this, though, such content gets a significant number of viewers.

What I also found interesting as I went to the YouTube page on MLMs is the increasing number of videos that are targeted to men. Instead of haircare and vitamins, these MLMs profess to sell cryptocurrency and insurance, and they are no less scammy.

Through all of this and in a relatively short period of time, the anti-MLM movement has had an impact on the industry. It has gotten the attention of the MLMs, the FTC, the media, and the masses.

What some in the anti-MLM movement have also done is highlight the similarities between MLMs and cults—not like Jonestown and Heaven's Gate, but the more everyday cults discussed in this book. Understanding the crossover between these two concepts has accelerated awareness of what they are and how we might be sucked in.

PART III
INFLUENCERS AS "CULT LITE"

7

INFLUENCERS MUTATE FROM CONTENT CREATORS TO CULT BRANDS

Before discussing how influencers work as personified brand cults, I need to define who and what influencers are—a task that is harder than you might think. You may have a favorite influencer, say, Rachel Hollis or James Charles or Mark Manson. But ask a dozen people who their favorite influencer is, and you'll get a couple of dozen answers. Some people follow Charli D'Amelio for her dance and lifestyle videos on TikTok. Others love to watch David Dobrik give away luxury cars on YouTube or avidly follow Coffeezilla's video essays on crypto scams. Influencers run the gamut from kidfluencers like the McClure twins or Ryan Kaji of Ryan's World, to Orthodox Jewish TikTokers, like Miriam Ezagui, who explains the intricacies of her faith to Jews and non-Jews alike, to food evangelist Jamie Oliver, to hatemonger Andrew Tate.

The Internet Advertising Bureau (IAB), the industry's leading digital advertising association, defines influencers as "those who are deemed to have the potential to create engagement, drive conversation and/or sell products/services with the intended target audience. These individuals can range from being celebrities to more micro-targeted professional or nonprofessional 'peers.'" What these people have in common is that they have successfully developed a brand identity that engenders trust among those who follow them. Advertisers have learned to tap into influencers, who can help sell products without looking like they are selling anything. You also may have noticed that influencers work in niche categories, what marketers call "verticals." These can be beauty, travel, lifestyle, family and parenting, and so on. Defining content and creators by category allows marketers to find customers who are more likely to buy their stuff. Just like cable channels are defined by their audiences—ESPN for sports fans, Food Network for cooking, Bravo for young women—influencers have their specialties, but with a twist. An influencer's followers are a much more narrowly defined audience and they are more highly engaged because they can interact directly with the influencer. These audiences are also online, which means advertisers can access specific demographic information about whom these individual followers are and behavioral data about how they shop, what they watch, what websites they frequent, and what products end up in their carts.

Periodically rumors pop up that influencers are a fad. Don't believe it. Advertising agencies are gobbling up influencer marketing agencies, and they wouldn't do that if they believed this was a dying trend.[1] The industry is morphing, though, and you will see how as we continue.

In this chapter, I look at the influencer marketing ecosystem, explaining who they are, how advertisers work with them, how they make money, and how these structures set influencers up to be what I am calling "cult lite." This intricate network fuels what content is made and what drives influencers in their quest to make a living. What undergirds all of this is social media.

A LITTLE SOCIAL MEDIA HISTORY

Social media influencers can trace their roots back to the early 2000s, with the rise of platforms like Friendster (2002) and MySpace (2003). During this early internet era, users accumulated followers by sharing content and connecting with friends, family, and like-minded strangers. People posted on these sites for connection, not for commerce.

The shift to full-fledged influencer economy would take a few more years and a few more upgrades in technological functionality. These sites had nowhere near the level of video, music, and graphics we think of today. This was before Web 2.0, when the internet came to be defined by user-generated content, ease of use, and participatory culture. This was also before broadband, with its super-fast transmission speeds, was widely available, when webcams were not standard features on laptops, and the iPhone was still several years away.

YouTube launched on Valentine's Day 2005. It started humbly as a place to post family videos like a trip to the zoo, the first video ever posted on the site. By the end of its first year, the site was attracting eight million daily views. Late the following year, Google acquired YouTube as viewership had grown to twenty million users and one hundred million videos.[2] This turned out to be an incredibly smart move on Google's part; today, users watch one billion hours of YouTube videos, and 720,000 hours of content are uploaded to the site daily. Video bloggers (vloggers) began to take off on the site, producing the platform's first personalities like Michelle Phan, who did makeup tutorials (content that is now a site mainstay), and LonelyGirl15, who appeared to be a homeschooled teen but turned out to be an actress with an entire film crew and a thriller script behind her.[3]

The launch of YouTube's partnership program in 2007 marked the advent of influencers as we know them. Suddenly individuals could "monetize" their content by having advertising placed next to it, just like running ads during *The Bachelor* or the Super Bowl. And just like with traditional media, the amount of money made is based on how big the audience is, making YouTube advertising revenue incredibly lucrative for people with a huge follower base. Early mega-influencers like Tyler Oakley and Joey Graceffa demonstrated the potential for social media personalities to shape not only consumer trends but popular culture. And let's not forget that Justin Bieber was discovered on YouTube in 2008.

In a later adjustment to the partnership policy (2017), the company allowed *any* video creator to earn money from running ads next to their videos—without having to be popular or, more importantly, vetted. This will become an issue as content turned more nefarious.[4] But in the meantime, it was a big win for YouTube, which got tons more content from lots of smaller producers, and it cost the company next to nothing.

Facebook reached a million users by 2005, but it wasn't until 2006 that the platform became available to people outside of college campuses. From 2006 to 2007, the site grew from twelve million to fifty million users worldwide. Although Facebook is the largest social media platform, its users are also the oldest. In the United States 55 percent of users are older than thirty-four years of age, versus TikTok, where 62 percent of users are younger than twenty-nine. Because of this older demographic, Facebook advertising tends toward professional, educational, or inspirational. Celebrities like Will Smith and international footballers like Cristiano Ronaldo are the top influencers here. Unlike Instagram, the site discourages brand partners. That's because when influencers make money from brands, that means advertising that doesn't end up in the pocket of Meta, the parent company of Facebook (and Instagram). And while Instagram gets the influencer glamour, stodgy old Facebook is pulling in the cash—58 percent of Meta's ad revenue versus Instagram's 42 percent.[5] Facebook, first to last, is designed to gobble up visitors' data so that that information can be used to sell highly targeted ads to brand companies as well as to small entrepreneurs who are dependent on the platform.

Twitter "hatched" in 2006 and became a site for influencers who were facile with the written word, like journalists and academics. Originally introduced as text only with a limit of 140 characters, users had to be pithy with their communication. Had I written this book at an earlier time, there would be a longer discussion here about the importance of this platform. Certainly, in its day Twitter—rebranded as X, though no one calls it that, not even the company's marketers—had serious social and cultural impact. The hashtag was one of its defining features, which was adopted across social media as a tool for aggregating content. This symbol enabled activists and citizens to mobilize and create awareness for causes, including #ArabSpring, #BlackLivesMatter, and #MeToo. Former President Trump and the insurrection are part of Twitter's history and are discussed in a later chapter. After its purchase by Elon Musk, though, Twitter morphed into a cesspool of right-wing conspiracy theories and hate speech, making it an inappropriate choice for corporate marketers who didn't want the latest fashions or discounted airfares being sold next to crypto scams and beheadings. Advertisers left X in droves and ad spending, which had been the company's only source of revenue before Musk started selling blue checks and subscriptions, dove by 55 percent during the first year. Purchased for $44 billion in 2022, the platform was valued at $15 billion a year later.

Instagram was founded in 2010 and quickly became the platform of choice for influencers. Users capitalized on the platform's visual nature and beautifying filters. Although early posts were grainy and not all that interesting, Instagram became a place for cultivating carefully curated feeds that showcased aspirational lifestyles, fashion trends, and travel experiences, or, more succinctly, fitness, food, and fashion. This marked the emergence of a new breed of influencers characterized by their ability to seamlessly blend content creation with brand partnerships, thereby generating lucrative revenue streams. Product placement—Charli D'Amelio drinking Dunkin' Donuts coffee or English soccer player Becky Sauerbrunn wearing Adidas apparel—continues as a standard practice. Facebook purchased Instagram for $1 billion in 2012. What has kept Instagram powering along as the platform of choice is the company's ability to copy new competitors that attempt to encroach on its leadership position, including adding disappearing video Stories to compete with Snapchat and Reels to compete with TikTok.

Another important milestone in influencer history is the creation of Patreon (2013), a site where "patrons" can pay for monthly subscriptions or exclusive content, replicating the way artists were paid during the Italian Renaissance. Truth is, unless producer/influencers have large followings and high-paying brand deals, they weren't, and still aren't, making a ton of money. Patreon provides a means for a consistent revenue stream for content creators.

TikTok was introduced in 2017 and became hugely popular in the United States in 2019 in no small part because of its ease of use and the ability to grow a following much more quickly than other sites. Known for short videos (including a lot of dance content), the platform today allows for ten-minute videos and includes videos on everything from politics to DIY tutorials to try-on hauls. The platform's duets (side-by-side videos) and stitch feature (a short snippet followed by commentary) allow creators to combine their videos with others. This helps build connections and aids in growing follower counts. Creators can also go live, either alone or with others. Originally an app for young users, it has gained appeal with older users, producing a number of "granfluencers," older influencers like ninety-three-year-old Grandma Droniak, who has twelve million followers who listen to her daily grandmotherly advice, and The Old Gays, five gay guys with seven million followers who are activists for the LGBTQ community in a most entertaining way.

The mystery of TikTok is its algorithm. It is "hyperpersonalized," connecting users to content based on interactions. This specialization increases opportunities for what feel like personal connections, leading to word-of-mouth marketing and driving influence on a level never seen before. Those connections—true or not—power the popularity of one of the site's most popular hashtags, #TikTokMadeMeBuyIt. This drives home the message that these sites aren't about informing the public or giving voice to the voiceless. They are about pushing products and ideas, and influencers are the promotions' mouthpieces. According to Aspire, an influencer marketing firm, 80 percent of users claim that TikTok helps them find new products and brands. TikTok is so popular among younger folks that they prefer it over Google as a search tool when looking for things to buy,[6] and there are rising concerns about TikTok leading to increased debt among millennials and Gen Z because of its "infinite loop of shoppertainment," a marketing term used by TikTok to promote the platform to advertisers.[7] We see in a later chapter that TikTok influencers' abilities to make you buy are not as powerful as everyone has been led to imagine.

Lots of other apps and sites exist, but they don't have the staying power—or more importantly the promotional power—of Instagram, YouTube, and now TikTok. Pinterest is more of a search engine than an engagement site. Six-second video app Vine lost out to Snapchat, which lost out to TikTok. Periscope disappeared when live streaming became a standard feature of Facebook, Instagram, and TikTok. Clubhouse and

BeReal caused a stir for a minute and then seemed to disappear. Same is true for the apps that were supposed to replace Twitter, like Bluesky, Spoutible, and Mastadon, though Threads (owned by Meta) seems to be gaining some traction.[8]

In sum, the most essential influencer platforms, in order of importance, are Instagram, TikTok, and YouTube. A key reason why these lead the pack is because people overwhelmingly engage with video content over the written word or static pictures, a trend that has been growing during the last decade, driven both by broadband and the ubiquitous use of cell phones. Remember, this is all about getting people to engage with the material so that more ads can be sold. The average number of engagements—likes, comments, shares—reaches into the thousands on TikTok and YouTube; on Pinterest, it is a few hundred. I would be remiss if I did not also at least mention Substack and Reddit as sites for raising new voices, though these sites tend to be more political than commercial.

The impact of influencers and social media more broadly is substantial. Prior to social media, we didn't use the internet all that much. We might have looked up a recipe, searched for information on Google, or checked out a blog post. We weren't tied to our phones the way we are today. In 2011, U.S. users spent 6.8 hours *per month* on social media. Today, we spend 2.5 hours *per day*. Checking our phones is the first thing we do even before we get out of bed and the last thing we do before we go to sleep. Of themselves, influencers would not have the clout or capabilities they do without the platforms to support them and the marketers to finance them.

WHY MARKETERS WORK WITH INFLUENCERS

> Influencers link brands with their communities. Influencers act as thought starters within their communities and have the ability to foster 1:1 connections that people crave. By leveraging influencer relationships to build a sense of belonging and community with other like-minded consumers, brands can build and nurture customer relationships and boost customer loyalty—which is more important now than ever.
>
> —Aspire, *State of Influencer Marketing 2023*

Influencers are a boon for marketers in so many ways. First, these online personalities have created relationships—ostensibly trusting, authentic relationships—with their followers. These relationships develop in this way because interacting with someone through social media is personal, engendering emotional connections that traditional media does not. Rather than looking at a television screen from across your living room, you are watching and interacting with someone that you are literally holding in the palm of your hand. You begin to feel like you are talking face-to-face with that person, because he or she speaks directly into the camera. These "authentic" connections make influencers perfect brand ambassadors, selling everything from beer to belief systems. Research from *Variety* found that teens were more connected to influencers than to celebrities because the influencers weren't being managed by a public relations machine. Their ability to generally take more risks and be more daring in their humor makes them particularly relatable to this age group.[9] As a rule, people are more likely to buy from people they trust. If a brand partners with someone who truly likes and uses a brand, that creates what marketers call "social proof"—if this super-cool influencer likes this product—then I should use it too!

Second, initially used simply as mouthpieces, the mega-successful influencers today are content producers, some rivaling what you see coming out of Hollywood. That's why this category is now called the content economy, not the influencer economy. Content can be customized for the audience and for the brand, which leads to higher engagement levels. It could be as simple as posting a picture on Instagram but is more likely to be a complex, multiplatform, fully integrated campaign in which the influencer and brand work together to create a sales message that works for both parties. Think about that for just a minute: the content is so seamless that it is hard to distinguish between the brand message (the commercial) and the influencer. In essence, the influencer *is* the ad. The influencer is the product. The influencer is the cult brand.

Third, advertisers can quantify how many people interacted with the ads as well as how successful the influencer was in turning viewers into brand advocates or "brand evangelists." This ability to quantify the success or failure of an influencer's content can give incredible power to marketers, who can readily switch who they work with, since there are so many options available to them. The exception, of course, is influencers who have a large devoted following.

Finally, influencers can have a two-way conversation with their followers. Customers might interact with their favorite brand by going to that brand's TikTok page, but they are much more likely to leave a post or a comment or attend a live session with their favorite YouTuber or Instagram celebrity. That level of connection happens because influencers are relatable, they are entertaining, and they evoke emotion, unlike mascara or Microsoft.

Never forget that content creation—snagging followers and interacting with them—is all about generating profit. These influencers are, well, influential. They persuade you to buy something through the power of their personality, whether it is a product, an idea, or themselves. E-commerce—buying lots and lots of stuff online because the marketing funnel has collapsed and racking up credit card debt is as easy as hitting a link—is expected globally to reach $7.3 trillion—*trillion* with a *T*—in 2025.[10]

TYPES OF INFLUENCERS

When you think of an influencer, you probably think of someone who has millions of followers across several online platforms. Addison Rae amassed eighty-eight million followers on TikTok with her dance videos and has another thirty-seven million followers on Instagram, where she gets hundreds of thousands of likes on posts about traveling in Japan or picking up the latest bestseller. MrBeast has millions of followers across multiple platforms (210 million subscribers on YouTube, 90.5 million on TikTok, 44.9 million on Instagram), where he is known for his numerous acts of philanthropy, including giving away cash and cars, paying students' college tuition, or inviting people to help him buy out an entire store. Then there are celebrities whose followers have themselves been branded, such as Taylor Swift (276 million on Instagram) and her Swifties or Beyonce (319 million on Instagram) and the BeyHive. These megastars provide loyalty as well as media tonnage.

REBRANDING GWYNETH PALTROW: FROM OSCAR WINNER TO UPSCALE HEALTH AND WELLNESS INFLUENCER

Gwyneth Paltrow is what people today call a nepo baby. Her mother is Blythe Danner, an Emmy- and Tony-winning actress, and her father, Bruce Paltrow, was a TV producer and director best known for *St. Elsewhere*, a medical drama from the 1980s, featuring among others Denzel Washington and Howie Mandel. Ms. Paltrow became an actress in her own right, first appearing in films in the early 1990s and winning a Best Actress Oscar in 1999 for *Shakespeare in Love*, an award many thought she did not deserve. (An unethical marketing campaign by Harvey Weinstein is suspected to be behind this, as his blitzkrieg also led to the film beating out Steven Spielberg's *Saving Private Ryan* for best picture.[11]) Deserved or not, she has sustained her acting career for more than thirty years, most recently appearing in several Marvel films. She also has several famous family members, including Gabby Giffords and Rebekah Paltrow Neumann, the wife of Adam Neumann, who founded WeWork.

In the early 2000s, Paltrow began to take a turn toward promoting alternative health practices. Press stories abound about her detox diets and in what can only be considered a calculated move, she wore a backless dress to a movie premiere, which revealed large round red rings, evidence that she had participated in cupping, a healing practice that claims to help ease pain and increase circulation.

In 2008, Paltrow launched goop (the name is her initials with two Os in the middle), a lifestyle brand and e-commerce platform. The brand started as a weekly newsletter providing recommendations on travel, fashion, wellness, and food. Because she traveled for her work, she was able to showcase her favorite coffee or hotel from wherever she was jaunting about the world. She was doing what we now see influencers do on Instagram every day of the week.

Over time and as technology improved, goop evolved into a full-fledged brand selling a variety of products from skincare and wellness items to clothing and accessories—at astronomically high prices. In a recent post called "The Ridiculous but Awesome Gift Guide" sponsored by DeBeers (which is not obviously identified as sponsored content), you can find products like a bracelet for $29,400, a hand-painted tulip vase for $16,752, and a 24-karat gold vibrator for $15,000. Although there are cheaper items on the site, even a plain T-shirt goes for $145.

Goop is (in)famous for questionable product claims that have gotten the company into trouble. The most famous one is likely the jade egg. Women are supposed to heat the egg in hot water and then insert it into their vagina "like a tampon." Using the egg while doing Kegel-like exercises was said to increase energy flow while balancing hormone levels, regulating menstrual cycles, and helping with bladder control, or so they say. Lawyers in California didn't think so, slapping the company with $145,000 in civil penalties for making "unsubstantiated" marketing claims.

Creating controversy around goop is not an aberration. It is a feature, according to a report in the New York Times with the headline "How Goop's Haters Made Gwyneth Paltrow's Company Worth $250 Million."[12] The more anger she can foment, the more traffic she drives to the site. So not only was she ahead of the curve in making celebrities seem more accessible through social media, she also played on people's emotions to get them to promote her overpriced and sometimes dangerous products.

Today, goop is worth $250 million, and Paltrow has 8.4 million followers on Instagram.

Prosperous influencers seem to sprout out of nowhere. The reality is that most of them have been plugging away online for years. Before MrBeast started raking in million-dollar deals, for example, he spent more than a decade churning out YouTube videos. The belief that anyone can became "internet famous," however, is part of the mystique. These You-Tubers and TikTokers seem just like us and the technology is so easy to use! Believing that we can do what they do if only we had the time is key to their appeal. Everyone thinks he or she can be an influencer overnight. They can't. If they could, there would be no need for all the TikTok videos explaining how you can get thirty thousand followers in a week. It's bunk. The way to get followers is to have a unique point of view and post consistently over a long period of time.

But not all influencers have millions of followers, and they don't have to when they work with advertisers. The true value of influencers is in their ability to get their followers to buy into what they are selling, whether it is a product or themselves.

There are millions of influencers across half a dozen key platforms with followers ranging from a few thousand to many millions. The industry breaks them into categories based on the number of followers they have. These definitions vary widely across the marketing industry, but the following provides a usable rule of thumb:

- mega-influencer (1 million-plus followers)—this includes celebrities, though they are sometimes included in a separate category
- macro-influencer (500,000–1,000,000 followers)
- mid-tier influencer (50,000–500,000 followers)
- micro-influencer (10,000–50,000 followers)
- nano-influencer (less than 10,000 followers)—some agencies define this group as less than 5,000

Big brands with big budgets work with mega-influencers, which is much like hiring a celebrity. Most marketers don't have that kind of budget, and even if they did, these big-time content creators probably wouldn't work with them. That's because content producers are as concerned about protecting their personal brand as they are with making money.

Given the issues with the celebs, marketers pivoted toward working with smaller influencers. Micro-influencers have been the most popular group for the last five years. Their audiences are well-defined, and they tend to have loyal fan bases. Also popular are nano-influencers, who have a few thousand followers and can provide personalization while being, well, cheap and compliant. According to an article in the *New York Times* touting the rise of the nano-influencer, "Brands enjoy working with them partly because . . . in exchange for free products or a small commission, nanos typically say whatever companies tell them to."[13] For pennies or a product sample, these smaller influencers provide higher engagement rates, the percentage of interactions a post receives, while seamlessly selling workout tights, nutritional supplements, or cereal.

TWO POPULAR INFLUENCER AD TYPES

Brand Ambassadors

Brand ambassadors make money by offering discounts through an affiliate link. One company that uses this type of advertising is Gymshark, a workout apparel company that scouts social media looking for potential ambassadors. It's like what lululemon has been known to do in the real world—offering free leggings to yoga instructors so they will recommend them to their students. The ambassador posts numerous pictures from the "haul" of products they get from the company. These posts feel authentic, and followers can ask questions of someone they already know and like.

Paid Partnerships

Seamless campaigns combine an influencer with a brand whose content is a natural fit. Chrissa Sparkles, for example, is a Filipina designer, Pilates teacher, and entertainer. One of her "bits" is acting out different Barbies. Go to her website, and what you see is pink, pink, and more pink. It should be no surprise that this would be the perfect match for furniture company Joybird, which created a line of Barbie Dreamhouse furniture in conjunction with the *Barbie* movie. Chrissa Sparkles created sponsored videos as well as pictures at the company's showroom, which solidified her brand while promoting products for someone else.

Paid partnerships are more likely than affiliate links to be labeled as commercial content.

So, the thinking goes, if one influencer is good, then two—or ten or twenty—is better. This is where influencer networks and platforms come in. Both services help marketers find groups of influencers that they can work with, at more or less the same time, to amplify a campaign message. Grouping influencers in this way is kind of like a television network sending out a commercial to hundreds of stations all around the country. But instead of people seeing the commercial through their TV screens, they see commercial content presented by one of their favorite influencers in a much more personal and individualized way.[14]

Influencer networks act like traditional talent agencies, except instead of connecting an actor to a film project, they connect an influencer with a brand. Influencer networks, with names like Upfluence and Viral Nation, do this matchmaking with more advanced influencers whom they vet for the advertiser. Influencer platforms automate this process. Brands can choose influencers and vice versa. Through a simple online platform, influencers can find out what the campaign needs to say, how often they need to post, and the dates of the campaign.

The easiest way to think about it is like a dating site. The brand is looking for X, the influencer can provide X, and their mutual interests are brought together through the online platform. McDonald's, for example, was looking to increase store traffic and "drive consideration"; that is, to make people think about this fast food restaurant when they are deciding where they want to eat. McDonald's created the "Trick. Treat. Win!" promotion to drive traffic to restaurants in the weeks leading up to Halloween. To do that, the network "activated 20 African-American Influencers between the ages of 18–35 over a four-week period." These influencers had to create a blog post as well as post multiple times to Facebook, Instagram, and Twitter. The content that did well was then more heavily promoted throughout the internet by the company, using paid advertising. This campaign led to "540k incremental visits to McDonald's, +23% incremental lift in store traffic, 82.4k engagements, and 98% positive brand sentiment."[15]

What most people don't know is that tens or hundreds of influencers are simultaneously presenting similar content all over social media. Even if consumers are aware of paid influencers, few are likely aware that influencers are being *assembled* to promote products to them. Based on my conversations with influencer marketing salespeople, although the networks tell influencers to note that they are being compensated for their work—as they are required to do by law—this is not always tracked.

This doesn't only happen in the commercial space. Influencers—and influencer platforms—are increasingly used in politics. Stories about influencers being paid by political entities first appeared in the popular press in 2016. It wasn't until Michael Bloomberg's 2020 presidential primary campaign that there was broad press coverage about this practice, because it led to controversy. Being a billionaire, he spent tens of millions of his own money on traditional advertising, but he needed something to help him look cool and appeal to younger voters. For that, he turned to influencer platform Tribe, where he offered $150 per post to nano- and micro-influencers. At the time, this was not common practice by politicians. Per *The Daily Beast*, "No other high-polling candidates . . . said that their campaigns have ever paid influencers to create content for the campaign, or for influencers to post such content on their own channels in exchange for money."[16] Bloomberg was lambasted for the practice, particularly because his "stop and frisk" campaign was out of step with young voters who saw that policy as a precursor to the endless murders of Black men at the hands of police.

Since then, influencers have become an essential tool in the political marketers' toolbox, and they are used on both sides of the aisle. On the left, influencer networks include companies like @Advocacy, Vocal Media, Social Currant, and People First (formerly Main Street One, the influencer arm of political marketing firm Main Street).[17] On the right side, there is Urban Legend,[18] Today Is America, and Turning Point USA, which has an in-house ambassador program. And, just like brands, political campaigns are tapping into micro- and nano-influencers.[19] Yes, because of their better engagement numbers, but also because they are more likely to have local followings, and as we know "all politics is local."

One important difference to note between influencers who are selling products and those who are selling politics: political influencers do not have to say they are being paid. That's because their content is considered political speech, which falls under the purview of the Federal Elections Commission (FEC). The FEC requires disclaimers to identify the paid nature of political content in "general public political advertising," but *it does not regulate online content*.[20] You have no clue whether someone you follow online is espousing the truth or an opinion that has been bought and paid for.

HOW INFLUENCERS MAKE MONEY

By 2021, more than fifty million people considered themselves to be influencers. However, only two million of those made a full-time career out of it. That's because although their lives may look glamorous, a lot of that is smoke and mirrors. In her book, *How (Not) to Get Paid for What You Love*, media scholar Brooke Duffy recounts spending years following and interviewing influencers. Most of them worked ungodly hours to make their life look effortless. They might be given an expensive handbag or a seat at a fashion show (so they could post about it online), but they didn't get a whole lot of cash. Yet they kept working and working in the hope of eventually living the life they presented, what Duffy calls "aspirational labor." We could say the same about women caught in MLMs.

Influencers, like others in the gig economy, make money through a hodgepodge of revenue streams. However, brand deals by far are the main sources of income. According to influencer agency NeoReach, almost 70 percent of creators make their money from brand deals. A little more than 7 percent make money from ad revenue, and the rest is made through creating their own brand, using affiliate links, courses, and a limited few make money from subscriptions and tips.

The bottom line is that making money as an influencer comes down to getting lucrative deals with marketers and some limited largesse from platforms. To give you an idea of how this works, let's look at some numbers. Bear in mind, the bigger the follower count, the more money an influencer makes.

Brand Deals

Starting with Instagram, influencers can earn from $75 to $10,000 per post, depending on their following and engagement rates. Mega-influencers with millions of followers can command even higher rates, from $100,000 to even $1 million for a single post. In 2022, for example, soccer player Cristiano Ronaldo reportedly earned $2,397,000 per post and Selena Gomez pocketed $1,735,000.[21] On YouTube, mid-tier influencers can earn from $1,000 to $10,000 for a sponsored video, with the largest influencers earning $20,000 or more. TikTok is paying the least, with even its top creators earning around $2,500 per post.[22] If you want to see how little this site pays, check out the TikTok money calculator.[23] Though not endorsed by the site, it does provide a framework for understanding what someone might earn based on the number of followers and likes a post receives.

As noted in the McDonald's example used earlier, brands may repurpose influencer content, which becomes an additional way to make money, and influencers will get paid for it, if they are smart enough to negotiate that into the contract. Or the creator may produce a picture or a video specifically for the brand—as advertising agencies used to do—which is posted on the brand's social media pages. This is known as creator generated content, or CGC

But working with advertisers isn't all it is cracked up to be. Although brands (and others) tout how much money you can make as an online creator, the truth is that most brand deals don't include a cash payment. *Only 41.6 percent of brand collaborations include cash.*[24] The table shows examples of payment amounts for influencers who are lucky enough to receive them.

Instagram versus TikTok—Payments for Macro- versus Micro-Influencers

Audience size	Instagram Story	Instagram Static	Instagram Carousel	Instagram Video	TikTok Video
Macro (750,000+)	$ 9,000	$25,000	$75,000	$30,000	$45,000
Macro (Average)	$ 700	$ 2,000	$ 4,063	$ 4,120	$ 5,133
Micro (10,000–100,000)	$ 4,500	$ 4,000	$ 4,500	$ 7,000	$ 4,000
Micro (Average)	$ 450	$ 650	$ 850	$ 1,500	$ 650

Created by author based on data from Collectively (2022).

Platform Revenue

In 2021, there was a push among the social sites to pay creators directly in an attempt to goose the amount of content on the sites as well as to motivate influencers to choose one platform over another. Meta (Instagram and Facebook) had a billion-dollar pool of money. YouTube was paying creators to post Shorts (videos that were fifteen seconds or shorter but now can be up to sixty seconds). Snapchat and Pinterest were also trying to tempt creators with cash.

All of this seems to have disappeared except for money from You-Tube, which is based on ad revenue, and TikTok, whose payouts add up to pennies. On YouTube, content creators get about 55 percent of every advertising dollar connected to their channels. So, if an ad costs $100, the creator makes $55. That sounds great until you realize how little is charged for an ad. On average, a creator makes $18 per one thousand views. This is why *Fast Company* noted that "96.5 percent of YouTubers make less than $12,140 (the federal poverty line)."[25]

TikTok had the Creators Fund, which paid small amounts to those who had at least ten thousand followers and one hundred thousand views in a month. The $2 billion fund was divided among those who reached these thresholds. As more people joined and more creators became eligible, the smaller the payoff for each individual person. Reports noted that $200 or less, like $20 or $30, was typical. In late 2023, TikTok introduced the Creativity Program, which rewards videos longer than one minute and claims to pay out twenty times what the original fund did. It is too early to tell if that is true.[26]

"HIDDEN" ADVERTISING AND THE FIGHT FOR AUTHENTICITY

What we have seen thus far is that content creators work to grow their following, perhaps to produce thought-provoking content, but ultimately to make a living. The way to do this is by connecting with advertisers who—until the influencers become successful in their own right—guide the creator in what the content should say.

I see this marriage of influencer and marketer as the natural extension of a trend that has ruled social media—covert advertising, or stealth marketing. Since the first days of television, people have not wanted to interact with advertising. They don't want their entertainment experiences interrupted by "a message from our sponsor." They don't want to watch an ad for Coke after spending $18 to go to a movie. Stealth marketing—marketing that the audience may not be fully aware of—has been the answer to this problem. On social media feeds, it is native advertising—ads that look exactly like a post that your friend or family member might send to you. On the *New York Times* or *Forbes*, it is branded content or branded journalism— an ad that looks like any other article posted by the publication. In influencer marketing, it's product placement—someone doing a makeup video who just happens to mention the brand of foundation they are using or an Instagram post on the balcony of a luxury Hilton hotel. More than any other medium, social media is about being connected—whether the personal connections behind the online interactions are real or not. The medium is very personal; as any social media coach will tell you, "social is about social." That is why marketers have turned to influencers with smaller followings. Those people engage with their audiences.

Simultaneously, most advertising online was becoming "programmatic," a fancy way for saying it was all done by computers. Today, there is rarely a human anywhere in the online advertising buying system. Influencers are discovered on platforms; they push out endless content, which is then married with persuasive design technology that leads to us spending more and more time online, which leads to more shopping and behavioral data for marketers and social media platforms to analyze. Creating content is now super easy, selling ads is lightning fast, and we are spending ungodly amounts of time online. All the labor is being done by creators and consumers, while these social media platforms make no content. As one influencer agency put it, "for the cost of one in-house photoshoot, brands can generate hundreds of pieces of diverse content by leveraging influencers, as well as other members of your brand community. . . . Think of these creators as individual content creation studios—they're often skilled in photography, videography, editing, creative directing, and much more." Talk about your win-win-win.

But for us, not so much. Although you may be aware of some advertising, research suggests that few know or understand the depth to which their data is collected or how little it is anonymized. Nor do most people grasp the full extent to which marketers can integrate online with offline behaviors or how they are using that against you.

When I ask my students if they understand how much of their data is being collected, they say they know and don't care. But then I ask if they understand that they may pay more money for health insurance if providers see lots of junk food appear in their newsfeeds. Or that they may be denied a mortgage because of digital redlining. Or, most relevant for impending graduates, they may not get a job because the opportunities they want will never be presented to them. Suddenly the story changes.

The advertising in social media is hidden because a lot of the influencers want it that way. The onus of ensuring that sponsored content is properly labeled often falls on the creator. Influencers are required to designate when content they post is sponsored. There needs to be #ad or #sponsored or #[brandname] partner or it is in violation of Federal Trade Commission (FTC) regulations. New rules also require that if video is used, the sponsorship notice must be audible. It also doesn't matter if the payment is in dollars or in product. If it is compensated, it is sponcon—sponsored content—and must be identified as such. Most influencers don't do this. The attitude is to beg forgiveness rather than ask permission because they know there is no way that the FTC can track all of the advertising that appears online. For creators, the bottom line is being authentic and when someone isn't, it comes back to bite them.

The "lashgate" controversy is a great example here. Beauty influencer Mikayla Nogueira demonstrated L'Oreal's mascara on TikTok, showing how the product lengthened her lashes. After showing herself using the product from a number of different angles, she finishes by claiming that the product is so amazing that she looks like she's wearing false lashes. Followers and other beauty pros pounced on this, saying they really were fake lashes.

The video quickly got close to twenty-five million views, and a number of people "stitched" her video, saying that she was lying. Some people said they were false lashes; others said she used lash extensions. Still others complained that although the video did use #lorealpartner, the hashtag was hidden under her user name and only visible for a few seconds—all tactics that are verboten in TikTok communities. The damage was done. Mikayla was called out for not being transparent, not being authentic, for not doing an "honest review."[27]

This controversy spawned the de-influencer trend, where creators told people to think twice before purchasing high-priced items and to check their materialism.[28] That lasted a minute, and last time I looked Mikayla had 15 million followers and 1.3 billion likes.

Another example of influencer backlash is connected to Shein, a fast fashion clothing company known for online haul videos—influencers trying on tons of clothing they got for a tiny bit of money. To help combat accusations of labor abuses, Shein took half a dozen influencers to their factory in China, all expenses paid. They had the influencers walk through a spotlessly clean factory where they met with the workers. The influencers posted videos and pictures of smiling workers and neat stacks of merchandise.

People didn't buy it for a minute! News stories quickly appeared everywhere from CNN to NPR, blasting not only the company but the creators. Shein was not only accused of labor abuse, but bad business practices by misleading the influencers who have been left to try and manage their tarnished reputations. The influencers are accused—rightly so—of not investigating the company before taking their "largesse." Although they took down TikTok videos, others stitched and dueted them, keeping the content alive with critical commentary attached.[29]

At the end of the day, the biggest risk for influencers—especially people with smaller followings—is maintaining the delicate balance between maintaining authenticity and making a living. But even doing their best might not protect them. Brands are looking beyond traditional influencers to find the most authentic. These can be longtime users who consistently promote a company or brand, loyal customers who "naturally" promote products and create online buzz, computer-generated influencers, and employees who produce behind-the-scenes content. Websites like Post-Beyond and Ambassify help companies activate their employees, enabling companies to better coordinate and curate preapproved employee content.

Executives at influencer platforms have been working hard over the years to get creators to include the required designations. William Gasner of Stack Influence told me it is "a baseline requirement." We also spoke about the need to inform influencers about changing rules and an appropriately more aggressive FTC, which has sent letters to influencers who do not properly label their content with warnings of possible fines of $50,120 for civil violations.[30]

But even with more stringent oversight, spotting sponsored content can get complicated for the consumer. Taylor Lorenz, a social media reporter who has worked with numerous top newspapers, has said that influencers use #ad in their posts or make their posts look like advertising even if it isn't sponsored. They do this because they want to make themselves more attractive to potential brand partners. I asked Katie Stoller, a longtime public relations pro and talent manager, about this. She said that she didn't see it happening but acknowledged the competition among influencers. "I've never had anyone tell me that, but there is a lot of competition especially in local areas. Like this holiday season? I've had a lot of chatter like 'oh my god, she got this deal' or 'this brand is doing deals with her and we haven't heard back from them.' So there is this competition of keeping up with the Joneses, of doing enough brand deals to show that you're working. . . . Maybe they got something gifted and instead of making it like it was gifted, they're making it seem like it was more of like a partnership." Claiming something is an ad when it isn't seems as doomed to backfire as not disclosing. First, if followers find out, it hurts the influencer's credibility, and, second, influencers can get real, admittedly unpaid, deals through a platform like Stack Influence, which works with smaller influencers and can help with building their skills in working with clients. Seems like a better bet to me.

Influencers, particularly those with smaller followings, don't have much power in this marketing and media environment, and they may not want to. Used in a synchronized manner, though, their content can affect what people think about and possibly what they purchase. Coordinated brand campaigns and irregular labeling of advertising makes the process deceptive and omits information. This does not let influencers completely off the hook. They are part of the persuasion system and have cultivated a following who look to them for ideas and possibly leadership.

All of this adds up to getting hooked.

8

GETTING HOOKED ON AN INFLUENCER . . . AND WHAT THEY'RE SELLING

Jimmy Donaldson, aka MrBeast, started posting videos to YouTube while he was in middle school. He grew up with a single mom who was a member of the military. This lifestyle meant that he had a lot of time on his hands, and being a shy, geeky kid, he started playing around with computers. It was the early days of YouTube (2012), and he posted a variety of videos, often with the help of his friend, Chris. Being bashful, though, he did not appear on camera for much of this content, instead doing things like talking over video game play.

After years of posting random videos, he began developing a following by making fun of how other YouTubers did their intros. The "worst intros" series led to Donaldson acquiring thirty thousand followers, which was good but nothing extraordinary. His first viral video didn't pop until 2017—five years after he began. The recipe for success turned out to be doing arbitrary and bizarre acts that no one thought to do because, frankly, they are just dumb. Donaldson sat in front of the camera counting to one hundred thousand, an event that took forty-four hours. Other stunts included things like twirling a fidget spinner for twenty-four hours, watching the same music video for hours on end, and reading every word in the dictionary. Crazy antics led to one million followers.

In 2018, he began working with a digital talent manager, and a year later, MrBeast—a moniker he had created early on—was a flat-out YouTube phenomenon. Not only was he reaching millions of followers, but every video he posted for a year reached more than ten million views.[1]

Stunts remain part of his repertoire, but today he is known more for his philanthropy. This content pivot began with the first video connected to a brand deal. The company, Quid, offered him $5,000 to make a video. MrBeast turned it down. He said he wanted $10,000 because he wanted to give the money away to a "homeless" person.[2] Dressed in gray sweatpants and flip-flops, he walked over to an unhoused man who stood on the median of a roadway holding a cardboard sign. Donaldson, with an envelope stuffed with $10,000 cash in his pocket, explained that he is a YouTuber who is starting a series about being nice to people. The man didn't believe him at first. When he realized that it wasn't a joke or a trick, he hugged Donaldson, and the two of them, plus Chris who shot the video from across the road, all headed out for dinner.

This video was followed by another with a charitable spin: MrBeast, again using money from Quid, tips pizza delivery people who come to his door several hundred dollars each. In a particularly touching moment, one man returns to Donaldson's house the next day and explains that because of this money, he could get someone else to work his shift and he got to spend time with his kid. These heartfelt videos propelled MrBeast's trajectory and established his practice of plowing advertising dollars into doing good for others, which in turn led to more content. "I want to use brands to allow me to help people," said Donaldson. And, of course, by helping them, he helps himself with a steady stream of revenue generated by the advertising in and around these YouTube videos.

Donaldson has been dubbed "YouTube's biggest philanthropist" and his giveaways get bigger as his follower count and brand deals grow. One example of these big events is #TeamTrees. He had the idea to plant one million trees. After doing some research, he realized it would be impossible, but being a guy who doesn't say no and because he was about to hit twenty million subscribers, he changed the objective to planting twenty million trees. He posted his idea on what was then Twitter and asked who wanted to help. He raised funds from Elon Musk and Twitter founder Jack Dorsey, as well as promotional support from other major YouTube influencers like PewDiePie and Mark Rober, plus hundreds of other lesser-known YouTubers, ultimately achieving this seemingly unachievable goal. He was creating community while doing good.

His online success led to an increasing number of offline ventures. The Beast Philanthropy channel presents only charity-related content and all money raised goes to running a food bank he started. That has expanded to a nonprofit organization he founded to provide "long-lasting relief to individuals suffering from homelessness, hunger, and poverty."[3] Plus, he started a burger restaurant and a gluten-free, plant-based chocolate brand.

With success came backlash. He has been accused of misleading followers because he promoted Refinery, a cryptocurrency scheme that led to people losing a significant amount of money.[4] More broadly, the videos he creates are "stunt philanthropy," or more derogatorily "charity porn." He is being criticized in the same way that we might criticize Mark Zuckerberg for trying to look generous for donating $150 million to assuage homelessness in San Francisco, when his company is instrumental in causing the problem. Although Donaldson does not cause homelessness and hunger, he has found a way to monetize altruism for himself, which comes off as virtue signaling and self-aggrandizing. When watching these videos, you also can't help but see the systemic economic inequities, not only in society broadly but between the recipients of the largesse and the now exceedingly wealthy white man.

This juxtaposition reached an inflection point when Donaldson asked his followers to go to their local Walmarts, where his Feastables chocolate bars were sold and fix the displays that were being decimated by customers. *Paper* magazine put it best when describing the disconnect that occurred:

> It's the intersection with a new level of late-stage capitalism that seems to have left a particularly strange taste in everyone's mouths. There's the obvious hypocrisy of a multi-millionaire YouTuber asking his fanbase to perform unpaid labor, but it's the way the act is postured as some sort of grassroots marketing campaign to promote his own line of chocolate bars that makes the whole thing feel like a deranged corporate social experiment or a relic of our dystopian present.[5]

This wasn't asking followers to help plant trees; this was asking followers to make his product look good so he could make more money. Even if the candy does raise some money for charity, it is Donaldson who decides which charity deserves his largesse—another point of privilege in late capitalism.

Unlike the people enmeshed in MLMs, the cognitive dissonance is not enough to break the spell—at least not yet. At 214 million subscribers and counting, MrBeast is the biggest content creator on YouTube, and his loyal following will buy seemingly anything the man has to sell, whether online or off.

INFLUENCERS AS CULT BRANDS

People follow MrBeast because he is a trusted brand, no different from McDonald's or Apple. He has a logo and a brand mythology, an intricate backstory that followers know well and relate to. Just as you anticipate salty fries and a Big Mac every time you walk into Mickey D's, you expect MrBeast to consistently produce content that is entertaining, perhaps informative, and very likely aligns with your beliefs. He is so good at creating and building his brand that Harvard created a business school case study about him.[6]

Despite the hoopla and Harvard, someone with a huge following like MrBeast can still be utterly unknown to people outside his sphere of influence. If you don't know who he is, don't feel bad. Until I started researching this book, I didn't either. That's because, in the context of social media, celebrity is different than in traditional outlets. The change in what constitutes celebrity began with cable dividing us into smaller and smaller groups. Digital parsed the population still further so that we are fed content that is explicitly individualized to our supposed wants and needs based on our on- and offline behaviors. Platforms have not only atomized us, but they are doing it at scale. To cater to advertisers, the population is sliced and diced so that we don't share the same content. We aren't all sitting down to watch *Grey's Anatomy* or *The Walking Dead* or *60 Minutes*. Instead, we connect with individual creators, viewing on our tablets and our phones as isolated individuals. You might love Jeffree Star because of his androgynous style and amazing makeup. Others might like Emily Schuman (@cupcakesandcashmere) because of her take on food and fashion. Each one of millions and millions of influencers have their own fans and followers who trust the personal brands that they have developed and nurtured over time, and with the trust comes repeat viewing and a sense of loyalty. It's no different than following the adventures of Flo in the Progressive Insurance commercials, except a lot more people know who she is.

Influencers, unlike brands, aren't static products or stodgy services. They are people and thereby fundamentally relatable. Leo Burnett, the famous Chicago advertising agency, built its philosophy on the idea that people don't relate to things, they relate to people. That's why they created characters for their brands, like Charlie the Tuna for StarKist, the Jolly Green Giant, and the Marlboro Man. Influencers do this one better. And because we are interacting with real, honest-to-goodness people, psychology plays a bigger role in why we connect with them and why they can become such a powerful influence on our lives.

Psychologist Christopher Chabris and psychology professor Daniel Simon in their book *Nobody's Fool: Why We Get Taken in and What We Can Do about It* explain a number of cognitive habits that might lead us into buying into a scam or an influencer. Key among them is truth bias: we assume people are telling the truth. This bias is amplified if it is someone we know. That's why there's the old saying, "the wife is always the last to know." Why? Because she believes her spouse wouldn't lie to her. Of course, truth bias does not preclude you from thinking someone might lie;

they do and they will. However, it is not our default position to think that, and confirming a lie takes a whole lot more effort.

Truth bias is particularly potent online. You choose people to follow, which, if you are a typical social media user, you will do for 151 minutes per day. You scroll quickly through the feeds, only half paying attention, and rarely stopping to fact-check what you are seeing. This is by design. Social media technology pushes you to think fast—with your emotions—not slowly with your rational mind. As you scroll some more, you see the same "fact" again and again and again, and you find yourself starting to believe it. This is how misinformation and disinformation spread, misinformation being false information that may not be meant to intentionally deceive, whereas disinformation is information that purposefully intends to deceive and manipulate. In short, psychology and technology work together to get you to accept what you see presented online.

There is also a particular type of content that solidifies trust: storytelling. A new study in the *Journal of Consumer Research* analyzed what "levers" influencers can use to increase engagement; that is, to get you to interact with them. These researchers analyzed 55,631 Instagram posts from 763 influencers. They found that telling stories about anyone they have close ties to—romantic partners, friends, family—aids in increasing audience attention. This "personal" storytelling increases the sense of authenticity and warmth, a sense of similarity between the viewer and the influencer, and may spark "viewers' interpersonal curiosity," the academic way of saying that we like gossip.[7] After reading this study, it struck me how true this is and how often storytelling is used. Comedian Sarah Silverman constantly posted about her dad, whom she called Schleppy, until he passed away in 2023. Miriam Ezagui, a leading Orthodox Jewish TikToker with almost two million followers, posts about her family life and religion, including periodically hosting conversations with her grandmother, Bubby, about her Holocaust experiences. Even MrBeast brings his mom into the act, with one of his earlier videos showing him handing her a check to pay off her mortgage.

Now, marry our default toward trusting people with what we know about cults—brand or otherwise. Cults have defining elements that marketers use to their advantage. These include a charismatic leader; a culture of persuasion, especially one that leads to thinking alike and shunning those who don't agree with you; deception; and exploitation—usually economic, but in traditional cults, it can also be sexual.[8]

Thinking about this as it relates to influencers, we can see the parallels and how social media is set up to perpetuate the use of cult tactics. By definition, influencers are leaders, and the ones with the biggest followings are extremely charismatic. They are looking to persuade you toward their thinking, usually in an attempt to get you to buy something. Often, the sales pitch is hidden and thereby deceptive. You are not being given all the information you need to be able to make an informed decision, a key cult tactic. Finally, while the form of exploitation may not be sexual or even economic in the traditional sense, minimally, you are being ensnared in the anxiety economy, paying with your time and mental health.

All of this is happening as social media technology is creating a world of in- and out-groups, at scale. Marketers—and religions and cults—have long defined who and what they are by defining who they are not. As discussed earlier, Mac users are *not* PC users. You are Starbucks *or* Dunkin', Methodist *or* Mormon. Members of the in-group are part of your tribe, you relate to them and give them preferential treatment. In cults, once someone has become part of the group, one of the steps is to separate him or her from nonmembers in order to solidify belief systems. In social media spaces, the algorithm is intended to give you the content you prefer, which, as you use the technology, will put you into more and more defined and isolating groups explicitly designed to perpetuate us-versus-them interactions. We saw this in stark detail after Hamas attacked Israel on October 7, 2023. Max Fisher, the *New York Times* reporter and author of *The Chaos Machine*, explained how this works on the *Offline with Jon Favreau* podcast:

> Your incentive [as an influencer] is the thing that is going to get people to watch my videos and that is *expressing the most fervent outrage at the other side*, articulating the conflict, not even as one of Israelis and Palestinians, but one of the influencers who share my views, who are good, and the influencers who have other views, who are pieces of shit, and we're going to get them in the comments. The message of these videos . . . is that you, the person on your phone scrolling TikTok, you're the protagonist of this conflict. It's about you. It's about how it makes you feel. And it's about you dunking on and owning the other side.[9]

The combination of charismatic leader, persuasion, deception, and separation into in- and out-groups with the end goal of having followers pay with anxiety, attention, and/or money is why I call influencers "cult lite." Influencers embody several fundamental elements of a cult, without extricating you from your day-to-day activities like a traditional cult would.

Let me be clear: Everyday influencers aren't maleficent and I'm not attempting to bash them. They are trying to make a living. I get that. I'm even sympathetic about how hard they have to work, and they do work hard. However, their need for income (and advertisers' desire for eyeballs, and the platforms' mandate to generate revenue) depends on you being reeled in to spend more time online than you should, all in the hopes that you will buy things you probably don't want or need.

DON'T I KNOW YOU?

The connections made between influencers and their followers add a layer of complication to how these creators act as brands. As people spend increasing amounts of time online, they begin to feel like they know and are friends with the people they follow. When social media began, the people you followed were people you knew, your friends, your family. Now those connections have expanded to a whole swath of people you have never met and likely never will, but you still feel personally connected to them. You check TikTok to laugh with Sarah Cooper, or Instagram to find out what your "friend" Jen Selter suggests as today's workout, or jump on YouTube to see what Peter Zeihan has to say about geopolitics. One-sided relationships between media personalities and their fans are what is known as parasocial relationships, a media phenomenon first written about during the early days of television. Although most people think these are fundamentally negative, that's not the case. Research has shown that "51% of Americans have likely been in parasocial relationships, even though only 16% admit to it."[10] Al Roker is America's favorite weatherman for a reason. People often feel the same way about their local weather personalities because they engage with them almost daily. Heck, for twenty-plus years, millions of women interacted with Oprah like she was their personal confidante coming to join them in their living rooms every afternoon like clockwork.

PARASOCIAL RELATIONSHIPS

Parasocial relationships exist when someone forms an emotional attachment to a media personality. This phenomenon was discovered in the 1950s when researchers found that audiences became invested in TV personalities.[11] Since this was happening through the TV screen, the relationship was one-sided. The viewer could become deeply devoted, but the media personality knew nothing about the follower.

Parasocial *interactions* are what most of us experience. These are of-the-moment engagements that we don't think about again after they're done. Parasocial *relationships*, however, are much more intense, especially on social media. The person may think about the influencer during the day and, unlike the television era, can continually check up on them online. A follower may even come to speak about the influencer as if he or she is a friend.

Parasocial relationships are not necessarily bad. They can be an important part of social development and identity formation, especially for adolescents who are more likely to establish these connections than adults. A 2017 academic study further noted that gender affects the parasocial relationship, suggesting "that boys were more likely to see celebrities as mentors, role models, or authority figures, while girls were more likely to imagine a friendship with media figures."[12] These connections can provide motivation and inspiration, as well as a sense of companionship and community.

Parasocial relationships become problematic when they begin to overtake one's life and real-world relationships. The object of attention becomes like an addiction, leading to isolation, loneliness, and anxiety. Such a relationship may also lead to negative comparisons, like wishing you had the influencer's audience, fame, or physique.

Connection to the influencer, in conjunction with digital technology, leads to more time on social media. The consequences of this tend to be increased spending and materialism, particularly among adolescents, and it can contribute to depression among older adults.[13]

With television, it was almost impossible to meet the source of one's obsession. Not so today. Meet Michael Brown aka Misha aka @dontcrossagayman. He is a white guy with a long face, round glasses, and a casual style. His job title is digital creator, and he has 713,000 followers on Instagram and 2.7 million followers on TikTok, which is his primary platform. Misha's content relates to everyday life, stories about family members, trips to a restaurant, or run-ins with a neighbor. There's a "hey girl" feeling to his content (in the gay way, not the MLM way), as if he has the latest gossip to tell you. Misha is a great storyteller, filling his tales with humor and snark, which is what makes him endearing and approachable. He is also brutally honest and calls out rude or abusive behavior, especially when it is directed toward the LGBTQIA+ community.

Unlike MrBeast, who obviously has someone shooting his videos, Misha's videos are straight to camera, like you are having a face-to-face conversation with him. People feel free to approach him in real life, and he is not averse to chatting and taking a selfie when approached in public.

But one day it went too far. A follower appeared at his house with no compunction about tapping on his front door. I'll let him tell the story:

> Let's talk about boundaries. I just had the craziest experience I've had since acquiring a following online. I just took my dogs for a walk, and I got home and I was holding their leashes. I was washing my hands. And I heard a knock on my front door, and I'm expecting some packages, so I just assumed it was those. But I open the door and there's a woman standing there. So I'm like, "Hello." And she said, "Hi, Misha. I'm one of your followers."
>
>   Bitch, it took me a minute to comprehend what she just said. I said, "Oh, how do you know where I live?" Turns out, she saw me walking my dogs and decided to follow me to my home. So I said to her, I feel like this is inappropriate and you've overstepped a boundary and I would like it if you'd leave. And she got really upset. She told me she's followed me for a really long time. She said, "I thought you love your besties," and then she threatened to make a video about me to expose how I'm fake. So I told her, I said, "I am asking you to leave my property or I'm going to have to call the police." And this bitch stood her ground in my doorway and told me that I pretend to be a good person and then said that "Your stories are fake. You probably can't even come up with a good insult." I said, "Well, why don't you start eating your makeup? Because then at least you'll be pretty on the inside. Get off my property." Besties, out in public, all good. In my home? Please don't.[14]

Having a follower show up at an influencer's house and the influencer saying, "who are you?" is the very definition of a parasocial relationship. It is also what brings influencer culture to the level of cult—it is extreme, and it is unhealthy.

You might be thinking, isn't this just an overly zealous fan? The key difference is that fans love, love, love the celebrities that they follow, but they do not believe that they have a relationship with that person. You might wait after a concert or a Broadway show to get an autograph or a selfie, but you don't think Josh Groban or Taylor Swift is going to go out with you and your besties for coffee or a cocktail.

#TIKTOKMADEMEBUYIT, OR DID IT?

If you spend any time on social media—and even if you don't—you have probably heard of the hashtag #TikTokMadeMeBuyIt. The hashtag had eight billion views in January 2022. Less than two years later, that number was eighty billion and growing. That sounds astounding, but let's stop for just a second. That's eighty billion *views*, which on TikTok simply means that the video played for at least one second. It means that the creator of the video knows how to create a hook—a sound, movement, or comment—that gets people to stop scrolling for literally a second. It doesn't mean they watched the video or even a good part of it. It also doesn't mean that eighty billion people posted a video with the hashtag. So although it sounds like an impressive number, it probably isn't relevant. But it is terrifically good marketing.

Since researching #TikTokMadeMeBuyIt turned out to be a fruitless starting point for understanding if influencer marketing is effective, I pivoted to follow the money. If we can understand the revenue flows in this marketing ecosystem, we can better understand how influencers impact you. We saw this in the last chapter in terms of how influencers get paid, how that impacts the kind of content they create, and how they interact with brands. Here, I dig further into how effective they are in leading you to buy. This turned out to be far more interesting than I originally thought.

Let's start with some data. In 2024, U.S. marketers are estimated to spend $5.89 billion on influencer marketing. That spending is a small part of the $75 billion spent on social media advertising, an even smaller part of the $364 billion in overall U.S. ad spending, and an infinitesimal percentage of the $1 trillion spent on advertising globally. Of those ad dollars, Instagram gets $2 billion. Next is TikTok with $1.2 billion, followed by YouTube and Facebook, both of which are expected to crack the billion-dollar mark.[15] This explains why Instagram remains the influencer platform of choice, for now.

An issue with researching a nascent category like influencers is that you must rely on the industry to supply the data, and most of that is marketing hype because they are working to grow the business. They will say things like "91.7 percent of marketers use influencer marketing," and when you look closely at the data, you find that it is based on 307 of the influencer marketing firm's clients, people already predisposed to use it. One influencer agency report noted that 52 percent of marketers spend more than $200,000 annually, 7 percent spend $100,000 to $200,000, and 12 percent spend $50,000 to $100,000. Those numbers are a pittance in the advertising world, and they ignore the fact that 30 percent of advertisers aren't even participating. These are also strangely arbitrary price points to slice and dice the numbers.[16] A bit better is information from the Influencer Marketing Hub, based on a survey of 3,500 brands and marketing people. According to its figures: *43 percent of brands spend less than $10,000*; 22 percent spend between $10,000 and $50,000; 14 percent spend between $50,000 and $100,000, and 11 percent spend more than $500,000. This last category tripled in size over the last year.[17] Some of that may have been fueled by the 2023 actors and writers strikes. With no new TV shows and the inability to hire union talent for the better part of a year, marketers had to look at alternatives to TV for ad placement, and they had to find nonunion talent.

But even with that boost, you have to wonder why so many advertisers are spending so little. A lot of that has to do with how effective they believe, or pretend to believe, nano- and micro-influencers are. Paying for a MrBeast can cost millions. Use one or two thousand nano-influencers who have committed followings, and it costs marketers next to nothing. Most payment for them is in the form of "seeding" or "gifting," a veiled way of saying that these companies will give influencers free product but won't pay them for their labor. Advertisers are consciously using this tactic to keep costs down as they wait for this form of advertising to prove itself, and, let's be honest, they do it because the market has become saturated with smaller, easily substituted players.

This sucks for influencers. Advertisers claim they aren't spending more money because there is no standardized method to establish that a purchase occurred based on having seen influencer content.[18] Some research, however, suggests it is effective. A study from marketing company Tinuiti found that "nearly two-thirds of Gen Z beauty shoppers reported seeing or hearing about a new beauty product on social media that they later went on to purchase, with more than half reporting doing so in food and beverage and nearly half in over-the-counter health."[19] Pew Research looked at adult social media users and found that three in ten "say they have purchased something after seeing an influencer or content creator post about it on social media. When looking only at users who *follow* these accounts, that number rises to 53%."[20] It appears, then, that influencers are using cult tactics as a one-two punch: sell you on them and then sell you on stuff.

I still couldn't shake the notion that we should know more about the connection between influencers and sales. Given that we are talking about advertising in digital spaces, these numbers should be available and they should be granular. For example, we know that Meta (Instagram's parent company) knows your interests, your habits, and your purchases. That information is collected on its own platform, but it also tracks you through any site that has an Instagram icon, meaning virtually everywhere. It can also connect what you do online with your offline activities, and it can do all this with mindboggling accuracy.[21] One study found that even if you don't spend time on social media, the platform can create a profile that is 95 percent accurate.[22]

The whole point of data collection—which has been going on for decades at this point—is for platforms to be able to sell your profile to advertisers while purposefully tapping into our vulnerabilities to manipulate our perceptions and emotions. That manipulation is intended to lead us to take a desired action—vote or not, compare ourselves to influencers, and so on. These companies know whether their marketing works. They are not, however, screaming it from the rafters when it comes to influencers. This means one of three things: it is smaller than they want anyone to know; marketers may be tracking something other than sales; or a gatekeeper is protecting it, meaning the platforms aren't sharing it with advertisers unless they pay, and pay handsomely, for it. My strong guess is the last.

Since Meta won't ever give us access to its data, let's look at how effective influencers are at making us buy another way—by looking at conversion. Conversion is when you take action after having seen an ad (go to a website, sign up for an app, purchase a product). The *conversion rate*, the number that advertisers use to assess marketing success, is a percentage based on the number of people who took an action over the number of people who saw the ad. So if one hundred people saw an ad and five people went to a website, the conversion rate is 5 percent.

There are a lot of numbers out there about conversion rates, and they are all over the map based on which social media platform was used and the number of people who follow an influencer. Most are in agreement, though, that influencer marketing has about a 1 percent conversion rate, though bloggers have higher numbers at 2.3 percent.[23] One marketing consulting company compared different forms of digital advertising options and found that the *conversion rate to sale* for influencer marketing was 1.1 percent; the only thing lower was display ads (0.7 percent), and you know how rarely you interact with those. Far more effective were paid social (2.1 percent), organic social (2.4 percent), and email (2.8 percent).[24] Those influencer numbers don't seem great, but they're not terrible when you consider the typical conversion rate is less than 4 percent, and 1 percent of a whole lot of influencers can lead to a whole lot of product sales.

But marketers and platforms rarely talk about sales. It's softer numbers, known as KPIs, or key performance indicators. During the early days of social media, no one could figure out whether advertising on the platforms worked. Marketers had to find something to quantify so they could justify spending their client's money. Quantifications became likes and shares and comments, derogatorily dubbed "vanity metrics." These same fuzzy numbers are used today when it comes to influencers. Adrienne Lahens, the head of TikTok's global business, in talking about the effectiveness of the platform, said, "brands are seeing a 26% lift in brand favorability, a 22% lift in brand recommendations."[25] That may ultimately lead to sales because the product is top of mind or because it becomes part of the consumer's consideration set. Even on the business part of its website, which is a sales tool to other marketers to buy advertising, the content is obtuse. I went to the TikTok business website to look for sales numbers in case studies based on (1) creator content and (2) attribution (where the website visitor came from that led to sales). It came up as "no result."

When platforms can't, or won't, talk about sales conversion, they turn to anecdotal evidence. On TikTok, Converse used 2,900 creators for its "Creative All-Star Series," which led to "*16.86 million impressions* and *1.8 million clicks . . .* [which] drove a *9.22% engagement rate* and a *75% uplift in brand recall.*"[26] That's a lot of eyeballs, but I don't see sales. Instagram touts the example of Daniel Wellington, a watch brand that grew into a $228 million business in three years because of influencer gifting and user-generated content. No matter what those platforms say, though, and especially TikTok because it is so influencer driven, influencer marketing has not been proven to be consistently successful in selling products. When it does, like Chipotle's #GuacDance, it is because it has some other marketing tactic attached to it. In this case, Chipotle increased sales (dollar figures not given) because it was giving guacamole away for free during a very short time frame (six days). As Sofia Hernandez, the global head of business marketing for TikTok, admitted, "what the industry thinks today is that TikTok is pretty much an awareness play," meaning that when you see an influencer promote a product—just like when you see an ad—it introduces you or reminds you about a brand, but they aren't getting you to buy.

Looking at case studies on influencer agency and influencer platform websites confirms this. The McDonald's campaign that led to 540,000 more store visits was the only one I found that included statistics related to conversion, and that case is several years old. Instead, agencies overwhelmingly exclaim about the large number of impressions (the number of people who saw an ad), engagements (likes, shares, comments), and "influencer media value," which is an estimate of what it would cost an advertiser to invest in paid advertising. The companies use language like "we drove traffic," which resulted in purchases, but they don't include hard numbers.

This is not to say that influencer marketing doesn't ever work. Campaigns that boast sales figures are executed with mega-influencers, similar to traditional celebrity advertising, or through the use of a gazillion nano-influencers. For example, Dunkin' Donuts (a company with a large following in its own right) has a long-term paid sponsorship deal with Charli D'Amelio, a TikToker with more than 144 million followers. Dunkin' created a drink called the Charli and connected it to the hashtag #CharliX-DunkinContest. This campaign "led to a 57% increase in app downloads on launch day," an increase of 20 percent in cold brew units on the first day and 45 percent on the second day. This is combined with a brand ambassador program made up of the company's employees posting to their accounts, which gives the content an added push. When Animalhouse Fitness introduced its product MonkeyFeet, an admittedly odd-looking device that allows you to lift weights with your feet, the company used an influencer gifting campaign on TikTok and Instagram. The campaign activated 1,471 influencers who created more than 3,700 posts, leading to $7 million in revenue, and the company rose to the top 1 percent of Shopify's fastest-growing companies.[27]

That the sales were generated on Shopify is an important element here, because what has been shown to work broadly when it comes to influencers is affiliate marketing. We saw this take off in 2022 when Amazon launched its first "Prime early access" sale. Influencers were plastered across social media promoting the special deals available for a forty-eight-hour period. In addition to using the hashtag "PrimeEarlyAccessSale," almost every creator prompted their followers to go to a link in their bios for their curated "Amazon storefront." Influencer content was boosted by user after user rushing to grab cheap leggings or new makeup and then posting about it in response to the influencer's post. What made this effective was that the videos all contained a prompt to go to their "Amazon storefront." Up until now, affiliate marketing and influencer marketer were not the same thing, but don't be surprised when they become increasingly conflated.

Case in point: TikTok Shop launched in late 2023 as the app's answer to Amazon's affiliate program. It marries influencers to shopping, all within the app, enabling consumers to buy without being redirected to an outside website. More than two hundred thousand brands and independent sellers use this feature to promote their products. Aligned with this in-app shopping mall is an affiliate program in which influencers can make commissions when promoting TikTok Shop merchandise. According to *Ad Age*, "creators have been sharing videos about the earnings they've received through this commission-based content, ranging from hundreds to even thousands of dollars per week," also noting that it is "TikTok's plan to position itself as a destination for shopping."[28]

Truth is, influencers are all about "younger" demographics. Millennials and Gen Z, the demos advertisers care most about, increasingly rely on influencers to make their purchase decisions. According to an independent survey, 20 percent of adults made a purchase based on influencer recommendations and 43 percent said an influencer was instrumental in their decision, even if they weren't the sole reason for the purchase. If you look at the same numbers for eighteen- to twenty-five-year-olds, 75 percent of respondents said, "recommendations from influencers impact their decision to make a purchase," and 40 percent made purchases directly through an influencer's storefront. Similarly, Pew Research found that 72 percent of Gen Z follow influencers, and 43 percent have bought something based on their recommendations. For millennials, the numbers are 44 percent and 33 percent respectively. In short, Gen Z relies on influencers the way older generations rely on product reviews.[29]

The question is: will they keep doing that if the platforms become one big shopping mall populated with big-name talent making high-quality content on one end and a slew of nano-influencers making hyper-niche content on the other? We don't know. What we do know is that first to last, the platforms control the show. What works for them right now is to do whatever they can to get everyone on the hamster wheel of staying on top of trends. TikTok, in particular, has emphasized this from the get-go. Young people want to stay on top of trends—FOMO, you know—but so do creators and advertisers. Partially this is pushed through trending music or trending filters that are supposed to miraculously boost your follower numbers. But the real reason is that some of the biggest viral moments happen serendipitously and not necessarily with an influencer. You may remember the Grimace trend, in which people pretended to drink a purple milkshake from McDonald's and proceeded to promptly pass out. This was started by a micro-influencer named Austin Frazier with a ten-second video. People went crazy with it, the same way people went crazy with the Ice Bucket Challenge.[30] Another example was when a woman named Danielle (@danimarielettering) posted a video showing that her car had burned to a crisp. However, her Stanley cup was still intact, and when she shook the cup free from the cupholder, you could still hear ice rattling inside. (It may or may not have been ice, but it made for good video to say that it was; the video has 89.9 million views as of this writing.[31]) In response, the president of Stanley posted a video on TikTok saying the company was going to buy her a new car.[32] Danielle now has 101,000 followers and 9.3 million likes, 8.8 million of which are from that single video. Danielle may now be the new spokesperson for Stanley cups, but she is not an influencer.

Influencers are part of a system that gets us to buy. In traditional media, there was something called effective frequency. That was how many times a person needs to see a marketing message before he/she understands it and in turn decides to buy. That number used to be three. Today, the thinking is that someone requires between seven and thirteen touchpoints—times when you have interacted with a brand—before you decide to buy. Influencers, for most people, will be one of those touchpoints.

New research shows that users are posting less content but consuming more of it. They feel they can't compete with influencers who post high-quality content supported by an entire production team who make it look perfect but effortless.[33] In an interesting turn of events, it isn't just users who are starting to pull away from platforms. After more than a decade of churning out daily material, influencers are burned out. They just can't do it anymore, which is why so many are turning to opportunities beyond influence and social media. Given this, what we will begin to see are more high-end, mega-influencers dominating the brand deals and a whole bunch of nano-influencers appealing to specific psychographics and a winnowing down of the influencers in the middle.

THE MEGA-CULT

The winner in this scenario is the one who holds the purse strings—the platforms. While social media sites are growing, they treat their visitors well. They treat their creators even better because they need to have content to sell to advertisers. Once they get the business clients onboard, they find a way to extract as much profit for themselves as they can. Cory Doctorow called this enshittification.[34]

We can see this happening now with streaming video services and TikTok. Netflix and Max promised ad-free viewing experiences, and we can still watch commercial free but we have to pay through the nose. Same is true of TikTok, which has flooded its site with advertising.

This is not the only way the system is set up to fail. Although internet enthusiasts talked about the long tail of the internet, they were quiet about what Clay Shirky called the "power law distribution." This is a business strategy in which companies can profit from selling a few items to a lot of customers instead of selling popular items to lots of people. Think of this in terms of Amazon: It can sell a few copies of really obscure books to people, and it doesn't cost it a lot of money. If it can sell a few copies of thousands and thousands of obscure books, it can make good profit. Brick-and-mortar bookstores could never do that. They simply don't have the space. As for Shirky, he wrote, "In systems where many people are free to choose between many options, a small subset of the whole will get a disproportionate amount of traffic (or attention, or income), even if no members of the system actively work towards such an outcome. . . . This has nothing to do with moral weakness, selling out, or any other psychological explanation. The very act of choosing, spread widely enough and freely enough, creates a power law distribution."[35] So even though the system makes lots of options available, there will be a limited number of people that get attention.

The creator economy didn't democratize the media. Rather, a limited few reap the benefits while millions create content, ultimately putting money in the pockets of large corporations that no longer have to spend money to create the placeholder with which to surround the advertising.[36] It is the David Dobrik and the Kardashians and Donald Trump who grab the attention, solidifying their brands.

The umbrella cult in all of this is the platforms themselves.

9

FROM SKINCARE TO COACHING
TO CRYPTOCURRENCY

So far, we have been talking about social media influencers. Those influencers fall primarily into the three main buckets of fitness, food, and fashion. Persuaders, however, are not limited to improving your looks or your health, nor are they limited to online, interactive platforms, though these may be integral to getting their message out. Influencers can be academics like history professor Heather Cox Richardson, who writes the number one newsletter on Substack and hosts live events on Facebook. They can be activists and journalists, like podcasters Aubréy Gordon and Michael Hobbes of *Maintenance Phase*. They can be news personalities, like Tucker Carlson or Rachel Maddow, or celebrities, like Gwyneth Paltrow or Jessica Alba, both of whom expanded beyond acting to become entrepreneurs. Or they can be from the world of business.

I focus on this last one due to an explosion of hoodwinking in this area, which is often boosted by influencers. The other reason I focus on business is because influencers, finding it inhumanly hard to keep up with posting 24/7/365, have moved to the realm of business coaching, and most of it is as smarmy, deceptive, and cult-y as MLMs.

BUSINESS AND "BROFLUENCERS"

Sam Bankman-Fried, or SBF as he was known, was the guy to know in crypto. He is a Stanford-educated computer geek who at the height of his wealth—reported to be $16 billion—routinely dressed like a schlub in a T-shirt and cargo pants, with a mass of hair so unruly it looked like it hadn't seen a comb in a decade. He'd do television interviews while playing video games, either because he wanted to show he was so smart he didn't need to listen to the interviewer or because he had the attention span of a gnat. We really can't be sure. But by early 2022, he had built one of the largest cryptocurrency exchanges in the world, framing it as easy for the user, with the added benefit of raising money to make the world a better place.

Bankman-Fried started FTX, a cryptocurrency exchange to help consumers feel more comfortable trading this amorphous form of digital banking. For the uninitiated, crypto is money that you can't touch or see because it exists only on the internet, but you can use it to buy things, just as you would use cash or a credit card. Instead of a bank down the street, you store your money in a digital wallet on your computer or smartphone. Cryptocurrency is not issued by a government, and it is not regulated, which is why it is the currency of choice for international drug cartels. I've tried to learn more than this—stuff about mining and blockchains and price fluctuations--but my brain starts to spin, and that's with an MBA and a Ph.D. Now you understand why SBF could sell the need for FTX, and why people who got into crypto could be so easily fooled.

Nothing says "this product is for the masses" more than placing an ad on the Super Bowl telecast, which FTX did in 2022. A now famously ironic commercial showed Larry David of *Curb Your Enthusiasm* fame turning down one world-changing invention after another throughout history. In the final scene, David is in a large office sitting behind a desk. A guy who appears to be in his late twenties or early thirties, dressed in Friday-casual attire, sits across from him with cell phone in hand and says, "It's a safe and easy way to get into crypto." We didn't realize how wise Larry David was when he replied, "Neh, I don't think so."

Promotion didn't stop there. SBF was on the cover of *Forbes* and *Fortune*, and he was being compared to billionaire investor Warren Buffett. FTX logos appeared on the shirts of Major League Baseball umpires. Influencers promoted FTX as if it was a new burger joint you should try, never considering that it was a volatile investment vehicle. There was Steph Curry and Kevin O'Leary of *Shark Tank*, who disclosed he was a paid spokesperson during a CNBC appearance, but that's because it's a requirement of the network. Not everyone was forced to announce their affiliations, so they didn't. There was Tom Brady and Naomi Osaka, and that's just a few of the famous names that pushed what turned out to be a toxic investment product. These were the influencers for the masses.

Less well known was the phalanx of online financial influencers pushing FTX in an uncannily coordinated way. In his article, "How Social Media Influencers Fed Bankman-Fried's Cult of Personality," Chris Norlund, a former professor of international business, entertainment, and design, exposes the web of influencers who were being sponsored by FTX online. Many of the influencers were clients of an agency called Creators Agency, who "collaborated" to push FTX and SBF, likely making millions of dollars to do so. The article goes on to list about a dozen financial influencers, mostly mega folks with more than a million followers, and some with as many as four million. All of this struck Norlund as suspicious when he started tracking YouTubers posting videos about FTX. He put it this way:

> I knew something was up because suddenly all of these seemingly unconnected creators were talking about the same thing at the exact same time. That is: FTX is great and Sam Bankman-Fried is a genius. . . . Creators Agency assisted some of the most watched and influential channels in promoting what could turn out to be one of the largest financial crimes in history. And in so doing, it helped Bankman-Fried establish his reputation as a selfless billionaire and FTX's as a safe cryptocurrency exchange.[1]

We know now that repetition and parasocial relationships play a key part in ginning up belief in an idea and a leader. What also makes it work is the coordination by influencer agencies, which I dig into a bit more in the next chapter.

By the end of 2023, Sam Bankman-Fried was in jail for swindling people out of billions of dollars. The details of the case aren't relevant to this discussion. What is important for us to pay attention to is our willingness to believe those we perceive to be in positions of power. SBF was deceptive. Crypto is deceptive. FTX was the ultimate Ponzi scheme, leading to astronomical economic losses. As columnist Michelle Singletary wisely noted in the *Washington Post*, "Cryptocurrency investing is like going to a ritzy casino—the sights and sounds of winning don't mean the vast majority of people are richer than when they started playing. It's all part of the lure and illusion."[2] A perfect description of a cult that thrives in digital spaces.

SBF is not alone in his ability to work Wall Street, the press, and the public. Two high-profile examples of young entrepreneurs are Adam Neumann of WeWork and Elizabeth Holmes of Theranos. I debated including them here because even while they created cultlike companies, their influence wasn't as embedded online. However, they are products of the Silicon Valley mindset and will help further elucidate the idea of "brofluencers."

WeWork had all the makings of a cult. Neumann was a charismatic leader whose wife, Rekebah (Gwyneth's cousin), an early partner in the company, always seemed to be hovering in the background. News stories appeared throughout the mainstream press championing the company through its meteoric rise and increasing the hype without anyone knowing what was truly going on with the financials. As investments increased, WeWork office-sharing spaces seemed to sprout up everywhere. Single entrepreneurs were on the rise and looking for connections beyond what they could get at their local Starbucks.

Neumann was also a member of the Kabbalah Centre, having been introduced to it by his wife, and much of that organization's touchy-feely pseudo-spirituality infused the company. One of my master's students, Michael Bass, found himself employed by WeWork after it bought MeetUp, the online platform for organizing group gatherings. In his thesis, he explained that Neumann (an Israeli) envisioned the company to function like a kibbutz, a place of community and support. In 2008, its website home page said, "Now more than ever, creating opportunities for connection, promoting love and a focus on humanity is essential to empowering everything we do." The company would bring in guest speakers, like Deepak Chopra, to talk about spirituality and work. Michael was a fairly religious guy, and even he felt it was pretty woo-woo. To get a sense of how embedded this was in the company mandate, this is a post from one of the company's Instagram accounts in 2018:

> Our Mission is to elevate the world's consciousness by expanding happiness and unleashing every human's superpowers. Our Founder, Rebekah Neumann, sharing her thoughts on our collective purpose as human beings. Consciousness is the new cool! ♥ Link in bio for more on what we're building. #studentoflife #consciousness[3]

As the company continued to attract more and more investment money, Neumann's vision expanded to a more holistic view. Not only would the company be WeWork, but WeGrow (education) and WeLive (co-living), among others, so that the brand hypothetically encompassed all aspects of life. Less reported is that Neumann referred to WeWork operations as "WeOS," the company's "operating system for life." The company was designed to act like a digital space in the real world—using gamification and technology to invoke interactions—and Neumann saw social media, not other workspaces, as his competition.[4]

The sharp fall of WeWork began when the company announced its initial public offering (IPO). In conjunction with going public, a company has to produce documents showing its financials. Not only did the document reveal that the company was not making money, but much of it was written by Rebekah, who had more experience with Kabbalah than with financial disclosure documents. The IPO never went forward, Neumann was removed, and the company was restructured.

Through all of this, Neumann was deceptive in his business dealings, leading people to believe that he was doing something new and different when it was nothing more than a standard real estate venture. He abused his workers and kept them tied to the company with the lure of an equity payout that never happened, the same way NXIVM dangled scarves before its members. In an incredibly unjust Wall Street deal, Neumann was never charged, and he walked away with almost a billion dollars while his workers got nothing. The company filed for Chapter 11 bankruptcy in 2023.

Elizabeth Holmes, too, built Theranos as a cult through some of the most widely reported and ultimately dangerous forms of deception. Ms. Holmes claimed that she had created a device (called Edison) that could test blood on the spot, with only the smallest drop derived from a finger stick. She tightly controlled every aspect of the business because she had to; the device didn't work, and she couldn't afford for anyone to find out.

I don't think you can call Ms. Holmes charismatic, at least not from any presentations I saw. Poised yes, charismatic no. She modeled herself on Steve Jobs, dressing in black as he did. And she was young, she was pretty, she was (partially) Stanford educated, and the press loved the idea that Silicon Valley had finally produced a female-led unicorn. (A discussion about the male dominance of Silicon Valley and how women are denied access to venture capital funding is for another book.)

What she was able to do was to persuade an impressive group of older, powerful men to join her board. Board members included family friend George Shultz, who brought others to the table, including Jim Mattis, the former head of U.S. Central Command who later became secretary of defense, and former secretary of state, Henry Kissinger. Although it made sense to have some military connections on the board—because, if functional, the device would have battlefield uses—politicians far outweighed those with medical experience.[5] This was the crux of the hoodwink: people invested because they knew smart and important people were connected to the company. However, that none of those smart people had medical knowledge should have raised a red flag.

Once appearing on the covers of *Forbes*, *Fortune*, and *Inc.*, Elizabeth Holmes today sits in jail serving an eleven-year sentence. I'm really not sure why Adam Neumann isn't there too.

Now that we have looked at some examples, let me define brofluencers, a decidedly darker side of influence. The Urban Dictionary defines brofluencer as a "Person on LinkedIn who spouts quick fixes to make X better with no research, sourcing, or (sometimes) even experience. Not limited to male creators. Prevalent in the LinkedIn marketing community, but can sometimes be found lurking outside of it."[6] That definition doesn't go far enough. When I talk about the brofluencer culture here, I am specifically referring to it as it relates to "tech bros," usually white, usually male, and utterly immersed in the Silicon Valley ethos of move fast, break things, make as much money as you can, and leave the suckers holding the bag. Elon Musk, Mark Zuckerberg, Jack Dorsey—you get the idea. It is not limited to men, because it is a mindset not a gender. The influence is not limited, however, to LinkedIn. So I am modifying the definition for our purposes here: A brofluencer is any person with a Silicon Valley mindset promoting a product or service (usually online) who spouts quick fixes with no basis in research, no proof of success, and/or no evidence of expertise. This is done with the intention of misleading consumers for profit.

As we saw, "quick fixes" can include making investing in crypto easier or analyzing blood more efficiently. More broad and pernicious are the increasing number of influencers selling their "expertise" packaged as coaching and courses—and creating a cult following to do it.

THE RISE OF THE "COACH"

Tim Ferriss was instrumental in spawning the fake expert trend even before the rise of social media. Ferriss is the author of the *4-Hour Workweek*, a book that sold more than two million copies, was translated into dozens of languages, and spent four years on the *New York Times* bestseller list. Ferriss had worked as a tech entrepreneur but made his money selling supplements. His job and his wealth weren't making him happy, so he decided to reassess his life by taking a year off and traveling around the world. Right there, bells should go off in your head. Could *you* take a year off and travel around the world?

What you discover after reading the book is that it is about you paying other people so *you* can have a four-hour work week. He also says it costs nothing to write a bestselling book. Maybe, but only if you have the time, and really you only have time if you have money. The quintessential element to achieving a nonwork life is to generate a stream of passive income, the goal of any good tech entrepreneur.

Ferriss explains that your unending stream of revenue without any work comes in the form of an informational product—a course. Today, it would be an online course, a source of passive income for lots of today's coaches. He then proceeds to tell you how to scam followers by pretending to be an expert. He's claiming success can be achieved under the long tail theory. Of course, you'll have to find the people who are interested in that limited area in which you claim "expertise."

Since that book was published, untold numbers of people claim expertise in how to invest, how to improve our relationships, how to take the next step in your career, and so on. What we also see time and time again is that the "expertise" is flimsy, and the content is topline to appeal to the lowest common denominator. Much of it has been pulled from online sources, as Ferriss recommended in his book. The difference is that it has been repackaged and resold by an influencer. What you are paying for with these coaches is quite simply the marketing.

Andrew Tate is an extreme example of creating a consciously divisive online personality to sell repackaged content to guys who want to be just like him. Tate originally gained attention as a four-time world kickboxing champion. His fame was goosed by appearances on *Big Brother*, a show he was kicked off after a video surfaced of him beating a woman with a belt. To solidify his hardcore male bona fides, he appeared with other right-wing personalities and peddled misogyny. He made millions from what he admitted was a scam that he ran with his brother. Moving to Romania (he is American), he and his brother set up a webcam business in which models told "sob stories" to get men to part with their money.

In 2021, he started Hustle University, an online "university" that was supposed to teach men how to get rich and drive fancy cars just like Tate. It was an affiliate marketing/pyramid scheme that entailed signing others up by posting videos of Tate. Followers received a commission, and Tate ended up all over social media.[7] What they were selling was basic business information, not taught by Tate, for $49 a month. He also used the now-familiar tactic of retaining followers by shaming them if they threatened to quit and saying if the method didn't work for them, it was because they didn't try hard enough.[8]

In August 2022, Facebook, Instagram, YouTube, and TikTok shuttered Tate's accounts, claiming policy violations.[9] Simultaneously, Twitter permanently banned Tate from the platform. By the time the accounts were closed, Tate had 4.6 million Instagram followers and a YouTube audience of 740,000. There is little evidence that any of the university scholars made substantial money; there is ample evidence that Tate did.

Tate embodies the worst of what we are talking about here: anger-inducing content, a walled community where people support each other's beliefs, and a charismatic leader with the ability to influence large numbers of people. I wish I could say it ended there, but I cannot. He is now back on X, with more than eight million followers, and Hustle University has been rebranded as "The Real World Portal."

Tate is just one example of what has been dubbed the "male guru grift."[10] It is the male equivalent of luring women into MLMs, and like MLMs, these courses have consequences. To see what can happen, we look at Dan Lok, an entrepreneur who sells "courses" teaching how to be a high-end, luxury salesperson. One person who got sucked in because he wanted more in his life was Garrett, a hip young guy who wears a knit cap and a neatly trimmed beard. He was a teacher who decided he did not love his career choice. As the end of summer approached and he realized he had to get into the classroom again (which he admits was a low point for him), he decided to sign up for a class with Dan Lok, who claimed Garrett could quit his job and begin making six figures. The decision to make the plunge wasn't necessarily out of the blue. Dan Lok had been popping up on Garrett's feeds for a while, including being promoted by other influencers Garrett followed. All these people he trusted were recommending Dan Lok, though they weren't saying that they were getting paid to promote him. Long story short, Garrett was sucked into buying thousands of dollars of courses, invited into an inner circle, which led to spending more money, and never learned a useful skill. After six months, he came to realize that he had been sucked into this cult (his word) and he was $26,000 in debt.[11]

How Garrett was pulled into the course is an important aspect of how these course cults work. Like MLMs, the ads start appearing in the feeds of people looking to change their lives. Get-rich-quick schemers and crypto brofluencers appear on one another's shows, and because it's a guest appearance, like a celebrity promoting a new movie, it doesn't need to be flagged as promotional. It's simply two guys talking. But what this does for the viewer is provide social proof, a term coined by Robert Cialdini in 1984 in his book *Influence: The Psychology of Persuasion*. It means that we view behaviors as being more correct the more we see other people do it. If we think one beer brand is more popular than another, we'll pick that. Cialdini ran an experiment to try and encourage people to reuse towels in hotels. He tested different messages, and when the message said that more people reuse their towels, the response rate was 9 percent higher than when an environmental message was used.[12]

The more we see people acting in similar ways online—signing up for courses, promoting the promoters' work for them—the more we believe that is the right thing to do. One of the reasons we see the same actions over and over is that the influencers promote each other. This doesn't just happen with brofluencers; it has become standard practice. In *The Authenticity Industries*, an influencer talked about the tools she uses to boost her numbers, including "reciprocal shout-outs (i.e., tagging and recommending others to follow) and link-ups (posting on a coordinated topic)."[13] When more than one influencer starts talking about the same product, it provides social proof. This is not only done by influencer platforms and agencies, but is coordinated by the influencers themselves.

BRITTANY DAWN—BROFLUENCER IN LEGGINGS

Brittany Dawn is a painfully skinny, blonde, perfectly coiffed and styled influencer, the kind you see on Instagram every day. Based in Texas, she started on the platform in the mid-2010s and presented herself as a health and fitness expert offering "personalized nutritional guidance and individualized fitness coaching" plans ranging from $92 to $300 a month.

Some women followed her in hopes of losing a few pounds. Others were particularly attracted to Brittany Dawn because they believed she had special training in managing eating disorders because she used the hashtag #EDwarrior (eating disorder warrior). She claimed in YouTube videos that she had overcome her own weight issues with healthy eating and exercise. These videos and the persistent use of the hashtag led followers to believe she had ED expertise when she had absolutely none.

People struggling with eating disorders signed up for her program, only to be told to eat less than they already were. Those trying to get fit lost neither pounds nor inches, and getting emails saying, "you're killing it!" fell flat because they knew it was a lie, and they weren't getting the one-on-one attention they had paid for.

In 2018, plan purchasers started a private Facebook group—called Brittany Dawn Complaints—where they shared their workout and diet plans. They discovered nothing was customized for them; they didn't get the promised personal coaching or the promised phone calls. Infuriated, clients began asking for their money back, mostly to no avail.

As issues mounted, *Good Morning America* produced a segment about online health and fitness scams in early 2019. Brittany Dawn was the centerpiece. She tried to justify her actions—providing the same workout and meal plan, not responding to customers, and so forth—by saying that her business scaled too quickly. She simply couldn't customize plans for five thousand people. An *Insider* reporter was skeptical of that claim because the problems had been going on for years; she had plenty of time to correct them if she wanted to.

In 2022, the Texas Attorney General sued Brittany Dawn for fraudulent advertising claims. The suit didn't focus on her lack of credentials, either as a fitness coach or a nutrition expert. It was about false advertising. Lying on the internet isn't against the law; lying in advertising is. This strategy is increasingly being used to go after bad actors. You may remember that the Sandy Hook families used the same method to sue Remington. The $42 million judgment was not because its products (guns) kill people; it was because Remington advertised that the product helped make men more masculine.

The same year as the *Good Morning America* story, Brittany Dawn rebranded from fitness influencer to Christian devotee. The launch is announced with a cringeworthy YouTube video in which she proclaims, "Fitness and health are no longer my identity. My identity is in Christ." Now, she hawks religious one-day conferences for $125 per person or three-day events for $600 through her She Lives Freed website. Her content grew increasingly bizarre, including espousing QAnon conspiracies.

Like Adam Neumann, Dawn left a wake of hurt behind her but walked away virtually unscathed. Dawn settled the Texas State lawsuit, which led to a relatively minor payment of $400,000.[14] Pivoting to Christian influencer turned out to be a boon. She launched a podcast, *Chiseled and Called*, and her online presence is bigger than it ever was: she has 1.3 million followers on TikTok and more than 500,000 on YouTube. She even has a clothing line called Hazel and Layne. Instead of fake diet and fitness plans, she's selling family, faith, and false beliefs, all with a touch of fashion. The move from fitness to religion to conspiracist is, sadly, not uncommon, as we will see in chapter 11.

One last example is Vishen Lakhiani. Vishen is the bestselling author of *The Code of the Extraordinary Mind* (2016) and *The Buddha and the Badass: The Secret Spiritual Art of Succeeding at Work* (2020). He is also the founder of Mindvalley, an online learning platform "to support individual spiritual development and lifelong learning." The company's site offers approximately forty coaching programs covering topics like leadership, unlimited abundance, healing from heartbreak, and lots of stuff about focusing your mind and spiritual growth. Programs last between thirty and fifty days and entail listening to a twenty-minute daily lesson. One of the promotional videos boldly states, "According to the company, people are five times more likely to complete a course on Mindvalley than on any other educational platform due to scientifically backed tools, such as community motivation and daily micro learnings that condense complicated topics into easy to understand portions. Their learning approaches are based on neuro-science, peak performance, and speed learning techniques." A semiannual highlight for Mindvalley is "A-Fest," an event for wealthy and conscious entrepreneurs held in rotating exotic places around the world. This will set you back about $3,495 to $4,495, depending on how early you book, and you have to be a member of Mindvalley, which sets you back another $499 annually.[15]

Vishen's product is saturated in spirituality, and meditation is very much a part of the learning process. (Some have referred to him as a younger, more corporate version of Deepak Chopra.) Spiritual practices are not, however, for personal growth alone but to aid in increasing one's business efficiency. This is "on trend" these days as companies integrate meditation—not for health purposes but to improve productivity. Religion scholar Justin Henry explains Mindvalley's gestalt by saying that Lakhiani believes "the fully self-actualized entrepreneur . . . is one for whom 'the old model of work disappears,' wherein a 'job' or 'career' is not merely a means of financial subsistence but instead a vehicle transporting you to your 'vision board' image of yourself, generating meaningful and fulfilling experiences and relationships along the way."[16]

While researching Mindvalley, two stories came up again and again. In one, Lakhiani talks about being down on his luck after the dot-com bubble. Unable to find work, he took a job as a salesman making cold calls to at-torneys. Frustrated, he went online and discovers the Silva Mind Method while performing a Google search. After Lakhiani used this focusing tool, every lawyer he called was willing to listen and ultimately bought what he was selling. The other one showed Lakhiani claiming that he knew what a book said simply by waving his hand over it. I'd seen this before at the Kabbalah Centre, where teachers claim you don't need to know how to read Hebrew; simply scanning it with your finger provides all the spiritual knowledge you need. But people seem to love what he is selling because there is lots of social proof to back him up.

Mindvalley's marketing is aggressive and brilliantly segmented. On one social media platform, I saw ads about weight loss and fitness. On another, I saw one about how to guarantee my online course would be successful. Mindvalley also uses affiliate marketing assiduously. If you go on YouTube looking for examples of people who have taken classes, videos are posted with what appear to be critical headlines ("The Truth about Mindvalley: Are Courses Legit or Cult?"), but after a few minutes these quickly turn to how great the courses are. If you look in the video captions, you find the link for 15 percent off or even 40 percent off the coaching courses. And, like the Mormons, it is almost impossible to find anything critical about the company because so many videos are being pushed out by the devotees.

You can even become a Mindvalley certified life coach—without experience or expertise. According to the website, through a free webinar, you will learn (1) how to escape the nine-to-five and create true freedom (just like MLMs), (2) whether coaching is right for you, and (3) how to build your coaching business. Most important, you will learn "how to confidently coach anyone—even as a total beginner. Learn the proven four-pillar framework to facilitate massive breakthroughs and transformation for clients—even as a new and inexperienced coach."[17] And to overcome your concerns about the market becoming oversaturated, there's a video called "Breaking the Myth: Are There Too Many Coaches in the World?" To that I would say, "Yes, yes there are." Mindvalley does not agree.[18]

FROM CULT LITE TO BUSINESS COACH

The trend to move from influencer to coach has been growing during the last few years.[19] Much of this shift has to do with the burnout that influencers are dealing with after a decade or more of having to post every . . . single . . . day. The dangers of social media—anxiety, social comparison, invasion of privacy—are well documented when it comes to us, the viewers. Less studied is what happens to influencers over time. Every semester I have students who say they want to become influencers, and they are not alone: 54 percent of Gen Z and millennials say they would be interested in being an influencer, and 86 percent say they would post sponsored content if they were paid.

I try to explain to students what it takes. I found out the hard way and I don't consider myself an influencer. I use social media, primarily TikTok, as a new outlet for my message. I have no intention of making any money from posting online. But I found myself waking up at 5:00 in the morning with some new topic ideas or to figure out the flow of an argument for a post. Having worked with a few coaches (real coaches with expertise, who did help me), I was told that you have to post consistently in order to grow your audience, especially when you start out. It didn't have to be every day, but it did have to be consistent. I started out posting three days a week. Now I sometimes do it five days a week but rarely on the weekend. I can't imagine coming up with something new seven days a week for years on end. Sure, there's batch production—shooting content in one day and then posting it one day at a time—but even that requires planning, and what happens if there is a last-minute news event or a new trend that changes everything, and you have to create something on the spot?

In the same way that we are affected by likes and shares, influencers are motivated by how their followers respond to them. This is what is known as audience capture, "a self-reinforcing feedback loop that involves telling one's audience what they want to hear and getting rewarded for it." Influencers are motivated to produce content based on what audiences respond to.

One of the saddest stories I heard was about a young boy named Nicholas Perry. He started on YouTube as a skinny kid, a vegan violinist. Those videos didn't draw followers, so he knew he had to try something else. He began showing himself eating. Followers began to take note, but they also began pushing for more extreme forms of consumption. Over the years, his follower numbers grew, his views ballooned to more than a billion, and so did his waistline. He became a parody of himself and dubbed himself Nikocado Avocado. Although this is an extreme example, and he has moved away from this content recently, it is the force that keeps content creators on the hamster wheel.

More and more stories are coming out about influencers hitting the proverbial wall. Charli D'Amelio, the poster child for how to become a huge internet star, said she "lost the passion" in 2021, and she's not alone. Influencers with hundreds of thousands of followers, making thousands of dollars a month, have decided to tap out. You can find articles about TikTokers burning out and YouTubers calling it quits.[20] Influencers are overwhelmed by the constant need to create and the barrage of complaints from followers if they don't.[21] It's no joke. In one case, the "queen of the Mommy bloggers," Heather Armstrong, who was famous for sharing her life and her struggles with depression, committed suicide.[22]

A way around this is to either have your production team post content that doesn't require the influencer's input, or, more commonly, influencers are pivoting to become coaches. I'm sure you've seen these online. Ads for how to write a book in thirty days, or financial self-help telling you how you can retire by age fifty, or the more generic "life coaching," which is where former influencers seem to land. Many of these "experts" don't have a background in what they are training others to do, nor could they earn a license to coach, because they don't exist. The part that is beyond ridiculous is the growing bevy of twentysomethings calling themselves life coaches, asserting they provide value to their clients based on their vast life experience.

Coaching itself is not new. Dale Carnegie wrote *How to Win Friends and Influence People* in 1934, which spawned Dale Carnegie Training. Norman Vincent Peale wrote *The Power of Positive Thinking* in 1952, a belief so embedded in our culture that you can take online classes still today. What has fundamentally changed is the explosion of people who claim to be coaches and who also have the ability to bamboozle people into paying for these services at scale. There is so much concern about this phenomenon that it has gotten the attention of the Federal Trade Commission, even leading to one company being forced to cough up $2.5 million to pay back those who were harmed.[23]

As I see it, coaching is a rebranding of self-help. Maybe because more women have entered the workplace. Maybe because it is the out-of-work professional's gig-economy way toward entrepreneurship. Maybe it's because all you have to do to be a coach is to say you are one. Also, coaching has an important marketing advantage: whereas "self-help" was New Age–adjacent and mostly targeted toward women, "coaching" allows for a much broader prospective target audience that includes businesspeople and men—who also are likely to have more discretionary money to spend.

This refreshed strategy seems to be working. The percentage of coaches grew globally by 54 percent from 2019 to 2022, according to the International Coaching Federation (ICF). The ICF may sound like a reputable and responsible licensing body, but in truth it is a trade organization that promotes coaching as a profession and provides classes to wannabe coaches, which can be taken for $18,000 per a report on CNBC. Coaching is a completely unregulated industry and so ill-defined that trying to find numbers on how big it is range from $2.85 million to $14.1 billion.[24] That said, it's big and getting bigger. According to ICF's figures (derived through a survey done in conjunction with PricewaterhouseCoopers), there are 34,200 "coach practitioners" in North America, up from 23,000 in 2021. We have to believe that number severely undercounts the total, as this organization focuses on life coaches and not the panoply of other possible offerings.

What makes coaches more insidious than typical content creators is that they are telling you how to live your life rather than simply selling you a product. We saw this in the coaching that goes on in connection with multilevel marketing companies. Without the push toward toxic positivity, most women might never become enmeshed in groups, or at least they might leave them sooner. If you have picked up a book or found a podcast from motivational coaches, life coaches, or financial self-help coaches, you are probably at a vulnerable point in your life. It is at those times when marketers and cults are most likely to swoop in.

An example of an early influencer who turned her life experience into a coaching enterprise is Rachel Hollis. She started her career in event planning and later founded her own company, Chic Events, where she developed a list of high-profile clients. She transitioned to blogging, writing about parenting, relationships, and personal development. After a social media post went viral, she started writing self-help books, including the bestseller *Girl, Wash Your Face* (2018) and the follow up, *Girl, Stop Apologizing* (2019), both female empowerment books meant to help women overcome obstacles that were holding them back from true happiness and success. Motivational speaking, online courses, and personal development conferences followed, the last of which was done in conjunction with her husband.

Her husband, Dave, had been a Disney executive who left as his wife's career began to take off. In addition to conferences, he also wrote books, and as their empire grew, they did a podcast together. They presented themselves as "an average couple who had learned from their mistakes, and had chosen, altruistically, to share their lessons with the masses. They weren't educated counselors or scholars; they were a mom and dad who had taken the circumstances life gave them and turned them into something incredible," per BuzzFeed News. In a video launching their Rise Together conference for couples, they readily admit they have zero training and even laugh about this.[25] You see, in the influencer world, posting your happy, happy marriage is enough to translate into teaching others to do the same.

Hollis was at the center of a number of controversies, but one of the biggest was the couple's announcement that they were getting divorced via an Instagram post—two years after announcing their $1,795 couples weekend. The issue was that right up until that time, they had acted online as if everything was fine. Suddenly the brand was not as authentic as it appeared.[26] Today, Hollis is no longer on TikTok because of a firestorm she ignited related to comments she made claiming that she wasn't trying to be relatable and comparing herself to Harriet Tubman (really!). Although she continues on Instagram, where she has 1.5 million followers, it is interesting to note that she does not post video and she has turned off comments to her posts.

The success of someone like (pre-meltdown) Hollis and others, mixed with the pandemic, plus the need for a break led to an explosion in influencer turned life or business coaches in 2020.

When you start to look at a number of these, you begin to see the same thing—literally. Just like the courses repackaged by the bros, influencers are repackaging Instagram platitudes. Strikingly, almost to a one, the amount of money that they promise people will be able to make is $10,000 per month. Some of that will be from coaching (though they don't say where you will get your clients), and some of it will be coaches coaching other coaches, a variation of the MLM pyramid model.

Alyse Parker is featured in the CNBC life coach story and although she is presented as one of many examples of how to do it right, I see her as a cautionary tale. She started as a vegan YouTuber around 2015. In connection with that vegan lifestyle (branded as Raw Alignment), she espoused New Age-y mystical content and posted videos about why she doesn't wear makeup, how she dropped out of college and moved to Hawaii, and various aspects of her minimalist lifestyle. In 2019, her content transforms, and she's trying a carnivore diet, shaving her armpits for the first time in three years, and posting about "life updates." It is a rebranding she announces in a video called "Goodbye Raw Alignment. HELLO Alyse Parker."[27]

She is a successful influencer with an enormous platform across multiple social media touchpoints. As of this writing, she has 153,000 followers on Instagram, where most of her content is a few years old, and 667,000 on YouTube, where she has pulled back substantially on her content, posting only a few times in the last year. When she does post, she gets thousands of views and lots of comments. With that kind of following, if only a handful made the switch from follower to coaching client, she would have a thriving business with a fraction of the effort. That's not the part that bothers me.

There is no readily available evidence that Parker had any kind of training or education, and she admits as much to CNBC, "I don't hold any certification or degree in the realm of life coaching. I'm a certified health coach and the remainder is life experience, in this lifetime, past lifetimes, wisdom from trials and errors. . . . The way that I talk and the way that I embody the things that I share has just been absolutely all that people need in order to be like, 'That's who I want to support me. That's who I want to be my guide, because I see that they're walking the talk.'"[28] When this was recorded, Alyse was still in her twenties. Then and still today, the banner on her YouTube page is an illustration with aliens, crystals, and mushrooms—not something that necessarily inspires confidence.

When you go to her coaching site, there is no "about" page, no information page, nothing that will tell you anything about what qualifies her to give you advice. What you will see are seven boxes: three are for free downloads, one is for one-on-one mentorship (when I clicked the link, the scheduling platform was invalid), one to book a retreat in Hawaii (for which a shared room goes for $3,900), one is for an online self-guided course called "Higher Intuition" (which costs $222), and one to teach others how to be a coach (which can cost "as little as $199," plus additional discounts if you promote Alyse, but the price is never stated outright). The coaching section is interesting for another reason. Way in the FAQs is where you can learn that she has a certificate from IIN. IIN stands for Institute for Integrative Nutrition and according to its website, it is "the world's most respected nutrition and health coaching school with the largest global presence in health coaching."[29] Its courses are a mixture of nutrition and New Age, and it hosts guest faculty like Julia Cameron and Andrew Weill and offers a Chopra Coaching certification based on the teachings of Deepak Chopra. Like other schools of this sort, classes go for $5,000 or more.

You have to give it to Alyse. She checks all the boxes—retreats, coaching, and coaching coaches. But I wonder how well this is going for her. She started a new vlog in 2023 but posted only a handful of times. Her most recent video, seemingly an update about her life, was actually a brand ambassador post for LMNT electrolytes. The video also seemed like it was posted by someone who is floundering, not someone who could help others to be their best selves.[30]

Alyse Parker is just one in a sea of influencers changing their life strategies. Marie Ewold was a fitness influencer turned coach and like multilevel marketing posts, her Instagram is filled with pictures of her living the high life and drinking champagne.[31] She also has a podcast called "Make Bank with Marie." Top multilevel marketing salespeople who have made the switch to coaching abound on YouTube.[32] Lee Tilghman, a former wellness influencer, now coaches other influencers on how to leave the profession.[33] Danielle Ryan (@itsdanielleryan) has become a popular YouTuber based on her analysis of business coaching scams, many of which relate to former influencers.[34] All of this will have implications for social media, both in terms of content and in terms of job opportunities that these platforms provide.

But whether we are talking about life coaches or financial coaches or wellness coaches—and especially those who work online—we need to be aware of the psychological and technological mechanisms that are pushing us to buy, especially social proof manipulated by coordinated content.

It's all a game to push us toward anxiety—all to the benefit of the influencer.

Buyer beware.

PART IV

FROM "CULT LITE" INFLUENCERS TO SOCIAL MEDIA EXTREMISM

10

ALGORITHMS AND "ANGER" FUEL INFLUENCER EXTREMISM

Conservative mom Carol Smith signed into Facebook in the summer of 2019, listing her likes as politics, parenting, and Christianity. She followed pages for Donald Trump and Fox News. Within two days, Carol was directed to QAnon conspiracy pages. Even though she never interacted with these groups, Facebook persisted in pushing her toward pages filled with disinformation and hate speech. But Carol never got hooked by Q. Because Carol Smith isn't real.

"Carol" is one of many fake accounts researchers created to track how Facebook sends users down conspiracy rabbit holes. The company claims this happens to only the smallest percentage of users. However, a small slice of 325 million U.S. Facebook users is still millions and millions of people. (The extraordinary number of people pushing the same products or ideas on a platform is the reason why you think TikTok made you buy it).

In a TED Talk called "We're Building a Dystopia Just to Make People Click on Ads," sociologist and *New York Times* columnist Zeynep Tufecki explains that companies like Facebook, Google, and Amazon are in the business of capturing and selling our data and attention to advertisers. The more information these companies collect, the better the algorithms work to move you in the direction of buying. The way to get more data is to keep consumers online, and technology on these platforms works to do just that. She explains, for example, that when you go to YouTube, the site populates a list of recommended videos and even simplifies the task for you by automatically playing a video it thinks you would like to watch. This tactic is incredibly effective. In 2018, the company's chief product officer confessed "that more than 70 percent of the videos you watch on YouTube, is due to suggestions made by one of the service's AI-driven recommendations."[1]

But the platform doesn't just make suggestions. Professor Tufecki noticed something interesting about how the YouTube recommendation system works. She watched a Donald Trump video for research purposes. After she viewed it a few times, YouTube began to autoplay white supremacist videos, with each subsequent recommendation becoming increasingly more extreme. This wasn't limited to politics. When she looked at videos about vegetarianism, the next recommended content was for veganism. She quips, "It's like you're never hard core enough for YouTube."

Social media platforms pushing us toward more hard-core content is meant to elicit anger. Anger keeps us tied to our technology and generates more revenue for platforms and influencers. Using advertising to generate extreme emotion isn't new. Mark Bartholomew, author of *Adcreep*, writes about the rise of "shock advertising" over the last two decades. This so-called "shockvertising" captures the audience's attention by violating norms, such as using sex, profanity, or violence, all with the intent of triggering "negative emotions, particularly fear, anger, and disgust."[2] But it is very different to rail at your TV screen after seeing a commercial about how one political party or another is ruining democracy than it is to look at an online post and be able to immediately share it with thousands of people. Anger and algorithms are responsible for the division and extremism plaguing not only the United States but the world.

Political extremism is driven by conspiracy theories and here we look at how influencers use those theories and the tricks of social media, all in a cynical grab for attention. Just as all influencers aren't coaches or bros or multilevel marketers, not all influencers are extremists, but ignoring those who are is to our detriment.

EXTREME EMOTIONS DRIVE AD SALES

The mission of social media platforms is to maximize user engagement, no matter what the cost. Even while our teenage daughters are being harmed by Instagram and our democracy teeters on the brink of destruction, these privately held companies work at the behest of their shareholders (which include their founders and CEOs) before anyone else. Facebook knowingly feeds us "more and more divisive content in an effort to gain user attention & increase time on the platform."[3] Their business is so destructive that in late 2023, forty-one attorneys general, in a bipartisan move, sued Meta for building addictive tools that are detrimental to teens' mental health.[4] What is so brazen in all of this is that the company could easily tweak its algorithm so people would spend less time online, but it simply chooses not to. It locks us in, despite knowing that it is corralling billions of people into extremist echo chambers that gin up hate and anger, while trying to put a good face on its practices and saying that it cares about the world.

We saw this with abundant clarity when it came to vaccine information, even before COVID. In 2015, Mark Zuckerberg took to Facebook and said, "Vaccination is an important and timely topic. . . . The science is completely clear: vaccinations work and are important for the health of everyone in our community." Well, someone forgot to tell the algorithms. According to reporting from the *Guardian*, visitors on Facebook were pointed toward content that was primarily anti-vax propaganda. The same thing was true of YouTube, whose "recommendation algorithm steers viewers from fact-based medical information toward anti-vaccine misinformation,"[5] which we know leads people to stay online longer.

Facebook, Instagram, and YouTube have a massive incentive to tie us to technology—billions of dollars in advertising revenue. It is the fuel that drives digital media. Google (including YouTube) and Meta (including Facebook and Instagram) dominate the digital advertising marketplace.[6] In 2022, the two companies combined accounted for 48.4 percent of U.S. digital advertising revenue. Add in Amazon, and these three players control the digital ad market. Google and Meta's share fell below 50 percent for the first time since 2014, in part due to Apple allowing users to opt out of being tracked and in part due to increasing gains by Amazon, which is at 11.7 percent and is expected to continue to grow.[7] In a clever twist to maintain dominance, Meta and Amazon joined forces to "allow" Amazon customers to shop on Facebook and Instagram without having to leave the app. The catch for users is they must link their Amazon account to Meta's properties, in the same way Meta forced potential Threads users to sign up through an Instagram account. This venture helps both companies, as it keeps visitors on Meta apps longer, it increases sales for both companies, and it leads to more data and more sharing of data, though to what extent has not been divulged.[8]

If we look specifically at platform data, it gets interesting. Although Meta gets 7.6 percent of the "time spent viewing" in the United States, it gets a whopping 19.5 percent of the advertising dollars. Compare this with YouTube, which gets 7.5 percent of the viewing time (only slightly less than Meta) and just 5.8 percent of the dollars (about a third of what Meta gets); TikTok gets 3.7 percent of viewing time and 2.3 percent of the ad dollars. Per Insider Intelligence, "only Meta seems to have figured out how to transmute user engagement into outsize monetization."[9] The other sites are making money. It's just that Facebook retains advertisers through a combination of size, technology, and marketer inertia.

Network effects and cross-subsidization allow the mega-companies to preserve control of the industry, creating barriers to entry that other firms cannot overcome. "Network effects" occur when, as more and more people use a product, it increases its value. Let's take Facebook. As more people joined the platform, it became harder not to join as well. One woman told me that her friends knew more about what her adult son was doing than she did because she wasn't on Facebook. If your friends and family are all there, you feel compelled to be there, too, or risk feeling left out of the community. Network effects account for why numerous possible competitors have not been able to break the Facebook stranglehold. The value of the platform is in the people and transferring three billion people is next to impossible. It's also why alternatives to Twitter have floundered. Another advantage is the ability to cross-subsidize. This is when "one arm of the firm reduces the prices of a service or good (even providing it for free), but another arm raises prices in order to make up for those losses."[10] More simply, it is price shifting. In *Platform Capitalism*, political economist Nick Srnicek provides the example of Google giving email away for free to build an audience but generating revenue through charging advertisers on its search engine and elsewhere. Amazon Prime Video is cross-subsidized because it comes "free" with a Prime subscription. Facebook used Instagram to launch Threads, which was ad free. You get the idea.

In the United States, where these companies are based, they can bulldoze forward with these practices because regulation is all but nonexistent. What protects them more than anything else is Section 230 of the 1996 Communications Decency Act, which states, "no provider or user of an interactive computer service shall be treated as the publisher or speaker of any information provided by another information content provider." Under this regulation, social media platforms claim that they are not publishers like newspapers; they are only technology companies. So while you can sue a newspaper for libel if it lies about you, the same is not true of Facebook. The regulation was put in place when the internet was new and regulators did not want to impede its growth. Today, however, with the unwieldy use of algorithms and AI, you would be hard pressed to say that social media platforms are not making editorial decisions. The fact that we are all in information silos fundamentally argues against that. But because Section 230 exists, lies and disinformation and conspiracy theories are allowed to thrive.

We get sucked into this anger and advertising machine by persuasive design. YouTube uses recommendations, as does Amazon. Instagram, Facebook, Twitter (X), and TikTok use infinite scroll, a mechanism whereby there is no natural stopping point, as you would have with a television show, movie, or a book. You endlessly swipe through the feeds because it is designed to be that way. This is combined with intermittent variable reinforcement. Remember that this works like a slot machine: Most of the time you won't get what you want, but every now and again, you will get a like or a comment or recognition that leads to a dopamine hit. And if you do put down your phone, notifications are there to reel you back in.

While you are scrolling along, you are focused on what you perceive to be a genuine connection to your friends, family, or influencer. Rarely do you pause to ponder how technology plays into what you see and what you don't, what content of yours gets seen, and which is hidden from view. As Max Fisher explains in his book *The Chaos Machine*, "Online, the platform acts as an unseen intermediary. It decides which of your comments to distribute to whom, and in what context. Your next post might get shown to people who will love it and applaud, or to people who will hate it and heckle, or do neither. You'll never know because its decisions are invisible. All you know is that you hear cheers, boos, or crickets."[11] In short, you have no control over how your posts get seen or the content that is fed to you.

But what you do see seems like popular information. You want to show others that you are in the know, so you share it, further boosting its popularity. Or, it might be anger-inducing content, which you are also likely to pass on to your friends and followers. In *Contagious*, Jonah Berger outlines why we want to pass content to other people, making it go viral. He uses the acronym STEPPS: Social currency, Triggers, Emotion, Public, Practical value, and Stories. Much of this is not earthshattering. We like to share so that we look cool or so that people will turn to us as the go-to person for the latest info. This is social capital, what we used to call "water cooler talk," and it gives us standing within our group to know what Stephen Colbert said last night or what the hottest new Netflix series is. Storytelling has a long tradition, and earlier we talked about the importance of it online. Narratives evoke emotions, and the two emotions that Berger highlights are anger and awe, which are the most potent. When you are surprised and amazed by a new way to get corn off the cob or to whiten your shoes, you share that content because it wowed you and it is practical advice—it's that "person in the know" thing. You might have been awed—for good or for bad—by the storming of the Capitol, or you might have been angered. Pushing this kind of content is purposeful. When Facebook ran its emotional contagion experiment, it found that negative emotions increased the more negativity we were exposed to. Research since then confirms that "negative words had a positive effect on click-through rate, while positive words had a negative effect on click-through rate."[12] Anger is proven to get people to take action, and that leads to more ad sales—democracy and mental health be damned!

INFLUENCERS GAMING THE ALGORITHM

In 2016, I first learned about a company called Social Chain. I was researching hidden advertising, and this company came up as an example of an organization producing seriously surreptitious sponcon. This was pre-TikTok and during the heyday of Twitter. Back then, the company ran an account on Twitter called Medieval Reactions, a meme-like account that used pictures from the Middle Ages captioned with pithy epithets related to life's hardships, especially those that might appeal to young people, who were the target for this content. In one example, there is a picture of Jesus, who looks like he is in pain, and the copy reads, "When you're the saviour of mankind and you pop in to check how it's going and you see america."[13]

The account was the brainchild of Cathal Berragan, who worked for Social Chain. Mixed in with the pithy quotes connected to medieval paintings would be a quote that was actually an ad. Advertising like this was uncommon. We were only just beginning to see the rise of native advertising, ads that are made to look indigenous to the sites in which they exist, what we think of today as in-feed ads, or branded content, videos or news articles that were in truth content that had been paid for to not look like advertising. Some of this was innocuous, like Netflix paying for a piece in the *New York Times* about women in prison, but some of it wasn't, like Shell paying for content about sustainability. Admittedly, Social Chain used #ad, but few people knew what that meant. Research showed that only 17 percent of visitors knew when they were interacting with sponsored content, and that included Gen Z, who admittedly were young at the time but were "digital natives" and professed to be wise to these tactics.[14]

The issue isn't merely that people don't recognize content as ads. The issue is that we approach information differently when we know someone is paying for it. The persuasive knowledge model is a theory that proposes that people develop a better understanding of persuasion the more they are exposed to it, almost like building a muscle.[15] The more you see advertising and understand that the content is trying to persuade you to buy something, the more agency you have in deciding how to respond to the sales pitch.

Within the model, there are targets (consumers), agents (the brand), and the persuasive attempt (the ad or the sales pitch). This is straightforward. You see an ad, and you know it is from a company trying to sell you something. Great. How you decide how to respond, however, is based on having knowledge related to who is communicating the information (the agent), what is being sold (the product), and whether you know if you are interacting with a biased message (is it sponsored content or not). You don't have to have knowledge in all three areas, but when you don't, you lean more heavily into one over the other.

Let's take the example of an influencer promoting a product. We can assume we trust the presenter, or we wouldn't be following him or her. Say, for example, the influencer is pushing an inexpensive lipstick or a cheap piece of clothing. In this case, you don't need much product knowledge, so you rely on your connection to the influencer. It's cheap, someone you "know" says it's okay, and you buy it. If you've never heard of a product or it costs more than you would normally spend, you might stop and wonder if relying on the influencer is enough. It depends on the situation, but if you are buying a $5,000 coaching package, you might want to rely more heavily on the knowledge that it is a biased message—an ad—than on the influencer, even if it is someone you have followed for a long time.

Now think about this in terms of a political candidate or a hot-button issue. Take someone like George Santos, the New York congressman who was expelled from office. No one knew who he was during his campaign, and the ads didn't have to be tagged as promoted because it was political speech. In this scenario, the system is designed for you to rely almost solely on the influencer. What if you saw someone post about pregnancy centers and he or she asked you to support these purported health clinics? Maybe you know that they are antiabortion clinics, but the name of these centers is designed to be deceptive. Might you have looked at it a second time if you saw hashtag #ad?

The issue is that you can only lean into your knowledge of persuasion if you know the content is sponsored. If you see #ad or #PaidPost, you can tap into what you know about the tips and tricks used to coax us to buy. You might remember that someone trying to rush you is a signal to think twice or say no. Keeping people off-balance and ill-informed gives the influencer the upper hand. And when it comes to politics, we couldn't possibly be wobblier.

Using obscured advertising is not the only thing that Social Chain did. It was one of the first agencies to manipulate trends in a concerted manner. Steve Bartlett, a U.K. university dropout, was the brains behind this company and what he did was brilliant and brilliantly horrifying at the same time. He found people who had large followings on social media. When he started the company in 2014, the term influencer didn't exist. He saw the value in getting multiple content creators to work in concert and harness their followers. In 2017, the company owned four hundred accounts across several social media platforms. Social Chain was using access to multiple content producers to manipulate the social media space, much the same way the Mormon Church influenced search engine optimization in the early days of the internet.

The speed with which a trend could be forced through the system is, frankly, terrifying. On an episode of *Vice*, employees of Social Chain demonstrated how quickly they could make a topic trend on what was then Twitter. The young creative team came up with the hashtag #AmericanVsBritish because Brexit and Trump were already in the zeitgeist. A few people sitting around a table with access to a couple hundred accounts were able to make their hashtag trend in *eleven minutes*. The *Vice* reporter wisely asks about the transparency, or lack thereof, of who is behind this hashtag and why it is suddenly so popular. There is nothing to denote that it was something other than a bunch of people sitting around causing it to trend because they could. And Steve Bartlett laughs and says, "It's exactly what you just described there. . . . There's a group of people that sit around, they come up with something, they post. That's exactly what you've just seen here. These are the people that before this, came together, were sitting in their bedrooms influencing all those trends. The only thing is now they do it here."[16] The laugh tells you even he doesn't believe that.

What Social Chain started a decade ago continues today on steroids. Influencer platforms coordinate the mass dissemination of content. Agencies oversee a cadre of influencers who work in conjunction with each other to push each other's content. Individual influencers work in engagement pods. And now, the savviest agencies go beyond coordination and key performance indicators to add data strategies for purposefully manipulating the algorithm.

Wired magazine featured a cover story about Ursus Magana, the founder of influencer talent agency 25/7 and a manager who plays the algorithm game with finesse. That 25/7's motto is "Influence the algorithm, not the audience" tells you everything you need to know. You, the viewer, are superfluous. It's all about the numbers and the Benjamins. Even the content itself doesn't matter if it cranks up the numbers. In one example, the agency's music scout discovered YoungX777 by reading his content data. One of his songs ("Toxic") didn't do well, but the five-second intro was turning up on TikToks of MMA fighters and weightlifters. Tapping into this defined and passionate audience, the agency does what influencer platforms do: it mobilized dozens of fighters with smaller followings to push the song. Some were paid, but some did it for free. Flooding the zone (a strategy popularized by Steve Bannon) led the app's algorithm to push the content into the feeds of workout content. Inevitably, those users began incorporating the song into their content, and so on, and so on.

Magana's agency works on two theories: "The first: Once a social media user hears an audio snippet nine times, it gets stuck in their head. . . . The second . . . the 10 percent rule, is that 10 percent of those earwormed users will end up tracking down the snippet's original source."[17] Over the course of a few months, "Toxic" was a hit on TikTok and Instagram Reels, leading the 10 percent rule to take effect. Less than a month later, the full song was nearing one million plays on Spotify.

The same methodologies are being used in politics and Turning Point USA (TPUSA) is just about the best at playing the political influencer game in support of conservative candidates. TPUSA has an "in-house" ambassador program, which includes lifestyle influencers and Republican communications professionals. They are paid with hotel rooms and given free access to Amerifest, its annual student activist conference. TPUSA works promoting influencers and integrating them into the broader conservative media landscape. According to reporting in *The Verge*, "the organization has onboarded and trained over 400 creators as brand ambassadors." Like commercial brand ambassadors, these influencers have large followings in their own right and use their platforms to disseminate conservative messages. Turning Point also has its finger on the pulse of data. TPUSA went through a messaging revamp in 2022, when it saw their content was not hitting home with young voters.[18]

Young voters have been their bread and butter, as TPUSA started by agitating between progressives and conservatives on college campuses. Today, it represents a movement that the Republican Party takes seriously. It shows full-throated support for Donald Trump, white grievance, and xenophobia. And in the latest spin, it has become outwardly misogynistic. "We need to bring them [women] back to the kitchen. To be honest they are happiest in the home," per a young white man at the 2023 Amerifest event. Even with those fringe perspectives, Tim Miller of *The Bulwark* has called them "the power center of the Republican Party."[19] He claims that the group helped remove the speaker of the house and made Trump the nominee, which Miller notes is anathema to what the D.C. Republican establishment wants. Its power is not limited to national politics. Based in Arizona, a key swing state, it has insinuated itself with the Republican Party there, supporting candidates like Kari Lake and other election deniers, and although these candidates didn't win, TPUSA and its influencers made these races much closer than they should have been. What TPUSA has done, and done successfully, is create a community (one might even say a cult) around patriotism and positioning its members as defenders of democracy.

This is not to say that its content is all on the up and up. In September 2020, a *Washington Post* investigation revealed a misinformation campaign funded by TPUSA. Teens in Arizona were paid to post to Facebook and Twitter questioning the integrity of the election. The campaign was intended to replicate the behavior of bots and trolls, using "the same or similar language posted repeatedly across social media . . . though nowhere disclosing their relationship with Turning Point Action or the digital firm brought in to oversee the day-to-day activity."[20] Dozens of accounts were suspended after the social media platforms were contacted by the publication.

HYPE HOUSES

Hype houses, or content houses, are residences where groups of ten to twenty young creators live together producing content around the clock. Members of the house work as individuals and as a group promoting each other's content, much in the same way that agencies coordinate their talent pool to boost each other's content.

Content houses started in 2009 with a group of YouTubers. The concept was so popular that candy brand Sour Patch Kids set up houses around the country for musicians. The houses were equipped with recording studios, and bands could use the spaces to rest while on the road or to write music. Stays were only a few nights and although there were no specific requirements, musicians would typically produce content that the brand would put on its Tumblr and YouTube. The musicians got a nice place to stay, and the brand got content and the connection to up-and-coming musicians, making it seem like a hipper brand.[21]

These group houses had a resurgence in 2020 with the onset of the pandemic and the explosion of TikTok.[22] The biggest and most well-known is Hype House (@thehypehouse), which has 20.8 million followers on TikTok and another 1.5 million on YouTube.[23] This house helped further the careers of online celebrities like Addison Rae and Charli D'Amelio, and although they moved on, the Hype House continues to produce content today.

Political hype houses exist on both sides of the aisle. In the lead-up to the 2020 election, TikTokers in tech and marketing united in "The House of Us" to mobilize young votes for the Biden-Harris ticket. The group was created by 99 Problems, a political action committee (PAC), and was a virtual house because of COVID. Content focused on issues of concern to Gen Z, like social justice, gun violence, and climate change.[24] There are also groups that function like a hype house, such as Gen Z for Change (@genzforchange), which incorporates the work of eight creators.

On the right, there was @republicanhypehouse, which promoted Donald Trump and conservative issues. This TikTok account no longer exists. It was banned from the site, because it was posting disinformation, specifically telling people that the 2020 Election Day would be held on two days due to the pandemic and that Republicans should go to the polls on November 3 (the actual day) and Democrats should "hang tight" and wait till November 4 (when the election would be over).[25] However, the spirit of the house lives on with the hashtag #republicanhypehouse.

I expect these houses—live or virtual—will reappear with a vengeance in the lead-up to major elections, since TikTok, Instagram, and YouTube have become the political outlets of choice for young people.

CONSPIRACY THEORIES, CULT MARKETING, AND INFLUENCERS

Nothing creates anger faster than pitting two sides against one another, and that's exactly what conspiracy theories do, because they set up an imaginary fight of not just good versus evil, but demonic forces and the white knights meant to stop them. In *A Culture of Conspiracy*, political scientist Michael Barkun defines it this way: "The essence of conspiracy beliefs lies in attempts to delineate and explain evil. At their broadest, conspiracy theories 'view history as controlled by massive, demonic forces.'. . . A *conspiracy belief* is the belief that an organization made up of individuals or groups was or is acting covertly to achieve a malevolent end."[26] Behind these conspiracies are four guiding principles: "(1) the universe is governed by design, (2) nothing happens by accident, (3) nothing is as it seems, and (4) everything is connected."[27] Like religion, conspiracy beliefs provide a unifying mythology so encompassing as to be able to explain everything.

But conspiracy theories do more than this. In *Wrong: How Media, Politics, and Identity Drive Our Appetite for Misinformation*, political science and media professor Dannagal Goldthwaite Young explains that these theories fulfill our basic human needs of comprehension, control, and community.

She says that conspiracy theories help us "connect the dots" (comprehension), are more likely to be believed by people who feel powerless (need for control), and fulfill our desire to connect (community). Of the last she writes, "Conspiracy theories increase in-group cohesion while emphasizing the threat posed by an out-group. . . . [They] also efficiently reinforce social identity and mobilize the in-group toward action."[28]

Marketing books touting cult tactics have provided the recipe for pushing these ideas into the mainstream. One example is Michael Schein's *The Hype Handbook: 12 Indispensable Success Secrets from the World's Greatest Propagandists, Self-Promoters, Cult Leaders, Mischief Makers, and Boundary Breakers*. Schein is the founder of the marketing company MicroFame Media and, well, let's just say he isn't anyone I want to sit down for coffee with. I won't go through all twelve "secrets," but let me provide a couple of choice examples that have been co-opted in political circles.

First, Schein recommends "picking fights and making enemies."[29] He chose to fight with Gary V, serial entrepreneur and longtime influencer who has ten million followers on Instagram and another four million on YouTube. By providing a common enemy for Gary V's followers to coalesce around, Schein could draw attention to himself. He writes, "The single most important factor that determines whether something becomes a phenomenon or a flop is arguably the least understood—an ephemeral combination of manufactured drama, media manipulation, and behind the scenes maneuvering."[30] Creating drama produces in- and out-groups fomenting ever-increasing anger. One of the people he notes who does this to great effect is Donald Trump. Think of all the people he attacked, how they came back after him, and how that led his followers to rally around him. He used to attack celebrities, like Rosie O'Donnell, who would gladly fight back. Today, he uses the same strategy in his court cases, but it is against judges and other political personnel who cannot fight back. The strategy still works to rile up his base, because it feeds the narrative of a Deep State that is out to get him.

Another "secret" Schein espouses is to "perfect your packaging." He argues that it is not enough to package a product; you must package group identity around your product, which will lead to undying loyalty. I'd argue this is Schein repackaging tribal marketing, or psychographic marketing, which has been around for decades. Tribal marketing segments audiences based on shared beliefs, affinities, and interests, rather than demographics, which can be done with more specificity today because of the data collection that digital allows. Creating a tribe or a movement builds on the concept of brand community. The point that stands out as something most marketers don't do is to create a name that followers call themselves (think

"Swifties," or "anti-vaxxers" or "Trumpers"). This makes members feel part of something bigger while tying followers to each other rather than being anonymous, individual followers. Schein is not the only one who advocates this. The latest buzzwords for creating a marketing tribe are "identity loyalty." Identity loyalty imbues a brand with values that customers care about so it becomes "an extension of their self-perception and aspirations. It goes beyond transactional or emotional loyalty programs and taps into the fundamental human desire for connection, shared purpose, and self-expression."[31] This is the path to creating a brand cult, political or otherwise.

Finally, Schein recommends making your work "scientific," which you do by "always speak[ing] with complete certainty."[32] It doesn't matter if you are espousing complete nonsense. Act like you know what you are talking about, throw in some numbers to signal your credibility, and include scientific terminology and more sophisticated language. Even better, create your own jargon and use it over and over again. This strategy is at the heart of online conspiracy theories, and we look at Alex Jones shortly as a prime example of this.

Schein is a protégé, or at least a fanboy, of Ryan Holiday. He first gained attention for his work as the director of marketing at American Apparel. You may remember that the company's ads were racy and of questionable taste, showing teen girls wearing sweaters and underwear (no pants) sitting or lying on beds in suggestive poses. They were sexist and offensive, but they were also effective in grabbing attention, because he leveraged social media in its nascent days and significantly boosted the brand's visibility.

In 2012, Holiday wrote *Trust Me, I'm Lying: Confessions of a Media Manipulator.* There are two parts to the book: (1) how to manipulate the media and (2) why you shouldn't. He wrote the book as a warning about how easily the media can be manipulated in the era of digital and social media. Instead, marketers saw it as a how-to manual. Readers focused on how they could take advantage of media vulnerabilities, rather than focusing on how sensationalism, clickbait, and the drive for page views distort the news and influence public opinion.

In addition to creating fake accounts, fake comments, and fake traffic, Holiday provides a method for gaining attention and fake expertise that is strikingly similar to Tim Ferriss's: Start by placing a story in a small blog, preferably one with low editorial standards. That smaller blog becomes a source for large publications, which picks up the story, which in turn gets picked up by an even larger, more legitimate publication. Presto, someone with made-up credentials turns instant authority.

#PIZZAGATE—ANATOMY OF A CONSPIRACY THEORY

#PizzaGate was a conspiracy theory based on the notion that Hillary Clinton was sexually abusing children in the basement of a Washington, D.C., pizza parlor called Comet Pizza—a restaurant that, by the way, had no basement. Beyond the fabulousness of the story, the speed with which this blew through social media and the vitriol it engendered was unprecedented. So much so that one day a North Carolina man felt compelled to action, showing up in D.C. with guns blaring.

The conspiracy began on Reddit,[33] quickly wending its way through the internet. Reporting in *Rolling Stone* (in conjunction with the Investigative Fund[34] and Reveal from the Center for Investigative Reporting[35]) identifies the original #PizzaGate post as one that appeared on Facebook. It appeared on the site in late October 2016, the day after then–FBI Director James Comey said the bureau was reopening the Clinton email investigation. The investigation was being reopened because former Representative Anthony Weiner had been found to be sending pornography online, and his wife was an assistant to Clinton. The Facebook post, by a user going by the name of Carmen Katz, said, "My NYPD source said its much more vile and serious than classified material on [Anthony] Weiner's device. The email DETAIL the trips made by Weiner, Bill and Hillary on their pedophile billionaire friend's plane, the Lolita Express. Yup, Hillary has a well documented predilection for underage girls. . . . We're talking an international child enslavement and sex ring."[36]

The reporters didn't peg this poster as someone who would connect the dots of this conspiracy in the prism-like way it was done. They consulted a cybersecurity expert named Clint Watts, who explained that "Katz fits neatly into a well-worn blueprint for disinformation campaigns. For a story to gain traction, propagandists plant false information on anonymous chat boards, hoping real people will pick it up and add a 'human touch' to acts of digital manipulation."[37] The Facebook poster became an unwitting conspirator in this disinformation campaign.

From there, it gets convoluted as these things are meant to do. Police message boards and Facebook groups started posting. It then jumped to Twitter, where a user called Eagle Wings, who claimed to be a middle-age female air force veteran, posted about Clinton. Researchers determined this was a bot account, and it was one of many. Another likely bot Twitter account was @DavidGoldbergNY, which posted a screenshot of the original Facebook post. From the time of "his" post, "Pizzagate was shared roughly 1.4 million times by more than a quarter of a million accounts in its first five weeks of life."[38]

The story was picked up and boosted by right-wing sites like Breitbart and InfoWars. InfoWars at that time was reaching 7.7 million unique visitors a month. After a broadcast of Alex Jones's show on November 2, the story exploded. This, of course, led to more influencers like Betsy DeVos and her brother, Erik Prince, posting and tweeting about it.

On its face, it seems odd that the story was still being perpetuated *after the election*. On November 22, InfoWars produced a video called "Pizzagate Is Real" and continued to post more during the following weeks. If your party has already won the election, the only reason to keep pushing a fake story about Hillary Clinton is for cash. It was InfoWar's over-the-top content that led Edgar Maddison Welch to head to D.C. with an AR-15 semiautomatic rifle and a .38 handgun.[39]

Almost no one has made more effective use of conspiracy theories and disinformation than Alex Jones, both in terms of a political agenda as well as in lining his pocket. His "theories" have run the gamut from #PizzaGate to "Stop the Steal" to Sandy Hook. As for the last, he was successfully sued by the families whose young children were killed in the mass shooting at the Connecticut elementary school, leading to a $1 billion judgment against him.[40]

Jones started in late-night access TV in Texas in the 1990s. Back then, he and his outrageous ideas were fringe and most people thought he was a bit crazy. According to Houston attorney Mark Bankston, "You'd have to know things about lizard people or teleportation pads—these crazy, crazy conspiracy theories."[41] His delusions—then and now—may have to do with his narcissistic personality disorder, a diagnosis often attributed to cult leaders and one that entails a propensity for wild fantasies, a lack of empathy, and a tendency toward being manipulative.

Over the years, Jones developed quite the media empire for disseminating conspiracy. A talk radio show began in the late 1990s. InfoWars.com followed, as did documentaries and Prison Planet TV, a subscription streaming service where fans could access his films. By 2013, it was reported that he was making $10 million a year from subscriptions, DVD sales, and advertising related to his radio show and web content. More recent court documents show that he is worth between $135 million and $270 million.[42] However, most of his income is not from online advertising (though he does make about a million dollars a year from that). He makes most of his money from the sale of supplements.[43] On his Amazon storefront, he sold products like "InfoWars Life" branded "Super Male Vitality" drops and prostate health supplements. This makes perfect sense because of who his audience is. According to internet tracking site Similarweb.com, InfoWars reaches 6.1 million visitors per month. His viewers are 68.7 percent male, and although he used to skew young, now 45 percent of his audience is older than fifty-five; only 17 percent is younger than thirty-four years of age.[44] The site does not track race, but from all accounts, we can assume it skews heavily white. In short, the hate and the rage and the conspiracies comes down to selling vitamins to old men.

Multiple times, Jones has faced career death only to pop back up like a Bobo doll. The first time was after 9/11. He claimed the tragedy was an inside job by the U.S. government and not international terrorists. Turning a national time of mourning into a conspiracy theory was a bridge too far, and two-thirds of the radio stations that aired his show dropped him. His career might have ended there, except that the internet was expanding, and he moved online in the early 2000s. After threatening to kill Special Counsel Robert Mueller, social media sites deplatformed him in 2018. This had less impact on him than other personalities because he can reach people directly through InfoWars.com.[45] What hurt him more than Facebook or YouTube or Twitter was Amazon stripping him of sales privileges. Even the 2022 Sandy Hook case didn't stop him. Since deplatforming (except for X, which reinstated his account in late 2023), lawsuits, and regulations can't or won't stop him, he has every reason to continue to push out not only conspiracies, but increasingly more extreme conspiracies to keep his audience engaged . . . just like the YouTube algorithm.

The information would never get the kind of traction it does if it was up to Alex Jones alone. He is one hub, probably out of thousands, that became the central starting point for disseminating rage content. We see the same pattern play out with each new culture war issue, whether it's drag queen reading time, book bans, immigration, or anti-Semitism. A major player like Jones with millions of followers creates outrageous content, and then other good-sized influencers jump on board to increase their numbers. That content starts trending, and smaller influencers pile on, leading to an atomic bomb–like communication chain reaction.

Looking at QAnon, we can see more specifically how groups of people are mobilized to send information through social media spaces. Within the conspiracy framework, a believer's purpose is to discover who is pulling the strings. This is where QAnon was so evilly brilliant: he gamified the search for truth. "Q" would post a cryptic message (a "Q drop"), and it was up to the QAnon influencers and QAnon-based social media groups to figure out what the clue meant. Gameplay is perpetuated by telling players to "do your own research." The value in this as propaganda is that the players take ownership of the ideas they create, and the online groupthink gives the best answers a virtual pat on the back, further upping that content. Solving the puzzle as a group online also creates community, and the "eureka" of finding the answer and getting group approval supplies the dopamine hit.

Game designer Reed Berkowitz described Q as "gaming's evil twin. *A game that plays people*" (emphasis in the original), and the world of Q uses standard fictional game play.[46] He goes on to explain that in gameplay, designers need to account for the issue of apophenia, "the tendency to perceive a connection or meaningful pattern between unrelated or random things (such as objects or ideas)." When players make random connections that take them offtrack, the designer or "puppet master" can move them back in the right direction. The problem with something like QAnon is that there is no track, there is no endgame, and there is no puppet master, except in the heads of the believers. Q is purposefully sending players down rabbit holes—leading them toward apophenia—by directing attention to unrelated events.

What helps this message to spread is that a conspiracy theory has to be simple and QAnon's is. "QAnon's core belief is that a secret, pedophilic cabal of major news figures, celebrities, authors, billionaires, elected officials, and Democratic Party officials is conspiring to take over the world."[47] Former President Trump is fighting a surreptitious war against them, and he is the only thing standing in their way. Q, who supposedly has high-level clearance in government or is comprised of a group of people who do, gives "breadcrumbs" to entice people to guess how the cabal is working or working to be stopped. After influencers dissect the Q drop, the conspiracy spreads through hashtags that appear to be unrelated. The QAnon slogan "where we go 1 we go all" (wwg1wga) appealed to freedom-inclined people and #SaveTheChildren, a hashtag Q co-opted to avoid being kicked off social media, became a major draw for women.[48] Along with lifestyle and mommy influencers, top multilevel marketing salespeople posted (endlessly) about the conspiracy, but they did so through their large and compliant downlines. This phalanx of women sanitized QAnon, creating what religion and radicalization researcher Marc-André Argentino dubbed "Pastel QAnon," a conspiracy theory wrapped in pink and baby blue.[49] What started as a crazy conspiracy theory infiltrated society by morphing into content that was already being widely spread on conservative and right-wing social media.

But it didn't stop there. Adding religion to the mix added fuel to the fire.

11

RELIGION MEETS ONLINE EXTREMISM

Jessie Lee Ward (@imbosslee) was a superstar multilevel marketing (MLM) coach and influencer. She was thin, with long black hair, and a drill sergeant attitude reminiscent of Jillian Michaels from *The Biggest Loser*. Peppered between admonitions to "do whatever it takes" were subtle mentions of faith like "my energy is a GOD given gift" and "life is a blessing."[1] Using this combination of toughness and spirituality, Ward became internet famous for her business advice videos ("What's Wrong with Hustle Culture?" and "You Are Just Making Excuses"), which were shared with her 362,000 Instagram followers who called themselves the Leehive.

Trouble started when, as part of her coaching business, Lee took a group of clients on a Colombian retreat in January 2023. Participants were told they would be taking a two-hour hike. Instead, they were subjected to a brutal ten-mile trek, followed by rock climbing, and a midnight boat ride where they were required to jump into the freezing water. Topping off the by-now-fifteen-hour event was a night of sleeping on the beach, while shivering in their still-wet clothes. One client who suffered with diabetes became seriously ill during this escapade and had to receive medical attention.[2]

When I heard about this event, it felt like a combination of the Fyre Festival—the Bahamian bait-and-switch musical nonevent—and New Age coaches pushing their followers to unhealthy extremes. The most famous example is James Arthur Ray, one of the spiritual leaders who appeared in *The Secret*, the book and later film that popularized "manifesting" for a new generation. As part of a retreat, Ray's followers participated in a sweat lodge ceremony after fasting for several days. Three people died when they were forced to stay in the lodge to demonstrate their commitment to their spiritual practice. Ray was later convicted of homicide.

After stories about the Colombia retreat appeared on social media, Lee didn't back down. Instead, she stood her ground, much as James Arthur Ray had done until they slapped cuffs on him. Her Instagram post about the retreat said, in part:

> I absolutely made them walk 10 miles in direct sunlight without telling them where we would end up (sleeping on a beach instead of the 12 bedroom Villa) and for how long [in order] to see who places blame on people when they are at fault for not preparing themselves, who points fingers, who gets mad in discomfort, who uses words like "I can't" and who listens to the thoughts in the head instead of talking to themselves. Pain is in your MIND.[3]

The ruckus around the event might have persisted except that a new controversy arose: Ward announced in March that she had stage 4 colon cancer. Her oncologist recommended aggressive chemotherapy in the hopes of extending her life by a few more years. Ward took to Instagram, calling her doctors "one hundred percent pimps. Not of women, of chemo. They love that hoe. . . . I have never in my life seen such a strong and compelling sales pitch." Ward, instead, opted for holistic medicine and made sure to announce this to her hundreds of thousands of followers. She claimed she wasn't telling anyone what to do, yet online she provided her step-by-step program.[4]

The backlash was swift, especially from the anti-MLM movement, which made videos castigating Lee for promoting dangerous alternative therapies. It is one thing, after all, to choose this for yourself if you do not believe that chemotherapy is right for you. It is quite another to tell hundreds of thousands of others to do it, too.

Two weeks before her death, she continued to proclaim that the holistic process was working. However, on September 18, six months after she began her alternative practice, an Instagram post appeared with a picture of Ward in front of a purple background covered in stars saying, "Rest in Joy."[5]

Ward is not the first person to use alternative medicine to try and heal her cancer, and I'm sure she won't be the last. She is also not the only one to promote this path to a large following and cloak it in the language of faith and spirituality. In 2015, for example, Australian influencer Jessica Ainscough, who dubbed herself "The Wellness Warrior," was diagnosed with a rare form of cancer at the age of twenty-three. Like Ward, she decided she would forgo traditional medicine and chose instead to partake in the Gerson therapy, a process that has been widely debunked. Online she meticulously outlined her wellness journey, which entailed meditation, large doses of supplements, eating raw organic foods, and partaking of daily coffee enemas. She reached more than 1.5 million unique global visitors at the time of her death at the age of thirty.[6]

Connecting religion and spirituality with influencers has had wide-ranging, and often perilous, impacts from public health to political conspiracy theories. Religious and spiritually adjacent influencers don't use in-your-face evangelical tactics. Instead, they are extremely subtle, presenting what sociologist Nancy Ammerman called "lived religion." Seeing these influencers live their faith (or pretend to) works to establish a shared belief system that slowly develops over time, just like a cult. These long-established connections can set in motion dangerous consequences—as fifteen-hour treks and 1.5 million people hearing about daily coffee enemas might attest. In recent years, this has led to the alarming combination of New Age practitioners peddling not only alternative medicine but QAnon conspiracy theories in what is known as "conspirituality." The marrying of these extremes makes for a social media soup of conspiracy theories, spirituality, politics, capitalism, and "do your own research" individualism.

RELIGIOUS INFLUENCERS

I have been studying religious social media influencers for several years and what I found was that most of them, until recently, weren't particularly good at using the medium. Religious practitioners were also all over the map in terms of what their objectives were for going online.[7] To try and understand the landscape of religious influencers, I created a taxonomy to categorize these content creators: from those who sell faith itself to those who use faith to sell something else.[8]

So, for example, traditional religious leaders, like Pope Francis, use Instagram to reach younger adherents and to promote Catholicism, not so much by using a sales pitch as by demonstrating how he lives his faith. Another category, what I called "religious social celebrities," found fame on social media because of their religion. They are laypeople whose faith is front and center in their content, and it is mixed with another marketing vertical, such as parenting, food, or travel. Chaviva Galatz, for example, started by chronicling her conversion to Judaism and then added parenting advice. Elena Nikolova is a Muslim influencer who created Muslim Travel Girl in 2013 to provide information about Halal-friendly travel.[9] Today, social media celebrities who have found fame through religious content have exploded on TikTok with everything from Orthodox Jewish women explaining their practice to ex-evangelicals helping others deconstruct their (former) faith.

On the most consumerist end of the spectrum are a group I call "false profits." False profits are people who sell secular or sometimes spiritually based products while infusing religion—or the appearance of being religious—in their online posts. They sell everything from clothes to prayer books and, of course, coaching. It is their claims to faith, however, that draw followers to them. What makes them so potentially dangerous is that portraying oneself as religious or spiritual engenders trust in a way that almost nothing else can.

Sazan Hendrix, for example, is a fashion and beauty blogger and co-founder of Bless Box. Like secular subscription boxes, Bless Box contains beauty, health, and food products curated for the subscriber. The "bless" moniker is tenuous in its relationship to religion, much as SoulCycle has little to do with spirituality or meditation. On *Bless Blog*, for example, featured stories have titles such as "The Bless Guide to Saving a Manicure from Chips, Splits & Cracks" and "The Bless Guide to Beating Scalp Build-Up (& Getting Gorgeous Hair)," which are not topics one would read about in the Bible or Quran. Hendrix has 1.3 million followers on Instagram and another 518,000 on YouTube. She has an individual website (sazan.me) and one she shares with her husband (stevieandsazan.com), with whom she also has a podcast. A religious vibe subtly suffuses through her work. On Instagram, for example, she posted a picture of her daughter with the caption, "I can't help but look at this sweet angel and think wow God is SO good." Of course, this is all toward the goal of selling their book, their candles, and their online content so that they can increase their ad revenue.

Stop for a moment and realize that comparatively few religious influencers are using the medium to attract followers to true spiritual wellness. Instead, they are selling products and conspiracy theories just like their secular counterparts, the only difference being a mention of faith here and a tip of the hat to a higher power there. It is the personal nature of religion married with the personal aspects of social media that makes this so powerful as a tool of persuasion.

Let me be clear: I don't know whether the people I discuss here are religious or not, and that is not the point. What I am concerned about—and what we have already seen with MLMs and others who ply the prosperity gospel, toxic positivity, and so on—is that increasing numbers of influencers will use a religious guise to gain audience and engender trust. This has already had consequences beyond buying makeup or a prayer journal.

TEAL SWAN—THE SUICIDE GURU

Teal Swan is a stunningly beautiful tattooed woman with long black straight hair and piercing blue eyes. Her appearance in no small part accounts for her ability to draw people to her and to her content. In her YouTube videos, she is front and center, while hypnotic lights undulate behind her. Her voice is soothing and fairly monotone, as if she is taking you through a guided meditation.

Swan calls herself a spiritual leader, "a revolutionary in the field of personal development." She is also a cult figure who grew an enormous following online, a group that calls themselves the Teal Tribe. She started her career as an energy healer in a New Age bookstore in Salt Lake City, but her popularity took off when she began doing weekly videos on You-Tube in 2012. More than one outlet commented on her facility with search engine optimization (SEO), which is a marketing way to say she figured out how to play the algorithms. Key to this was producing controversial content—on topics like depression, suicide, and addiction—and lots of it, so her videos would appear when people used these search terms on Google.[10]

By 2013, she had attracted close to a million subscribers to her channel and her videos regularly garnered thousands of views. Live workshops followed and fans greet her à la the followers of Tony Robbins. For these events, Swan sits in a large wing-backed chair and speaks to the audience leaning forward, as if she has a secret to tell. A couch or a chair will be next to her, sort of like a late-night talk show set. Audience members breathlessly hope to sit in the chair across from her onstage, because it is the person in that seat who gets her undivided attention, even if it means an emotional evisceration.

What made this guru stick out from all the others was her belief in repressed memories and her seeming preoccupation with death. She claims her "therapy" (she is not a licensed therapist, which she readily admits) is about immersing people who come to her in the idea of death so that they can determine if this is an appropriate option for them. She has said that suicide is "our safety net or our re-set button that's always available to us," but claims she has people visualize a suicide experience so that they can realize that moving on with their lives is the best option. Remember, though, she is not a therapist. After two followers committed suicide, the BBC published an investigation in 2019 called "Teal Swan: The Woman Encouraging Her Followers to Visualise Death."[11] Reports followed in other publications and then the inevitable social media backlash occurred. She was never charged with a crime, and although there was some crisis management public relations to be done, Swan walked away more or less unaffected.

Today, she has millions of followers, including 1.1 million followers on Instagram, 1.7 million on YouTube, where she took down her suicide content and later was forced to remove her anti-vax content,[12] and 2.3 million followers on Facebook, though the content there seems to be re-posting content from other social media and ads for her meditation courses (it's only $27, which is 87 percent off!). It is hard to determine how much money she makes from her online content, but like Alex Jones, it appears to be a means of onboarding people to what she is selling, which includes coaching, retreats in Costa Rica for $5,000, premium content for $79 a month, meditation courses, her books, her frequency artwork (whatever that means), and a bunch of other tchotchkes.

CONSPIRITUALITY—RELIGION + CONSPIRACY + POLITICS

Conspiracies about using masks and vaccines became a hotbed of contention during the pandemic. This was particularly visible in the wellness community, where health, fitness, and notably yoga influencers proclaimed that people needed to "do your own research," a term made popular by the QAnon movement and a philosophy that a surprising number of wellness practitioners bought into.

Stephanie Baker, a sociologist who studies wellness influencers, has said that "the religious dimensions of wellness culture make it particularly susceptible to misinformation," notably because this content gets disseminated by online gurus. The path to indoctrination goes something like this: Someone decides to get healthier. His or her wellness journey starts with devotion to a diet or a lifestyle that leads to a transformation—a purification—that is realized through practices such as clean eating and juice cleanses and, perhaps, yoga. Physical purification progresses to an overall wellness lifestyle, which leads individuals to seek out a guru who can offer salvation and provide purpose and meaning to their life. Followers will mimic their guru's journey, which has been painstakingly presented via social media. The final step, similar to a religious conversion, is to evangelize the lifestyle to help others on their spiritual and wellness journeys.[13]

Like influencers-turned-coaches, newly minted gurus proclaim no expertise other than life experience. It is a badge of honor, a way to say that they are working outside the system to a group that eschews authority.

Jessica Ainscough on her blog wrote: "I'm not an expert. I'm not a doctor or a nutritionist. I'm a health coach. . . . I lead by example, I put my life-style out there. I show people what I have done to transform my life and kind of invite them to come along with the journey and take the parts that resonate with them." Of which Baker notes, "The key point here is that it's her journey . . . the journey is so prominent because that's their selling point. That's what markets the guru."[14]

Commercialism is fundamental to the New Age, which is "a hybrid of spiritual, social, and political forces, and it encompasses sociology, theology, and the physical sciences, medicine, anthropology, history, the human po-tentials movement, sports and science fiction. . . . There is no organization one must join, no creed one must confess."[15] Instead of an organized insti-tution, these ideologies are rooted in mind/body/spirit practices, which are facilitated through product purchases. From books and seminars to spiritual adventure travel and yoga classes, it is about purchasing spirituality. As I explained in my book *Brands of Faith*:

> New Age consumers end up on a hamster wheel, chasing after the next thing that will help them to improve themselves. Thus, while the New Age might have been a deeper search for meaning in the 1960s, today it has become what Jennifer Rindfleish (2005) calls "the commodifica-tion of the self." Raising your consciousness to improve the world has devolved for many into straightforward self-care. Within this system, in order to "get better," you must read the latest book or attend the next expo.[16]

During COVID, this translated into $8,600 necklaces on Goop, while yoga and wellness practitioners raked in the cash by telling followers "don't get vaccinated" and then selling them supplements, juice, tea, or essential oils.[17]

Susanna Barkataki is a yoga teacher in Los Angeles and an influencer with 110,000 Instagram followers. In a CBS News documentary about how the wellness community became a gateway for misinformation, she explained that the yoga community was particularly vulnerable to con-spiracy thinking during the pandemic because its philosophy is based on being open to new ideas, to be willing to explore alternative forms of health outside the mainstream. "I don't necessarily think people were anti-science to begin with, but with this upswelling of conspiracy theories. . . . They had questions about whether the government was protecting our wellness or not. They slid into being anti-science." Being anti-science led to ques-tions about the safety of vaccinations, and so shots were to be avoided in this body-focused and purity-minded culture. Simultaneously, Barkataki

explained that some of QAnon's phraseology meshed with yoga philosophies and beliefs. "It was so fascinating because they [QAnon] were using
words that spoke to me . . . phrases and hashtags like 'where we go one we
go all' . . . that sounds like the Great Awakening. I mean that's samadhi,
that's enlightenment," and she pegged a major shift toward QAnon beliefs
when the group started using the hashtag #SaveTheChildren, the same
thing that had occurred in other female-targeted communities.[18]

When spirituality and conspiracy theories collide in this way, it is
known as conspirituality. This concept was introduced more than a decade
ago by scholars Charlotte Ward and David Voas and gained considerable
renewed attention during the pandemic when a rash of New Age influencers began promoting conspiracy theories related but not limited to being
anti-vax.[19] It might seem counterintuitive for hippy-dippy, left-wing wellness folks to overlap with far-right, antidemocracy conspiracists, but it is
not so far-fetched if you consider that both cultures have a propensity to
question authority and share a strong distrust of institutions. Conspirituality,
then, posits that followers of the New Age who discover conspiracy theories about a malevolent secret group controlling the social order believe that
they have the power to protect against the looming totalitarian takeover by
ushering in the "new paradigm shift" foretold by New Age practitioners.
That paradigm shift is a belief in raising the consciousness of individuals
in order to change the world. "The new consciousness entails a unified
worldview—'we are all one'—and a belief in a higher power, though this
being need not be clearly defined."[20] The flexibility of this ideology allows
for false gods and fake gurus, and in the case of QAnon valorized Trump
as a religious strongman sent by God, an idea repeated endlessly through
online memes.

An influencer who checks all the boxes of conspirituality is Krystal
Tini. Krystaltini (@krystaltini) is a dancer, choreographer, and hair and
makeup stylist who has a few B-level acting credits on her résumé. She
began her influencer work with content about body and mind wellness—
lots of yoga, manifesting, and nutrition. Much of her early photography—
which was beautifully shot years ago but has seen considerable upgrade as
her following grew—is of her without clothes or scantily clad while doing
yoga or sitting on a beach. She has one shot (which she uses repeatedly) that
looks as if she's trying to replicate the famous Farrah Fawcett pose, with one
knee up and her hair flowing beautifully down her back. Glamour posts
like these rarely got a lot of traction, maybe a few hundred likes. Instead,
followers were drawn to content that was far less polished: Krystal sitting on

a chair in her bedroom, looking straight into the camera, and talking about New Age-y things like manifesting and how to eat healthy.

On March 13, 2020, Krystal posted static content telling her followers not to panic and claiming the media is the enemy. On March 30, 2020, Krystal's content takes a harder turn to the right when she posts a string of QAnon hashtags (#wwg1wga #qanon #qarmy #QPOST #calmbefore thestorm #truth #qdrops #coronavirus #truthseeker #truther #fakenews #msm), which is the only post she does this on.[21] Prior to this, she has one or two posts about being angry about the pandemic and taking vitamins, but she is still using her beauty shot photography.

On April 4, she has her first video about the pandemic, which goes viral (more than 480,000 views and close to 8,000 comments). It is an eleven-minute rant—truly a rant—that jumps from the why the lockdown is ridiculous to the pandemic wreaking havoc on the economy to how the mainstream media and the government are lying to the American people, and this is all being done as a way to stop Trump because nothing else has prior to this point.

True to yoga's antiauthoritarianism, she starts with the need to research:

> It's just like, we're all of us, around the world . . . in our country, just supposed to lay down and die at the expense of a fucking virus? This is not a pandemic by any means. If you don't realize yet that you are being lied to, about the numbers, about how you're catching it, about all of this, you need to seriously research, and research now.[22]

She spends a lot of time talking about people being complicit and letting their rights be taken from them. "At what point do we say we need to fucking stand up together and take charge of this whole thing? Our lives are being ruined, right before us. . . . What kind of sheep shit is this?" The use of the sheep meme was popular among conspiracy theorists as a way to say that people were following the herd without thinking.

Krystal backpedaled slightly, admitting that people were getting sick. However, that swiftly moved to whataboutisms in terms of all the other ways that our government and corporations are killing us, and this diatribe is something the community would certainly connect to.

> Where the fuck were all of you when people by the hundreds of thousands are dying during flu season? Do you walk out of your house with a mask wrapped around your face? . . . Do they [the government] care when millions of people annually die from cancer, heart disease, obesity?

If they gave a shit, half of those things that are in our food, . . . they'd be banned like other countries have. . . . So, if our government actually gave a shit to save lives, it would start with the food that we eat every single day. Tell me that I'm wrong. . . . Would you have all these crazy chemicals in Roundup? How many people got cancer because of Roundup? They're being sued by the billions. How many people get sick from powder, baby powder? Johnson and Johnson, they've been sued. . . . Our soaps, our lotions, our skincare products, the clothing that we wear, everything that is surrounding us is making us sick and slowly poisoning us to death. So, what makes you think that now all of a sudden they care about a virus that kills one in every 1,000 people? What makes you think that all of a sudden they care, that this isn't about something way bigger than a virus?

Later in the video, she hits this theme again: "They're already talking about the vaccine. . . . Are you kidding me? A vaccine? My immune system will fight it off just fine. Thank you."

Krystal complains about people losing their businesses, that "they" are lying about the death toll and falsifying death certificates, and she is concerned about the impending rise in depression and likely suicide and ultimately civil unrest. She calls for people to fight back to regain our freedom, asking, "Where are all of the Patriots that are in the Q movement?" She ends by saying why she has had to change her content: "I've always been a truth seeker. I've always wanted to teach people the truth about things, about food, about things that go on your body, your environment. And now it is political because we now have lost our freedom. So now it does become political."

For approximately the next two years, her content continues in this vein. Almost every video gets at least ten thousand likes and many get tens of thousands, but none is ever as viral as that first post. On Halloween 2020, seven months into the pandemic, Krystaltini posts a picture with static text that demonstrates how she continued to combine conspiracy theories and the tenets of the New Age paradigm:

My page is not shifting. But shifting gears is what i have to do for the time being and those that know, know. → Look for those who have vanished as I have previously mentioned. Many are unable to sleep. Unable to focus. Lost. Scared. Alone. But just know, there is a greater force in the Universe that hears us, feels our pain, and recognizes those who need uplifting. . . . We must do so and be conscious of the energy we are putting out there, as our power in shifting the frequency of the planet is up to us. . . . By you shifting your perception you will either help elevate others, or attract those who are on the same plane of life. Do not allow others negativity to bring you down, especially now! There is always a way out.[23]

By early 2022, after almost two years of anger and fighting, her videos are not getting the same kind of numbers that they had gotten previously. Later that year, Krystal's content starts to look more like it did prior to the pandemic, but it is still tinged with digs at the media, calls to not become complacent, and reminders to followers that they have awakened and to never forget that they are being lied to. The emphasis, however, is on the paradigm shift: "One can never change the outside world without first changing the inside world, for it is the inside world where all things originate."[24] There is also an obvious visual change to her Instagram page— it has a defined aesthetic (pink and white) and labels in a scripted font that say things like: "Manifesting Monday," "Abundance Mindset," and "Shifting Anxiety." She has a Campsite.bio, a listing that is similar to Linktree, connected to her account, and hers is longer than any I have ever seen. Some of the older links are to videos about the dangers of 5G. There is also a link to Krystaltini TV, which was a video venture that appears to have fizzled. The rest of the links are for products that she has created herself like yoga mats, affiliate links, and "nourish my soul" retreats, where attendees can share a tent for $2,300 for four nights. The top link is for X39 pain patches, a product of Amare, a health and wellness MLM.

I couldn't help thinking, after watching so much of Krystal's content, how much it was like Jessie Lee Ward's. There were times when I began to get the content confused, especially after Krystal dyed her hair black and started recording from her couch instead of her bedroom. It's all "pull yourself up by your bootstraps" and "don't believe what you read" individualism. Krystal believed in political conspiracies, and Jessie thought the medical establishment was trying to con her. Both believed in faith and a higher power, and while I can't determine if Krystal made much money beyond brand deals and speaking gigs during COVID, in the end, they both bought into capitalism—New Age or old.

THE PROBLEM WITH FINDING BELIEF ONLINE

Religious and political beliefs tap into what we fundamentally believe and, by extension, who we fundamentally are. Although we may not think of these things as being marketed and sold to us, they most definitely are. I have long argued that religion is a product that can be sold like any other item in the capitalist marketplace. This is not an extraordinarily new idea. There was "church merch" in the Middle Ages. What was new about marketing religion in the 1990s and the early 2000s was the use of sophisticated marketing techniques such as personal interviews and psychographics, such as "Unchurched Harry," the middle-aged, middle-class white guy whose wife went to church but he didn't. In tapping into these techniques, in particular, megachurches of two thousand congregants or more could draw the previously unaffiliated into the fold.

But social media changed the game, and the methods for selling a Bless Box or latest TikTok trend are now used to promote ideologies. It does so with dire consequences. Here's why. First, algorithms push what is most popular, not necessarily what is the most trustworthy or most beneficial. We have seen how algorithms can be manipulated when groups of people work together to make content trend. Wittingly or unwittingly, millions of people pushed the conspiracy of QAnon because of the hashtag #SaveThe Children, which became the tipping point for people to support this fakery and move it further and further to the top of the attention funnel. In the case of Teal Swan (see textbox on page 179), connecting her spiritual content to words like "depression" and "suicide" were fundamental in driving her follower numbers. Knowing how to optimize search engine results is the gateway to online success—preacher or packaged good.

Whoever is the best marketer wins. Even if a group has good intentions, its importance gets overblown, leading to skewed perceptions. Take breast cancer and pink ribbons. Because this icon became so ubiquitous, people came to believe that it was the leading cause of death for women when it isn't. It attracted so much attention and money that it drew charitable donations away from charities who were in more desperate need.[25] The same thing happened with the Ice Bucket Challenge. When that was the internet trend of the moment, ALS donations skyrocketed, while donations to other charities took a dive. As for religious content, you hear about televangelists like Joel Osteen or T. D. Jakes before you'll hear anything about secular humanism. If marketers are perhaps less scrupulous, they benefit by producing exorbitant amounts of content, which blocks out criticism and competition, much like Mindvalley and the Mormon church. And remember, most people online mentioning faith are not doing so for your spiritual development. They are using it as a branding element.

There are far too many ways in which religion, politics, and technology overlap to cover them all here. The idea I do want to leave you with is that it is not only consumer packaged goods companies that have sophisticated databases for targeting prospects. Churches, church marketers, and political organizations also tap into this data.[26] Just like traditional marketers, religious and political groups determine who their users are, gather as much information as they can about them, and then try to find new prospects by tapping into third-party data. Third-party data is information collected about consumers by research companies who then sell that data to marketers of all stripes. In consumer marketing, Acxiom is likely the most well-known data broker. For religion, it's Gloo. In a video that is no longer available on its site, Gloo explained what they do:

> Imagine a data platform designed to help you improve the lives of individuals, the health of families, and the vitality of communities. Insights from Gloo is the first big data platform centered around personal growth and development. It provides a 360-degree view of your audience with a privacy-protected database that includes more than 2,200 data points for nearly every U.S. consumer. Every point of data moves you one step closer to understanding the needs of your current people and those in your surrounding community so you can reach them with the right message at the right time. That could be people battling substance use and mental health issues or young people seeking their spiritual path. Maximize your capacity to change lives by leveraging insight from big data so you can understand the people you want to serve, reach them earlier and turn their needs into a journey towards growth.[27]

Two important points to note about this (once you catch your breath over the fact that this company you have never heard of has 2,200 data points about you): Just like cults, religious institutions tap into people when they are "battling substance use and mental health issues," as well as other vulnerability points like divorce or a death in the family, and, yes, this can be discerned through online data. The second thing to know is that Gloo is funded by the ultra-right-wing Koch brothers, who are also behind the "He Gets Us" advertising campaign promoting Jesus. This campaign is not simply a hip, highly produced series of black-and-white commercials, but an intricate web of marketing, courses, and data collection.

As marketing and technology work together, a number of psychological factors kick in. First, we have social proof: that's when we see others give approval to content, and so we click the like button because it looks like something we should be part of as well. This is similar to the chameleon effect. This is the idea that when we enter into a new social situation and we're not sure about how to act, we hold back to see what the rules are and follow what other members do. Or, what if the marketer uses gamification, like Q did? Gamification plays on intermittent reward, the Vegas slot machine technique that keeps us coming back for more.

All of this is going on while you are being pushed into more extreme content and an endless state of anxiety. According to Ramesh Srinivasan, an information studies professor at UCLA: "The best way to feed someone's anxieties is to not just echo what their existing anxiety is but to reinforce it with something worse, something a little more hardcore."[28] Tapping into our fear, anxiety, and loneliness—all of which were in abundance during COVID—is what former Google ethicist Tristan Harris calls "the race to the bottom of the brainstem," and it is what digital technologies are designed to do. On Instagram, for example, the technology will hold back likes. Based on online behavior, it determines when the best time is to release the likes in a burst in order to get you to spend more time online.[29]

This is not just psychological. It is physical. When you put down your phone, your adrenal gland produces cortisol, which triggers a fight-or-flight response. Dr. Larry D. Rosen, author of *The Distracted Mind: Ancient Brains in a High-Tech World*, explained it this way to *60 Minutes*, "What we find is the typical person checks their phone every fifteen minutes or less. And half of the time they check their phone, there's no alert, no notification. It's coming from inside their head telling them to. 'I haven't checked Facebook in a while . . . I wonder if somebody commented on my Instagram post.' That then generates cortisol, and it starts to make you anxious. And eventually your goal is to get rid of that anxiety, so you check in."[30] He also notes that putting down your phone doesn't solve the problem, because you can't shut off your brain: "Our phones are keeping us in a continual state of anxiety."

In *Unwinding Anxiety*, Judson Brewer explains that fear plus uncertainty equals anxiety. He goes on to say, "When uncertainty abounds, we get anxious and start scratching that itch that says, '*Do* something.'"[31] Doing something during COVID meant going online to look for answers. The more time we spent online, the more we were divided into information silos, often pushing us away from science-based, data-backed information and toward conspiracy theories designed to provide easy answers, a sense of surety, and a relief from anxiety. This was the extreme of the never-ending anxiety loop: anxiety—search for release—pick up your phone—get anxious again.

Political conspiracy theories are fundamentally about fighting evil, about destroying the dangerous cabal that is trying to ruin our world. Here, we saw New Agers mostly fighting back by promoting anti-vax conspiracies, which was bad enough. For those who fully supported QAnon and other right-wing groups, the protest and the violence went much further—and much further offline.

As noted throughout this book, although people have moved away from traditional religious institutions, they are no less interested in a cogent worldview. Instead of finding community and spiritual sustenance within traditional religious institutions, people have increasingly turned to everything from weight-loss programs to popular culture to radical political movements. In our search for good, our anxiety, anger, and loneliness have been turned against us by "politically and financially motivated opportunists who have weaponized the community-building capabilities of social media."[32]

We must never forget that whenever we are online, we are part of a marketing research project, we are immersed in a shopping model, and we are being programmed—all for capital gain.

12

CLIMBING OUT OF
THE ONLINE RABBIT HOLE

Caleb Cain was from a rural part of West Virginia, a state with the third–highest poverty rate and *the* highest percentage of drug use in the United States. Like the state, he didn't have a lot of prospects, making him the type of alienated, vulnerable person a cult looks to target. He dropped out of college and did what a lot of young people do: He started spending time on YouTube in search of guidance and self-help.

His video search led him to Stefan Molyneux, a "men's rights advocate" who presents a mix of dating advice, practical tips, and philosophical topics. The content seemed innocuous but wasn't. Caleb was engaging with someone the Southern Poverty Law Center describes as "a libertarian . . . [and] alleged cult leader who amplifies 'scientific racism,' eugenics and white supremacism."[1] Of course, the algorithms didn't stop with Molyneux. Caleb was pushed to other conservative content, like comedian Steven Crowder and Paul Joseph Watson, a right-wing conspiracy theorist who was ultimately barred from Facebook. The more he watched, the more Caleb felt part of a new community, and the more he was slowly moving away from his existing beliefs.

The men in these videos have perfected a facade of fatherliness and acceptance, which is particularly alluring for a generation that feels like they have inherited a world without constancy. Gen Z grew up in the wake of September 11 and bore the fallout from the recession of 2008. Climate change and active shooter drills are a steady drumbeat in their lives. Their vivid historical memories are of the murder of George Floyd, the January 6 insurrection on the Capitol, and a global pandemic. Their lives have been a permacrisis, "a term that perfectly embodies the dizzying sense of lurching from one unprecedented event to another, as we wonder bleakly what new horrors might be around the corner."[2] Millennials share a similar

191

perspective. When these generations lash out at baby boomers, this is why. They don't remember a time when jobs and families and social institutions weren't built on quicksand.

Conservative, conspiracy-laden content offers a sense of assuredness that feels like stability in a decidedly unstable world. It replicates the us-versus-them mentality of cults and the internet. The "us" is Western civilization (read: white men). The enemy is identity politics, feminists, cultural Marxists, and immigrants who are tearing down basic social structures. Caleb was immersed in this world—what he termed a "decentralized cult"—for five years before he got out and became a vocal critic.

Like those enmeshed in multilevel marketing (MLM) ventures, it wasn't one thing that led him to turn his back on right-wing extremism. Rather, over time, he questioned what he was seeing. Doubts were instigated by a rise in content from left-leaning YouTubers, notably Natalie Wynn of ContraPoints, who hack the system by replicating the aesthetic of the conservative creators while explaining that Western culture wasn't under attack. One horrifying event also helped break the spell: the massacre of fifty Muslims in Christchurch, New Zealand, which was streamed in real time around the world.[3]

Caleb is not alone. You might remember the testimony of Stephen Ayres in front of the U.S. House Select Committee to Investigate the January 6th Attack on the United States Capitol (aka the January 6th Committee). He sat in front of the congressional panel looking very much like the average Joe he is. He wore an inexpensive blue suit, his red hair was cropped short, and he sat with his hands crossed in front of him, seemingly overwhelmed by where he found himself. In his testimony, he describes himself as the guy next door, "a family man and a working man. Worked at the company, a cabinet company up in northeast Ohio for going on twenty years. You know, family is my life . . . camping, playing basketball, playing games with my son."[4]

He goes on to explain that he ended up at the Capitol because he had been drawn in by social media. "I was . . . pretty hard-core into the social media, Facebook, Twitter, Instagram. I followed, you know, President Trump, you know, on all the websites, you know. He basically put out, you know, 'come to the Stop the Steal rally,' you know, and I felt like I needed to be down here." When he found out some of his friends were attending the rally, he decided to tag along. He listened to Trump's speech on the Ellipse in D.C. and was driven by anger to head to the Capitol. He believed the election was stolen, not only because the former president said so, but because it was information he had been exposed to, "a lot of the stuff he [President Trump] said he already put out in tweets. I've already seen it and heard it before."

Mr. Ayres was arrested for illegally entering the Capitol and subsequently lost his job and his home. After January 6, he said he deleted his social media accounts. His advice to others: "I felt like I had . . . horse blinders on. I was—I was locked in the whole time. Biggest thing for me is take the blinders off, make sure you step back and see what's going on before it's too late."

As these examples attest, almost anyone who is continually exposed to disinformation can be in danger of sliding into the conspiracy swamp. Continual repetition *without competing perspectives* replicates the grooming process of a real-world cult. Isolation into information silos doesn't occur by algorithms alone. Believers start severing ties with anyone outside their group, and their friends start to drift away. We probably all know someone who has been drawn into one of these conspiracies and rather than seeing them yammering on, we unfriend them or block them, if only for our own mental health. The algorithms may start the silos, but we solidify them. Separation from alternative points of view is a basic indoctrination tool of cults and the online environment is set up to do this. As cult expert and author of *The Cult of Trump*, Steven Hassan has said, "We're on our phones 10 hours a day. People are up all night getting fed YouTube videos. . . . You don't need a compound anymore."[5]

In addition to being siloed, two other factors contribute to indoctrination online. First, social media pushes popular content, so we see the same messages over and over and over again. This produces a psychological phenomenon called the illusory truth effect. Repetition leads your brain to respond faster to repeated information because it feels familiar. In *Foolproof*, social psychology professor Sander van der Linden, explains, "the brain will imbue claims that we know or have seen before with a higher truth-value,"[6] which was certainly the case with Ayres. Couple that with truth bias, our natural inclination to believe that people tell the truth, and this becomes dangerous in the hands of influencers with ulterior motives. Second, the technology is designed to keep you connected to the screen in order to keep the ad dollars flowing—or to sell more manly vitamins. The longer we stay connected to the screen, the more information we are exposed to—real or not—and the creator on YouTube is making money from the advertising either way. Cult leader, conspiracy theorist, MLM coach—it's all the same money and power grab.

Being drawn into the conspiracy theories is not, however, only a digital issue. While younger folks get drawn in online, legacy media like talk radio and Fox News foment hate among older demographics. In the 2015 documentary, *The Brainwashing of My Dad*, Jen Senko explains how her father moved from JFK Democrat to right-wing extremist. It all began when he lost his job, and his new position required a three-hour commute. Rush Limbaugh became his daily companion. Over time, he added himself to conservative email lists and became a regular consumer of Fox News and a walking 24/7 receptacle for hate and misinformation. One day he fell ill, becoming bedridden for an extended time. While incapacitated, his wife blocked Fox News from their cable box and unsubscribed him from the emails. Separated from the constant haranguing, he no longer had the fodder for his hate and began to return to his pre-Limbaugh self.

What we see here is the implementation of cult techniques on a colossal scale. The fallout from the mass indoctrination by high-control groups includes the killing of elementary schoolchildren in their classrooms, the attempted kidnapping of a governor, and a barely thwarted attempt to take down democracy, just to name a few. So how do we get out of this?

The first step is to realize that the implementation of cult indoctrination tactics for political radicalization purposes via social media is not only an individual issue, but a societal problem. One of the leading voices in the anti-cult movement is Diane Benscoter. In the 1970s, she was a wide-eyed teenager who didn't fit in anywhere but desperately wanted to make a difference in the world. While in that vulnerable state, she joined the Unification Church (the Moonies) and remained a member for five years until she was "deprogrammed" by a former member of the group. In hopes of helping others escape from cultlike groups, Benscoter became first a deprogrammer and later found Antidote (antidote.ngo). The organization is a bit different from others in the field because it sees psychological manipulation as a public health issue rather than as an individual concern. In an appearance on CNN, she explained that the psychological manipulation that occurs with political radicalization is similar to cults, and we need to broaden our understanding of cult tactics:

> People have these ideas of what a cult is . . . if you point to the techniques, the tactics that are used, they're exactly the same. . . . People are vulnerable. We live in a time where it's hard to understand this world. Technology has made a huge change, much like the Industrial Revolution. So anytime when there's social unrest, I think people are more vulnerable, and there's fear and there's anger about what's going on in the world. And people want easy answers to life's questions, and they get sucked in. . . . They get constantly fed by all these media sources . . . the main messaging that cults do, which is us versus them, because if you

can first divide people into us versus them, and you can make the other side evil and wrong . . . then eventually what you can do is weaponize your side.

Fighting indoctrination, then, has to occur on both the societal and the individual level.

THE CONSPIRACY THEORY PYRAMID

If you don't know Abbie Richards by name, you have likely come across her **Conspiracy Theory Pyramid** (conspiracychart.com), which went viral in 2020. Abbie is a computer scientist, former comedian, and brilliant TikToker (@tofology) who has 523,000 followers and 5.8 million likes.[7]

The interactive infographic is an upside-down pyramid that categorizes multiple levels of conspiracies from those "grounded in reality" to those "detached from reality." At the skinny bottom are actual conspiracies, true events like Watergate and Big Tobacco lying about cancer. The next section is called "we have questions," which includes things like UFOs and whether Jeffrey Epstein killed himself. This is followed by the "unequivocally false, but mostly harmless" segment where you see "conspiracies" like the "*Titanic* never sank" and "Elvis lives." The next level gets more dangerous, because it moves into denial of reality, with mis- and disinformation, like Wayfair trafficking children and climate change is a hoax.

The widest part of the pyramid is the "anti-Semitic point of no return." This section includes QAnon, George Soros, and the Protocols of the Elders of Zion, among many, many more. This is where conspiracy theories become the most dangerous, because they promote hatred and violence against marginalized groups.

HELPING INDIVIDUALS EMBRACE REALITY

At the risk of sounding like an influencer-turned-coach, let me say again that I am not a therapist or a cult specialist. However, I am a researcher by trade and training, and I know enough to turn to the experts when I am out of my depth. What those experts agree on is that there is no quick fix. Getting people to rethink who they are requires a combination of approaches: hearing the stories from others who have left a cult; being listened to without lectures, blame, or shame; and as sappy as it sounds, the most important ingredient is love. Just as with MLMs, not only are these people walking away from their belief systems, but they are also walking away from their community and support systems. The soon-to-be former cult members need to know they will not be alone. The good news in all of this, according to cult expert Janja Lalich, is that most people do break away from cults, and the group death rituals of Jim Jones and Heaven's Gate are the exception, not the rule.

Steven Hassan, as noted earlier, is another leading authority on cults. Interestingly, like Diane Benscoter, he was a member of the Moonies in the 1970s. After being extracted from the group, he began a career explaining how mind control works, which he has been doing for more than forty years. One of the first things he says is not to disparage the organization or attack the leader. It's kind of like when you get divorced, and you don't want to bad-mouth the other parent in front of your kids. That person is part of them, just like the cult belief system is part of the member. Others have said not to attack the belief system because of confirmation bias, the idea that we favor information that confirms what we already believe: "Some cognitive and political scientists . . . hypothesize that because of confirmation bias, corrective information can backfire—that trying to convince someone that their falsely held belief is wrong actually causes them to dig in to those false beliefs even more."[8]

Instead, says Hassan, explain that what the person has been involved in is a mind control program. To help illustrate this to people caught in a cult, he created the BITE model of authoritarian influence. BITE entails four types of control: Behavior, Information, Thought, and Emotion. He uses this framework in conjunction with the influence continuum. One side of the continuum is healthy influence, in which you have unconditional love and free will, and on the other, there is hate, doctrine, and fear.[9] As he said in a TED panel about breaking people free of QAnon, "Learn about brainwashing and mind control and other cults. Talk to critics and former members. . . . Understand this is not mystical . . . the brain wants to find meaning in meaningless things. That's its function. We filter things to have an organized reality."[10] Undoing misinformed beliefs won't happen overnight. Research suggests that it takes sixteen months from the time someone first thinks about leaving a cult until the time that they actually do it.[11]

When I began to think about this in relation to the anti-MLM movement, I wondered whether its success in helping people break away from these cultlike companies could be replicated for other high-control groups. Maybe, but it will likely be more difficult. That's because anti-MLMers can attack the problem with a coordinated effort. People searching for MLM content found themselves stumbling on anti-MLM content—the anti-MLMers had played the algorithms. What made it work was that those still in MLM started seeing content that began to increase the doubts that they already held. MLMers talk about it as cognitive dissonance. Janja Lalich describes it as cult members putting their doubts on a shelf, and slowly but surely the shelf gets too heavy until it breaks.

An anti-conspiracy or anti-cult movement will have a harder time because the topics are more diverse. It is the same problem the environmental movement had. Do we save the whales? The polar bears? Are we supposed to focus on deforestation in the Amazon or promote recycling? Once the issue was honed to the singular "climate change," which is the bottom-line concern, awareness of the problem was heightened though sadly not solved. Right now, there is increasing awareness of cults and cult tactics and cult content, especially podcasts but also on social media. However, there is no coordination, and it appears to be a different problem when it is all of a piece. Sites like #igotout have the right idea. It provides resources and a place where people can tell their stories. But the information stays on the site. It has to be in places where people stumble onto it, because people in a cult don't think they are in a cult. Until the message is coordinated and individuals are angry enough to produce continuous content, it's not scalable.

WHAT WE NEED IS LARGE-SCALE, SYSTEMIC STRUCTURAL CHANGE

Cults have existed for millennia. They have not, however, always had access to worldwide communications technology or the ability to bring together large numbers of people for nefarious purposes.

Social media companies aid extremism, and they know it. They could very easily change their algorithms, but they don't because it will impact their bottom line. Meta, Google, and Amazon make up an oligopoly that has undue influence on our communication, our relationships, and our politics. You might also include Apple on that list. When companies will not change of their own accord, regulations must be applied. The Department of Justice (DOJ) brought a lawsuit again Google in 2023 for antitrust issues. At the time of this writing, there has not been a decision in that case, but this is exactly what should happen when companies manipulate the system with monopolistic practices. The Supreme Court broke up Standard Oil in 1911; it's time to break up the communication cartel.

The DOJ shouldn't have to do this alone, but so far other regulatory bodies have been utterly impotent. Year after year, social media CEOs get dragged in front of Congress and nothing happens. The excuse we hear consistently is that technology changes faster than the legislative process can keep up with it. Sure, that's true, but a fundamental overhaul to Section 230, the part of the Communications Decency Act that allows social media companies to claim that they are not responsible for the content that appears on their platforms, is in the hands of this governing body. *Forcing the platforms to be held accountable for what they send out into the world would change the content in a heartbeat.* And it has to be Congress to own this, because the Supreme Court has taken a pass.

In 2023, the Supreme Court had an opportunity to make adjustments to Section 230, when families of those murdered by ISIS sued the social media companies for having "knowingly allowed ISIS and its supporters to use their platforms and 'recommendation' algorithms as tools for recruiting, fundraising, and spreading propaganda; plaintiffs further allege that these companies have, in the process, profited from the advertisements placed on ISIS' tweets, posts, and videos." The unanimous decision, written by Clarence Thomas, stated, "It might be that bad actors like ISIS are able to use platforms like the defendants' for illegal—and sometimes terrible—ends. . . . But the same could be said of cell phones, email, or the internet generally." This statement on its face demonstrates that the justices have no idea how technology works.

These cases involved Facebook, Twitter, and Google. But TikTok is no better. Media Matters research found that transphobic videos moved visitors on to extremist content, and there is a rising group of TikTok influencers spreading Christian nationalism, an ideology that promotes a white, male-dominated, Christian-based theocracy.[12] The fastest fix to the divisive content online is the elimination of Section 230. It has outlived its usefulness. Period.

The other way to get to the root of the problem is to go back to where we started at the beginning of this chapter. Under late-stage capitalism, we live in a commodified world of yawning excess and income inequality. We have a generation without jobs, without affordable education, without hope. We have the largest income disparity ever. We've obliterated the middle class and full-time employment is increasingly harder to find and will likely get harder with the advent of artificial intelligence replacing any number of jobs. Massive "layoffs" occur in companies from Amazon to Hasbro, often privileging shareholders at the expense of workers.

Late capitalism is built on the notion of individualism, and with that we have become lonely and isolated. People don't go into the office anymore, so there are fewer opportunities for human interaction. Since COVID, more college students take classes online. When we get on public transportation or in an elevator, we reach for our phone. The idea of the third place—not home or work, but a third space for engaging with others—is nowhere to be seen.

There are some obvious simple fixes here. Massachusetts passed the "tax the rich" law, which was a 4 percent annual surtax on those making more than $1 million. This tax increased revenue by $1.5 billion in one year, helping to pay for improvements to the public transit system, universal free school meals, and tuition-free community college, among others.[13]

You know something's up when millionaires around the world are begging governments to tax them. In November 2023, British multimillionaires projected the message "tax our wealth" on the treasury building. They are calling for a 2 percent tax on those making more than £10 million, which could contribute £22 billion to the country's coffers.[14] In 2020, millionaires were asking to be taxed to help pay for costs associated with the coronavirus. There is even an organization devoted to taxing the rich called Patriotic Millionnaires.[15]

Just like getting someone out of a cult is a process, so too will be rethinking—reenvisioning—the world we find ourselves in. What I have discovered in writing this book is that cult tactics are not only fundamental to brands and influencers, they are the foundational principle to the technology that disseminates them.

Asking people to give up their cell phones and their social media is unrealistic. What is realistic is for us to work together to get our governments to protect us against a handful of companies with inordinate power. What is realistic is for us to make sure that we surround ourselves with a multiplicity of viewpoints. What is realistic is to consciously, and perhaps evenly lovingly, find ways to meet each other face to face.

EPILOGUE

The good news is that social media is dying. Really. It's done. Stick a fork in it. X is in a death spiral. TikTok has turned into a 24/7 shopping mall while living under the sword of Damocles, waiting for regulators to seal its doom. Facebook is becoming Amazon, and Amazon is trying its damnedest to become Facebook. The tech industry has suffered mass layoffs, and the Metaverse was a $10 billion bomb. Even Instagram is dying.[1] We have reached Doctorow's enshittification.

It's not me saying this. The headlines are everywhere: "Great News— Social Media Is Falling Apart" or "The Age of Social Media Is Ending."[2] Even *Adweek*, one of the bibles of the advertising business, ran a "Social Media Is Dead" headline.

I can hear some of you saying, "but all of these platforms are growing," and in that you would be correct. The overall number count continues to go up. But let's look under the hood.

Posting isn't fun anymore. People aren't posting as much as they used to.[3] Why? Because it's not fun when you are bombarded with advertising, swarmed by bots, and barraged by misinformation. Production quality is also a factor. When someone like MrBeast or Chiara Ferragni can produce top-of-the-line content, there is no way that smaller creators can compete. TikTok may say that down-and-dirty is fine so that it can get people to continue to churn out content, but that doesn't mean those posts will get any views. Same on Instagram, where it has become almost impossible to build a following. Getting views and likes and other engagement is what gives people the dopamine hit. No dopamine, no fun.

Influencers are too burnt, too big, or too willing to take a brand deal. The influencer landscape is changing. Some of the biggest names are burnt out and moving on. There is a growing chasm between mega-influencers and nano-influencers. We already see advertisers either making huge brand deals with the big online stars or working with nano-influencers, who get paid bupkis. The problem, according to several insiders I spoke with, is that nano-influencers are making deals with dozens of products. When they become that much of a shill, marketers don't want to work with them.

Social media has become second-rate TV. Social media started as social networking. It was a place to connect with far-flung family and perhaps reconnect with friends you had lost touch with. Today, you see post after post of what you don't want to see, which has forced out the content you do want to see, like pictures of your friends or dogs romping in the snow. Creating a community of three billion people was absurd on its face, especially in light of Dunbar's theory, the idea that we can maintain relationships with no more than 150 people. But platforms needed content and they got it by baiting creators with money. That growth strategy led to social networking morphing into social networks where the goal was to amass followers and turn ourselves into our own mini broadcast channel.

Brands are becoming media channels and subcultures.[4] Working under the premise that you may never see a commercial again, marketers are desperate to become integral to your life. The prevailing theory is that every brand will have to become a media company. Red Bull was a forerunner in this regard, with its media house producing digital, TV and film, print, and music. Brand subcultures will be an extrapolation of brand cults, creating rituals and shared experiences for users of the product.

The fact that social media is in decline is the best news ever. It was never the internet alone that handcuffed us to our phones. It was always social media. And now, social media is, after two decades, no longer delivering on its promise. The platforms have lost their "social" utility, and they have no one to blame but themselves.

Truthfully, Facebook and the rest won't disappear. But they will change. What we know from history is that "older" technologies don't die; we transform the way we use them. Radio, for example, used to have dramas. When television came along and presented that material better, we used radio to listen to music. In the same way, we will use the social media behemoths differently. According to Gartner research, "A perceived decay in the quality of social media platforms will drive 50% of consumers to abandon or significantly limit their interactions with social media by 2025."[5] People are already turning to smaller platforms to socialize with people they know. Direct messaging, groups chats, and Discord channels have become the social media of choice. Social media will be used as the shopping mall it was always intended to be, super-serving the advertisers who have always been the end customer.

But as social media declines, we still need to be vigilant. Brands progress in their cult tactics. There will still be influencers—of all stripes—who will be charismatic cult leaders. And, yes, there will still be good old-fashioned religious cults.

We are not helpless here. In fact, we have the upper hand, if we are only willing to utilize it. Advertisers want our eyeballs, and we decide if we want to give marketers our time and attention. As they say in the social media biz, here are some tips and tricks:

1. If you think about the cell phone in your hand as anything other than a shopping mall and a 24/7 spying machine, you are thinking about it the wrong way. Before you pick up your phone, and especially before you get on to social media, be mindful that what you have in your hand is a not communication device but a tool backed by a multibillion-dollar industry designed to steal your privacy, your money, and your peace of mind.

2. Spend time in spaces where you control the content. Technology is not the problem; social media is. Watching movies, doing research, chatting with your friends is not what will draw you into a cult-like situation. It is spending time in a space where you do not control the content with which you are interacting.

3. Call your elected officials and tell them to stop playing around the margins and eliminate Section 230. Congress needs to stop creating dangerous legislation and eliminate Section 230. The latest proposed regulation, the Kids Online Safety Act (KOSA), presents itself as a way to protect young people online while in truth acting as a form of censorship and a means of eliminating the access of much-needed information to marginalized youth. Having worked in corporate America, I well know that unless companies are forced to be responsible, they won't. You have to hit them in the pocketbook. If we want to hold social media companies accountable, we need to put regulations in place to do that.

4. Use social media against itself. I know this might sound crazy, but even the mommy influencers—some of the fiercest influencers around—want a safe environment for their content. And here, too, we can gain the upper hand. What if there was a social media blackout day? What if, for just one day, everyone froze their social media accounts and made their content unavailable? The platforms

would have to pay attention. More difficult would be going after Meta and Mark Zuckerberg, but a coordinated campaign might let the company know that Congress is not the only one who cares. I'd start by using the footage of Zuckerberg apologizing on the House floor for allowing kids to be bullied . . . and worse.

5. If anger and anxiety is what you don't want, focus on what you do want. Think about it. Why would you move into a community where everyone attacks one another? You wouldn't. So let's envision the community we do want—one with hope and support. If that's the community you seek, either find technology that is not based on advertising or maybe just go outside.

But whether it is the cult of capitalism, the cult of colleges, or the cult of Silicon Valley, we don't have to allow our emotions and our frailties to become tools of the market. We can finally open our eyes and stop being hoodwinked.

NOTES

INTRODUCTION: HERE A CULT, THERE A CULT, EVERYWHERE A CULT CULT

1. The page is unrelated to the company.
2. Chantal Fernandez, "Inside Lululemon's Unconventional Influencer Network," *Fashionista*, November 2, 2016, https://fashionista.com/2016/11/lululemon-ambassadors.
3. Deja Riley, *YouTube*, September 19, 2011, www.youtube.com/c/DejaRiley.
4. MLMs use a pyramid design in their company sales structure. Chapters 3, 4, and 5 examine the landscape of MLMs.
5. Alex Rawitz, "Lululemon's Influencer Marketing Strategy Explained," Influencer Marketing Platform for Lifestyle Brands, March 31, 2023, www.tribedynamics.com/blog/influencer-marketing-spotlight-lululemon.
6. David Z. Morris, "Does Crypto Still Care about Elon Musk?" *Consensus Magazine*, May 11, 2023, www.coindesk.com/layer2/2022/07/22/does-crypto-still-care-about-elon-musk/.
7. Matt Binder, "Elon Musk Says He Never Told People to Invest in Crypto. Here's What He Has Said," *Mashable*, June 21, 2022, https://mashable.com/article/elon-musk-never-told-people-to-invest-in-cryptocurrency.
8. Rachelle Bonja and Luke Vander Ploeg, "A Conversation with a Dogecoin Millionaire: An Update," *The Daily*, December 29, 2021, www.nytimes.com/2021/12/29/podcasts/the-daily/dogecoin-cryptocurrency.html.
9. Glauber Contessoto, "I've Lost Nearly $3M on Dogecoin," *Newsweek*, June 24, 2022, www.newsweek.com/dogecoin-millionaire-cryptocurrency-price-crash-bitcoin-1717417.
10. During the seventeenth century, cults were religious sects or groups that venerated a figure, deity, or object. Two centuries later, cults were expanded beyond religion to include ideas like "cult of success" or "cult of personality." It

was only during the late twentieth century that the word became pejorative in the mass media related to leaders like Charles Manson and the events connected to Jonestown (1978), Waco (1993), and Heaven's Gate (1997). More recently, cults are connected to fandom—cult film or cult products. (Philip Deslippe, "Past the Pejorative: Understanding the Word 'Cult' through Its Use in American Newspapers during the Nineties," *Implicit Religion* 24, no. 2 [2021]: 195–217.)

11. See *Black Ops Advertising* for an in-depth explanation of these practices.

12. E. J. Dickson, "Meet Andrew Tate, the Ex-kickboxer Red-pilling the Angry Young Men of America," *Rolling Stone*, December 11, 2023, www.rollingstone .com/culture/culture-news/andrew-tate-tiktok-hustlers-university-1397797/.

13. If you want to go deep on this, check out the podcast *Conspirituality*, which covers a different topic every week.

14. Jessica Rapp and Emma Chiu, *The Anxiety Economy*, ed. Hester Lacey (The Innovation Group, 2019).

CHAPTER 1: THE CULT TRAP

1. Sharlene Hesse-Biber, *The Cult of Thinness* (New York: Oxford University Press, 2007), 14.

2. According to cult expert Janja Lalich, "More than two-thirds of cult members are recruited by a friend, family member, or co-worker." (See www.ted.com/talks /janja_lalich_why_do_people_join_cults#t-174.) Being recruited by someone with whom you have a relationship is much harder to resist.

3. George Wright, "NXIVM: 'Why I Joined a Cult—And How I Left,'" BBC News, April 13, 2019, www.bbc.com/news/world-47900242?ocid=socialflow _twitter.

4. Lorne L. Dawson, *Comprehending Cults: The Sociology of New Religious Movements* (Oxford: Oxford University Press, 2013), 100–103.

5. In 2022, this content producer faced considerable backlash for plagiarizing others' materials. It's a bit overblown and Blair Kristy, the person behind iilluminaughtii, has explained and apologized. All that said, the content is well researched and worth a watch.

CHAPTER 2: CULT-Y BRANDS AND BRANDED CULTS

1. Direct Selling Fact Sheet, December 20, 2016, www.dsa.org/docs/default -source/advocacy/direct-selling-fact-sheet.pdf.

2. Albert M. Muniz and Thomas C. O'Guinn, "Brand Community," *Journal of Consumer Research* 27, no. 4 (2001): 412–32, https://doi.org/10.1086/319618.

3. Muniz and O'Guinn, "Brand Community," 412.

4. Douglas Atkin, *The Culting of Brands: When Customers Become True Believers* (New York: Portfolio Trade, 2004).

5. Matthew W. Ragas and Bolivar Bueno, *Power of Cult Branding* (New York: Random House, 2002).

6. "Survey Finds Disordered Eating Behaviors among Three out of Four American Women (Fall, 2008)," UNC Gillings School of Global Public Health, February 11, 2015, https://sph.unc.edu/cphm/carolina-public-health-magazine -accelerate-fall-2008/survey-finds-disordered-eating-behaviors-among-three-out -of-four-american-women-fall-2008/.

7. Sharlene Nagy Hesse-Biber, *The Cult of Thinness* (New York: Oxford University Press, 2007).

8. The Gathering, "The Gathering of Cult Brands," YouTube, October 7, 2014, www.youtube.com/watch?v=SeoB2qJpNyA.

9. This was two years before the release of the blockbuster movie—which itself became a cult phenomenon.

10. Barbie,"Barbie and Nikki Discuss Racism," YouTube, October 7, 2020, www.youtube.com/watch?v=RCzwoMDgF_I.

11. B. Joseph Pine II and James H. Gilmore, *The Experience Economy* (Boston: Harvard Business School Press, 2011).

12. John Berger, *Ways of Seeing: Based on the BBC Television Series with John Berger* (London: British Broadcasting Corp., 2012).

13. Megan, "15 Ways to Use Sensory Marketing in 2023," Brandastic, November 17, 2022, https://brandastic.com/blog/sensory-marketing/.

14. "The Science of Sensory Marketing," *Harvard Business Review*, February 17, 2015, https://hbr.org/2015/03/the-science-of-sensory-marketing; "Scents Make Sense: Using Smell in Marketing and Retail," ANA, May 13, 2022, www.ana.net /miccontent/show/id/aa-2022-05-scent-in-marketing.

15. "Sensory Marketing: The Power of the 5 Senses in Retail," Kendu, June 1, 2021, www.kendu.com/retail-news-trends/sensory-marketing/#:~:text=Due%20 to%20the%20constant%20need,point%20of%20difference%20among%20stores.

16. This is the idea of the therapeutic ethos. See T. J. Jackson Lears, "From Salvation to Self-Realization: Advertising and the Therapeutic Roots of the Consumer Culture, 1880–1930," *Advertising & Society Review* 1 (2000).

17. Max Fisher, "Disinformation for Hire, a Shadow Industry, Is Quietly Booming," *New York Times*, July 25, 2021, www.nytimes.com/2021/07/25/ world/europe/disinformation-social-media.html.

18. Craig Timberg and Isaac Stanley-Becker, "Cambridge Analytica and the RNC Suppressed Black Voters in 2016," *Washington Post*, September 28, 2020, www.washingtonpost.com/technology/2020/09/28/trump-2016-cambridge-ana lytica-suppression/.

19. Robinson Meyer, "Everything We Know about Facebook's Secret Mood-Manipulation Experiment," *The Atlantic*, August 5, 2021, www.theatlantic.com/

technology/archive/2014/06/everything-we-know-about-facebooks-secret-mood
-manipulation-experiment/373648/.

20. Georgia Wells, Jeff Horwitz, and Deepa Seetharaman, "Facebook Knows
Instagram Is Toxic for Teen Girls, Company Documents Show," *Wall Street
Journal*, September 14, 2021, www.wsj.com/articles/facebook-knows-instagram-is
-toxic-for-teen-girls-company-documents-show-11631620739.

21. Neil Patel, "12 Genius Ways to Apply Emotional Marketing to Facebook
Ads—Neil Patel," Neil Patel (blog), 2017, https://neilpatel.com/blog/emotional-
marketing-to-facebook-ads/.

22. Seb Joseph, "The Rundown: Google, Meta and Amazon Are on Track
to Absorb More Than 50% of All Ad Money in 2022," Digiday, February 4,
2022, https://responsema.org/digital-marketing/the-rundown-google-meta-and
-amazon-are-on-track-to-absorb-more-than-50-of-all-ad-money-in-2022/.

23. Chris Adams, "What Is Persuasive Design?" Modern Analyst, n.d., www
.modernanalyst.com/Careers/InterviewQuestions/tabid/128/ID/4925/What-is
-Persuasive-Design.aspx.

24. Many of his ideas have been noted by others before him, but I use this here
due to its succinctness.

25. Startup Grind, "How to Build Habit-Forming Products," YouTube, March
10, 2017, www.youtube.com/watch?v=-jXM4NymIcA.

26. This has also been exacerbated by the effects of COVID lockdown.

CHAPTER 3: THE COLLEGE CULT: A CASE STUDY

1. Douglas Belkin, "Who's at the Door? College Officials Delivering Your
Acceptance in Person (Sometimes with a Dog)," *Wall Street Journal*, February 13,
2018, www.wsj.com/articles/whos-at-the-door-college-officials-delivering-your
-acceptance-in-person-sometimes-with-a-dog-1518375304.

2. In addition to ranking universities and graduate schools, *US News* ranks everything from nursing homes to countries to vacation destinations (www.usnews.com/
rankings).

3. Note: the cost of education is not included in the *U.S. News* rankings, thus
colleges have no incentive to keep their price tag low.

4. Alison Go, "Baylor Pays Freshmen to Retake SAT," *U.S. News and
World Report*, October 15, 2008, www.usnews.com/education/blogs/paper-trail
/2008/10/15/baylor-pays-freshmen-to-retake-sat.

5. Richard Pérez-Peña and Daniel E. E. Slotnik, "Gaming the College Rankings," *New York Times*, January 31, 2012, www.nytimes.com/2012/02/01/educa
tion/gaming-the-college-rankings.html.

6. Amanda Waite, "A New Way to Apply to College Simplifies the Process,
Promotes Equity & Access," Coalition for College, August 1, 2022, www.coalition
forcollegeaccess.org/news-announcements/apply-coalition-on-scoir-launch.

7. Cathy O'Neil, *Weapons of Math Destruction: How Big Data Increases Inequality and Threatens Democracy* (New York: Crown Books, 2016).

8. As long as at least one school to which the students are applying requires the SAT or the ACT, students have to take it. Since they have those scores, they send them to the colleges that no longer require it.

9. Melissa Korn, "Some Elite Colleges Review an Application in 8 Minutes (or Less)," *Wall Street Journal*, January 31, 2018, www.wsj.com/articles/some-elite-colleges-review-an-application-in-8-minutes-or-less-1517400001.

10. Jon McGee, *Breakpoint: The Changing Marketplace for Higher Education* (Baltimore: Johns Hopkins University Press, 2015), 13.

11. Bill Hussar, Jijun Zhang, Sarah Hein, Ke Wang, Ashley Roberts, Jiashan Cui, Mary Smith, Farrah Bullock Mann, Amy Barmer, and Rita Dilig, *The Condition of Education 2020* (Washington, DC: National Center for Education Statistics, May 19, 2020), https://nces.ed.gov/programs/coe/pdf/coe_cha.pdf, 127–32.

12. Eric Hoover, "Application Inflation: When Is Enough Enough?" *New York Times*, November 5, 2010, www.nytimes.com/2010/11/07/education/edlife/07HOOVER-t.html.

13. Jeffrey Selingo, "Colleges' Endless Pursuit of Students." *The Atlantic*, April 10, 2017, www.theatlantic.com/education/archive/2017/04/the-business-of-college-marketing/522399/.

14. Gregor Aisch, Larry Buchanan, Amanda Cox, and Kevin Quealy, "Some Colleges Have More Students from the Top 1 Percent Than the Bottom 60. Find Yours," *New York Times*, January 18, 2017, www.nytimes.com/interactive/2017/01/18/upshot/some-colleges-have-more-students-from-the-top-1-percent-than-the-bottom-60.html#:~:text=At%2038%20colleges%20in%20America,the%20entire%20bottom%2060%20percent. When it comes to the top-drawer schools, there's not a lot of room for diversity—racial or economic. After having accounted for legacies, athletes, diversity candidates, and increasingly "development admits" (wealthy donors who are not alumni), there is very little room for anyone else.

15. John Quinterno, *The Great Cost Shift: How Higher Education Cuts Undermine the Future Middle Class* (Demos, 2012).

16. APM Research Lab Staff, *What Americans Think about College: Government Funding and Assistance* (APM Research Lab, 2019).

17. Dominic Russell, Alan Smith, and Carrie Sloan, *The Financialization of Higher Education* (Roosevelt Institute, 2016).

18. To see data visualization of social listening related to a Nespresso campaign, see www.brandwatch.com/wp-content/uploads/2019/05/Campaign-Analysis-5-Minute-Guide.pdf. Examples of companies that perform social listening are Brandwatch (www.brandwatch.com/) and Hootsuite (https://hootsuite.com/industries/higher-education), which has specialization in working with higher education.

19. Mara Einstein, *Black Ops Advertising: Native Ads, Content Marketing, and the Covert World of the Digital Sell* (New York: OR Books, 2016).

20. Will Patch, "Social Media for College Search in 2022—Niche," Niche, August 24, 2022, www.niche.com/about/enrollment-insights/social-media-for-college-search-in-2022/.

21. Gil Rogers, *The Maturation of Mobile and Social: The 2017 Social Admissions Report* (Digital Marketing Solutions for Education Institutions, 2017), 137.

22. Jo Littler, *Against Meritocracy: Culture, Power and Myths of Mobility* (London: Routledge, 2018).

23. Matt Taibbi, "The Great College Loan Swindle," *Rolling Stone*, June 25, 2018, www.rollingstone.com/politics/politics-features/the-great-college-loan-swindle-124484/.

24. Ryan Jenkins, "Generation Z versus Millennials: The 8 Differences You Need to Know," *Inc.*, July 19, 2017, www.inc.com/ryan-jenkins/generation-z-vs-millennials-the-8-differences-you-.html. "Gen Z & Millennials' Top 17 Favorite Celebrity List Reveals a Generation Gap," YPulse, September 11, 2019, www.ypulse.com/article/2019/09/11/gen-z-millennials-top-17-favorite-celebrity-list-reveals-a-generation-gap/.

25. Dr. Twenge has pulled back considerably on her moral panic around kids and screen time. Jean M. Twenge, "What We Know Now about Screen Time for Kids," *Deseret News*, March 8, 2022, https://www.deseret.com/2022/3/7/22965534/what-we-know-now-about-screen-time-for-kids-jean-twenge-igen-social-media.

26. Sarah M. Coyne, Adam A. Rogers, Jessica D. Zurcher, Laura Stockdale, and McCall Booth, "Does Time Spent Using Social Media Impact Mental Health? An Eight Year Longitudinal Study," *Computers in Human Behavior* 104 (March 2020), https://doi.org/10.1016/j.chb.2019.106160.

27. Ellen Bara Stolzenberg, Kevin Eagan, Melissa C. Aragon, Natacha M. Cesar-Davis, Sidronio Jacobo, Victoria Couch, and Cecilia Rios-Aguilar, *The American Freshman: National Norms Fall 2018* (Los Angeles: Higher Education Research Institute, 2019).

28. Benoit Denizet-Lewis, "Why Are More American Teenagers Than Ever Suffering from Severe Anxiety?" *New York Times*, October 11, 2017, www.nytimes.com/2017/10/11/magazine/why-are-more-american-teenagers-than-ever-suffering-from-severe-anxiety.html.

29. Paul Tough, "Americans Are Losing Faith in the Value of College. Whose Fault Is That?" *New York Times*, September 5, 2023, www.nytimes.com/2023/09/05/magazine/college-worth-price.html.

30. William R. Emmons, Ana H. Kent, and Lowell R. Ricketts, "Is College Still Worth It? The New Calculus of Falling Returns," Economic Research—Federal Reserve Bank of St. Louis, 2019, https://research.stlouisfed.org/publications/review/2019/10/15/is-college-still-worth-it-the-new-calculus-of-falling-returns.

CHAPTER 4: MLMS ARE PYRAMID SCHEMES, AKA CULTS

1. "Multilevel Marketing: Last Week Tonight with John Oliver," YouTube, 2016, www.youtube.com/watch?v=s6MwGeOm8iI.

2. You can also see the complete presentation from Bill Ackman here: www .businessinsider.com/bill-ackmans-herbalife-presentation-2012-12#-9.

3. *Direct Selling in the United States: 2017 Facts and Data* (Washington, DC: Direct Selling Association, 2018).

4. "Anne Coughlan Is Wrong on Herbalife," Fraud Files Blog, January 12, 2013, www.sequenceinc.com/fraudfiles/2013/01/anne-coughlan-is-wrong-on -herbalife/.

5. "Direct Selling Code of Ethics I DSA Business Standards," DSA, n.d., www.dsa.org/consumerprotection/code-of-ethics.

6. Nick Perry, "10 MLM Statistics You Need to Know," Fundera, January 23, 2023, www.fundera.com/resources/mlm-statistics.

7. This link provides access to the claims made against companies with documentation including marketing videos: https://truthinadvertising.org/evidence/ enagic-income-claims-database/.

8. Bonnie Patten, "Self-Regulation in the Direct Selling Industry: Can It Ever Be More Than Symbolic?" (2022 keynote address, Multilevel Marketing: The Consumer Protection Challenge, June 10, 2022), www.mlmconference.com/ conference-videos-copy.

9. Francie Diep, "Multilevel Marketing Has a 'Goodwill Ambassador' in the Classroom," *The Chronicle of Higher Education*, September 19, 2022, www.chronicle .com/article/multilevel-marketing-has-a-goodwill-ambassador-in-the-classroom.

10. Alissa Quart, *Squeezed: Why Our Families Can't Afford America* (New York: Ecco, 2019).

11. Federal Trade Commission, "Business Guidance Concerning Multi-Level Marketing," January 4, 2018, https://hbw.citeline.com/-/media/supporting -documents/rose-sheet/2018/01/180104-ftc-mlm-guidance.pdf.

12. Jon M. Taylor, *The Case (for and) against Multi-Level Marketing* (Consumer Awareness Institute, 2011), chap. 3.

13. Taylor, *The Case (for and) against Multi-Level Marketing*, chap. 7.

14. Federal Trade Commission, "Multi-Level Marketing Businesses and Pyramid Schemes," Consumer Advice, November 25, 2022, https://consumer.ftc.gov/ articles/multi-level-marketing-businesses-pyramid-schemes#pyramid.

15. "Key Information about Being an Herbalife Independent Distributor," Herbalife, September 8, 2023, https://iamherbalifenutrition.com/wp-content/up loads/2023/09/Typical-Herbalife-Independent-Distributor-Earnings_USEN.pdf.

16. "Income Disclosure," Forever Living Products, accessed January 16, 2024, https://foreverliving.com/usa/en-us/income-disclosurev.

17. "Income Disclosure Statement—Monat Global," MONAT, June 16, 2023, https://monatglobal.com/income-disclosure-statement/.

18. "Young Living 2023 U.S. Income Disclosure Statement," February 1, 2023, https://static.youngliving.com/en-AU/keyfiles/IncomeDisclosureStatement_International.pdf.

19. "Pyramid Schemes," New York State Attorney General, accessed January 17, 2024, https://ag.ny.gov/pyramid-schemes.

20. "Tupperware!" *American Experience*, February 9, 2004, www.pbs.org/wgbh/americanexperience/films/tupperware/#transcript.

21. This was also a time when abuse during self-improvement trainings was not unheard of.

22. Katie Dowd, "The Awesome Implosion of Bay Area's Biggest Pyramid Scheme," SFGate, December 15, 2022, www.sfgate.com/sfhistory/article/The-incredible-implosion-of-Holiday-Magic-16785971.php; Jake Rossen, "Sell-Shocked: The Pyramid Schemer Who Convinced His Targets to Climb into Coffins," Mental Floss, May 19, 2022, www.mentalfloss.com/posts/holiday-magic-pyramid-scheme.

23. Kschang, "Pyramid Schemes and Ponzi Schemes: Koscot Test and Howey Test," The Crime Wire, November 14, 2023, https://thecrimewire.com/money/How-Pyramid-Schemes-and-Ponzi-Schemes-are-Prosecuted-in-the-US.

24. Robert L. FitzPatrick, *Ponzinomics: The Untold Story of Multi-Level Marketing* (Charlotte, NC: FitzPatrick Management, 2022).

25. Anne Nelson, *Shadow Network: Media, Money, and the Secret Hub of the Radical Right* (New York: Bloomsbury Publishing, 2021).

26. FitzPatrick, *Ponzinomics*, 202.

27. *The Dream* (podcast), season 1, episode 7, "Lazy, Stupid, Greedy or Dead," October 29, 2018.

28. Dale Russakoff and Juan Williams, "Rearranging 'Amway Event' for Reagan," *Washington Post*, January 22, 1984, www.washingtonpost.com/archive/politics/1984/01/22/rearranging-amway-event-for-reagan/b3e74482-5ce0-4d20-9f98-ebdc9b4d4918/.

CHAPTER 5: AUNT SUSIE GOT SUCKED IN BY THE MARKETING . . . AND THE "HEY HUN"

1. Kate Shellnutt and Hannah Anderson, "The Divine Rise of Multilevel Marketing," *Christianity Today*, November 23, 2015, www.christianitytoday.com/ct/2015/december/divine-rise-of-multilevel-marketing-christians-mlm.html; Deborah Whitehead, "Selling a Dream: MLMs and the Rhetoric of Freedom through Fashion," in *Selling the Sacred: Religion and Marketing from Crossfit To QAnon*, ed. Mara Einstein and Sarah Taylor (London: Routledge, 2024).

2. Shellnutt and Anderson, "The Divine Rise of Multilevel Marketing."

3. "Beachbody Sees Gains," *Los Angeles Business Journal*, May 17, 2020, https://labusinessjournal.com/news/weekly-news/beachbody-sees-gains/; Abby Vesou-

lis and Eliana Dockterman, "How MLM Distributors Are Using Coronavirus to Grow," *Time*, July 9, 2020, https://time.com/5864712/multilevel-marketing -schemes-coronavirus/.

4. Kai Prins and Mariah L. Wellman, "Dodging Negativity Like It's My Freaking Job: Marketing Postfeminist Positivity through Beachbody Fitness on Instagram," *Feminist Media Studies* 23, no. 3 (2021): 1292–1308, https://doi.org/10.108 0/14680777.2021.1992645. This is one of the few studies that examines the work of MLM consultants. Most research is economic and policy related.

5. Jeff Wilson, *Mindful America: The Mutual Transformation of Buddhist Meditation and American Culture* (New York: Oxford University Press, 2014); Ronald E. Purser, *McMindfulness: How Mindfulness Became the New Capitalist Spirituality* (London: Repeater, 2019).

6. Matthew Harris, "Nick Sarnicola Co Founder of Visalus: Master MLM Recruiting Training—MIM Episode #32," YouTube, April 18, 2013, www.youtube .com/watch?v=bei86CyN3yI.

7. "What Happened to ViSalus? (Explained)," BehindMLM, November 23, 2020, https://behindmlm.com/companies/visalus/what-happened-to-visalus -explained/.

8. Shellnutt and Anderson, "The Divine Rise of Multilevel Marketing."

9. "The Email Heard Round AntiMLM!—Life after MLM Podcast: Episode 96 Unedited Video!" YouTube, 2022, www.youtube.com/watch?v=GnVfBRg0qJI.

10. Personal interview, August 9, 2022.

11. You can see more about her and her work on Instagram (www.insta gram.com/themlmpolice) and read more about her experiences at Elle Beau, the Anti-Blogger (https://ellebeaublog.com/2017/12/06/i-applied-to-attend-the -younique-foundation-retreat-i-really-wish-i-didnt/).

12. Allie Volpe, "What Happened When the MLMs Found Tinder," *Bustle*, January 10, 2022, www.bustle.com/wellness/mlm-recruitment-dating-social-apps.

13. Hannah Martin, "Thinking of Joining an MLM? Read the Truth behind the 'Income Opportunity,'" Talented Ladies Club, February 5, 2023, www.talented ladiesclub.com/articles/thinking-of-joining-a-mlm-read-the-truth-behind-the -income-opportunity/.

14. *Direct Selling in the United States 2021 Industry Overview* (Direct Selling Association, 2022), www.dsa.org/docs/default-source/industry-fact-sheets/dsa-2021g -ofactsheetv3.pdf?sfvrsn=51c6d6a5_3.

15. Marguerite DeLiema, Doug Shadel, Amy Nofziger, and Karla Pak, *AARP Study of Multilevel Marketing: Profiling Participants and Their Experiences in Direct Sales* (Washington, DC: AARP Foundation, 2018).

16. Marguerite DeLiema, Stacie Bosley, and Doug Shadel, "Multi-Level Marketing as 'Gig' Work: Worker Motivations, Characteristics, and Outcomes in the U.S.," *Journal of Labor and Society* 25, no. 1 (2021): 83–121, https://doi.org /10.1163/24714607-bja10029.

17. Stephanie McNeal, "Anastasia Beverly Hills Will No Longer Work with Rodan + Fields after a Ton of Fan Backlash," BuzzFeed News, February 7, 2020, www.buzzfeednews.com/article/stephaniemcneal/anastasia-beverly-hills-rodan -fields-mlm-backlash.

18. For a fairly exhaustive list, see MLM Truth: https://mlmtruth.org/master -list/.

19. Cruel World Happy Mind, "Tyra Banks Had Her Own MLM Makeup Line?! (It Failed)," YouTube, 2020, www.youtube.com/watch?v=6zXYHBCj4L Q&amp%3Bt=451s.

20. Mike McIntire, "Tax Records Reveal How Fame Gave Trump a $427 Mil-lion Lifeline," *New York Times*, September 29, 2020, www.nytimes.com/interactive/ 2020/09/28/us/donald-trump-taxes-apprentice.html.

21. Team Business for Home, "Hall of Fame MLM Celebrities—How to Handle the Pyramid Myth Objection," Direct Selling Facts, Figures and News, September 11, 2014, www.businessforhome.org/2014/09/hall-of-fame-mlm -celebrities/.

22. Pinterest is often used for its search properties and because it is valuable for search engine optimization; that is, it will help people find you on Google.

23. Decca Muldowney, "Yellow Tongue Strips Slammed as 'Scammy Miracle Supplement,'" Daily Beast, September 2, 2022, www.thedailybeast.com/mlm-elo mir-is-slammed-for-yellow-tongue-strips-they-claim-will-relieve-things-like -anxiety-and-joint-pain; "What You Should Know about Elomir," December 13, 2023, https://truthinadvertising.org/articles/what-you-should-know-about -elomir/#:~:text=UPDATE%2012%2F13%2F23%3A,to%20promote%20its%20 business%20opportunity.

24. Chiung Hwang Chen, "Marketing Religion Online: The LDS Church's SEO Efforts," *Journal of Media and Religion* 10, no. 4 (2011): 185–205, https://doi.org/ 10.1080/15348423.2011.625265.

25. Mara Einstein, "From Cause Marketing to Activist Branding," in *The Rout-ledge Companion to Advertising and Promotional Culture*, 2023, 211–23, https://doi .org/10.4324/9781003124870-23; Mara Einstein, "Pride Is Not Just about Market-ing: Support for LGBTQ Rights and Equality Goes Far beyond Brands," *New York Daily News*, June 25, 2023, www.nydailynews.com/2023/06/25/pride-is-not-just -about-marketing-support-for-lgbtq-rights-and-equality-goes-far-beyond-brands/.

26. "Nutrition for Zero Hunger," Herbalife, March 14, 2023, https://iamherba lifenutrition.com/global-responsibility/nutrition-for-zero-hunger/.

27. "National Park Foundation," Tupperware US, n.d., https://web.archive.org/ web/20230314174002/https://www.tupperware.com/pages/national-park-foun dation.

28. MONAT Global, "MONATions 2022 Recap," YouTube, 2022, www .youtube.com/watch?v=f-a3m0HwW34.

29. *(Un)Well*, season 1, episode 1, "Essential Oils," Netflix, 2020.

30. Brian Gill, "Brian Gill Unveils Marketing Initiatives at Younique Convention 2015," YouTube, 2015, www.youtube.com/watch?v=3JIW5BMJSY8.

CHAPTER 6: HOW TO BECOME AN EX-MLMER

1. *(Un)Well*, season 1, episode 1, "Essential Oils," Netflix, 2020.
2. Taylor Edgecomb, personal interview, August 6, 2022.
3. Simply Kelly Noelle, "Why I Quit My MLM from the Top .4%: My Story #ANTIMLM," September 19, 2022, www.youtube.com/watch?v=RP4vwEVphQI.
4. Simply Kelly Noelle, "Why I Quit My MLM from the Top .4%: My Story #ANTIMLM," September 19, 2022, www.youtube.com/watch?v=RP4vwEVphQI.
5. Not the Good Girl, "Why I Quit the MLM Industry at the Top: Anti-MLM Horror Story," May 21, 2020, www.youtube.com/watch?v=xzOt_Hmjcbo.
6. Not the Good Girl, "Why I Quit the MLM Industry at the Top: Anti-MLM Horror Story," May 21, 2020, www.youtube.com/watch?v=xzOt_Hmjcbo.
7. Norman Shaw, Brenda Eschenbrenner, and Daniel Baier, "Online Shopping Continuance after COVID-19: A Comparison of Canada, Germany and the United States," *Journal of Retailing and Consumer Services* 69 (November 1, 2022): 103100, https://doi.org/10.1016/j.jretconser.2022.103100.
8. "IBISWorld—Industry Market Research, Reports, and Statistics," n.d., www.ibisworld.com/united-states/market-research-reports/online-vitamin-supplement-sales-industry/#IndustryStatisticsAndTrends.
9. Talented Ladies Club, "Why the MLM Industry Is Dying Out (and Why That's Good News for Us All)," December 14, 2020, www.talentedladiesclub.com/articles/why-the-mlm-industry-is-dying-out-and-why-thats-good-news-for-everyone/.
10. "The Dream Drew Brees—and AdvoCare—Is Trying to Sell," ESPN.com, March 15, 2016, www.espn.com/espn/feature/story/_/id/14972197/questions-surround-advocare-nutrition-empire-endorsed-saints-qb-drew-brees.
11. Truth in Advertising, "Trial Court Rules Neora Is Not a Pyramid Scheme," September 28, 2023, https://truthinadvertising.org/articles/trial-court-rules-neora-not-a-pyramid-scheme/.
12. "FTC Puts Businesses on Notice That False Money-Making Claims Could Lead to Big Penalties," Federal Trade Commission, March 16, 2022, www.ftc.gov/news-events/news/press-releases/2021/10/ftc-puts-businesses-notice-false-money-making-claims-could-lead-big-penalties.
13. See the list of companies at www.ftc.gov/system/files/attachments/penalty-offenses-concerning-money-making-opportunities/list-recipients-mmo_notice_0.pdf.

CHAPTER 7: INFLUENCERS MUTATE FROM CONTENT CREATORS TO CULT BRANDS

1. Aleda Stam, "Stagwell Acquires Movers+Shakers," *Ad Age*, November 2, 2023, https://adage.com/article/agency-news/stagwell-acquires-moversshakers/2526506

2. Alexandra Sumar and Colleen Christison, "The History of Social Media in 33 Key Moments," Hootsuite, April 6, 2023, https://blog.hootsuite.com/history-social-media/.

3. Elena Cresci, "Lonelygirl15: How One Mysterious Vlogger Changed the Internet," *Guardian*, June 16, 2016, www.theguardian.com/technology/2016/jun/16/lonelygirl15-bree-video-blog-youtube.

4. Kevin Roose, "The Making of a YouTube Radical," *New York Times*, September 3, 2020, www.nytimes.com/interactive/2019/06/08/technology/youtube-radical.html.

5. Sara Lebow, "Facebook Still Generates Most of Meta's Ad Revenues, as Instagram Drives Growth," Insider Intelligence, December 21, 2022, www.insiderintelligence.com/content/facebook-still-generates-most-meta-ad-revenues-instagram-drives-growth.

6. "TechCrunch Is Part of the Yahoo Family of Brands," July 12, 2022, https://techcrunch.com/2022/07/12/google-exec-suggests-instagram-and-tiktok-are-eating-into-googles-core-products-search-and-maps/.

7. Iona Bain, "Is TikTok's 'Shoppertainment' Sales Model Pushing Gen Z into Debt? Just Look at the Numbers," *Guardian*, March 18, 2023, www.theguardian.com/commentisfree/2023/mar/16/tiktoks-shoppertainment-model-gen-z-debt.

8. Twitch, with its passionate gaming followers, is less relevant to this conversation.

9. Susanne Ault, "Survey: YouTube Stars More Popular Than Mainstream Celebs among U.S. Teens," *Variety*, August 5, 2014, https://variety.com/2014/digital/news/survey-youtube-stars-more-popular-than-mainstream-celebs-among-u-s-teens-1201275245/.

10. Karin Von Abrams, "Global Ecommerce Forecast 2021," Insider Intelligence, July 7, 2021, www.insiderintelligence.com/content/global-ecommerce-forecast-2021.

11. Rebecca Keegan and Nicole Sperling, "*Shakespeare in Love* and Harvey Weinstein's Dark Oscar Victory," *Vanity Fair*, December 8, 2017, www.vanityfair.com/hollywood/2017/12/shakespeare-in-love-and-harvey-weinsteins-dark-oscar-victory.

12. Taffy Brodesser-Akner, "How Goop's Haters Made Gwyneth Paltrow's Company Worth $250 Million," *New York Times*, July 30, 2018, www.nytimes.com/2018/07/25/magazine/big-business-gwyneth-paltrow-wellness.html.

13. Sapna Maheshwari, "Are You Ready for the Nanoinfluencers?" *New York Times*, November 12, 2018, www.nytimes.com/2018/11/11/business/media/nano influencers-instagram-influencers.html.

14. There are also multichannel networks (MCNs), which are only on You-Tube. They work like a cable TV system, in that the network brings together a number of YouTube creators. See Werner Geyser, "What Are MCNs for YouTube Creators (+ Top Multi-Channel Networks)." Influencer Marketing Hub, May 30, 2022, https://influencermarketinghub.com/mcn-youtube-creators/#toc-5.

15. Nader Alizadeh, "McDonald's 'Trick. Treat. Win!' Campaign." Linqia, October 25, 2022, www.linqia.com/customers/mcdonalds/.

16. Scott Bixby, "Mike Bloomberg Is Paying 'Influencers' to Make Him Seem Cool," *The Daily Beast*, February 18, 2020, www.thedailybeast.com/mike-bloom berg-is-paying-influencers-to-make-him-seem-cool-9?ref=author.

17. Stephanie Lai, "Campaigns Skirt Political Ad Rules by Paying Influencers," *New York Times*, November 2, 2022, www.nytimes.com/2022/11/02/us/elec tions/influencers-political-ads-tiktok-instagram.html.

18. Benjamin Wofford, "Meet the Lobbyist Next Door," *WIRED*, July 14, 2022, www.wired.com/story/meet-the-lobbyist-next-door/.

19. A. M. Goodwin, K. Joseff, and S. C. Woolley, "Social Media Influencers and the 2020 U.S. Election: Paying 'Regular People' for Digital Campaign Communication," Center for Media Engagement, October 2020, https://mediaengage ment.org/research/social-media-influencers-and-the-2020-election.

20. M. A. Amazeen, "The Rise of the Influencer Election," Truth in Advertising, March 2, 2020, www.truthinadvertising.org/campaign-2020-the-rise-of-the -influencer-election/.

21. Pallavi Rao, "How Much the Most Followed Instagram Accounts Earn on Posts," Visual Capitalist, July 20, 2023, www.visualcapitalist.com/cp/most -followed-instagram-accounts-earn-posts/.

22. Werner Geyser, "Influencer Rates: How Much Do Influencers Really Cost in 2024?" Influencer Marketing Hub, November 9, 2023, https://influencermar ketinghub.com/influencer-rates/.

23. Werner Geyser, "TikTok Money Calculator [Influencer Engagement & Earnings Estimator]," Influencer Marketing Hub, November 24, 2023, https:// influencermarketinghub.com/tiktok-money-calculator/.

24. Werner Geyser, "The State of Influencer Marketing 2023: Benchmark Report," Influencer Marketing Hub, October 30, 2023, https://influencermarket inghub.com/influencer-marketing-benchmark-report/#toc-10.

25. Michael Grothaus, "96.5% of YouTube Creators Don't Make above the U.S. Poverty Line," FastCompany.com., www.fastcompany.com/40537244/96 -5-of-youtube-creators-dont-make-above-the-u-s-poverty-line.

26. Nicholas Bouchard, "TikTok Creativity Program: How to Join the New Creator Fund," The Leap, November 10, 2023, www.theleap.co/blog/tiktok -creativity-program-beta/.

27. Asia Milia Ware, "Everything We Know about the Lash Drama on TikTok," *The Cut*, January 27, 2023, www.thecut.com/2023/01/everything-we-know-about-the-lash-drama-on-tiktok.html.

28. Faith Karimi, "Forget the Influencers. Here Come the 'Deinfluencers,'" CNN, June 1, 2023, www.cnn.com/2023/06/11/us/deinfluencing-tiktok-trend-explained-cec/index.html.

29. Jordyn Holman and Sapna Maheshwari, "Shein Flew Influencers to China to Help Its Image. A Backlash Ensued," *New York Times*, June 30, 2023, www.nytimes.com/2023/06/29/business/shein-influencers-backlash.html.

30. "Influencers Warned by FTC over 'Inadequate' Disclosures of Artificial Sweetener Promotions," NBC News, November 15, 2023, www.nbcnews.com/news/us-news/ftc-influencer-warning-disclosures-artificial-sweetener-promos-rcna125396.

CHAPTER 8: GETTING HOOKED ON AN INFLUENCER . . . AND WHAT THEY'RE SELLING

1. Julia Alexander, "MrBeast Changed YouTube and Launched an Entire Genre of Expensive Stunt Content," *The Verge*, October 25, 2019, www.theverge.com/2019/10/25/20924718/mrbeast-youtube-stunts-challenges-money-philanthropy-creators-morgz.

2. Curiosity Stream, "The Origin and Rise of MrBeast," March 19, 2022, www.youtube.com/watch?v=_Qq6sCvz4Z0.k.

3. "Beast Philanthropy Official Site—Help End Hunger," Beast Philanthropy, n.d., www.beastphilanthropy.org/.

4. Jorge A. Aguilar, "MrBeast's Fans Believe He Has Misled Them into a Refinable Crypto Scam," Gfinity Esports, May 24, 2021, www.gfinityesports.com/gaming-news/MrBeasts-fans-believe-he-has-misled-them-into-a-Refinable-crypto-scam/.

5. Matt Moen, "MrBeast Asks Fans to Clean up His Chocolate Bar Store Display," *Paper*, March 8, 2023, www.papermag.com/mrbeast-chocolate-bar#rebelltitem13.

6. Anita Elberse and Oliver Band, "MrBeast: Building a YouTube Empire," Harvard Business School Case 523-103, March 2023, www.hbs.edu/faculty/Pages/item.aspx?num=63941.

7. Jaeyeon (Jae) Chung, Yu Ding, and Ajay Kalra, "I Really Know You: How Influencers Can Increase Audience Engagement by Referencing Their Close Social Ties," *Journal of Consumer Research* 50, no. 4 (December 2023): 683–703, https://doi.org/10.1093/jcr/ucad019.

8. Caroline Thompson, "How to Get a Friend Out of an MLM," *Vice*, October 22, 2018, www.vice.com/en/article/43e573/how-to-get-a-friend-out-of-an-mlm-herbalife-amway-younique-?__twitter_impression=true.

9. *Offline with Jon Favreau* (podcast), episode 96, "The Truth about TikTok's Spin on Israel-Gaza," November 11, 2023, https://crooked.com/podcast/the -truth-about-tiktoks-spin-on-israel-gaza.

10. Angela Haupt, "In Defense of Parasocial Relationships," *TIME*, July 13, 2023, https://time.com/6294226/parasocial-relationships-benefits/.

11. Donald Horton and Robert Wohl, "Mass Communication and Para-Social Interaction," *Psychiatry MMC* 19, no. 3 (August 1, 1956): 215–29, https://doi.org /10.1080/00332747.1956.11023049.

12. Tracy R. Gleason, Sally A. Theran, and Emily M. Newberg, "Parasocial Interactions and Relationships in Early Adolescence," *Frontiers in Psychology* 8 (February 23, 2017), https://doi.org/10.3389/fpsyg.2017.00255.

13. Jayson L. Dibble, Tilo Hartmann, and Sarah F. Rosaen, "Parasocial Interaction and Parasocial Relationship: Conceptual Clarification and a Critical Assessment of Measures," *Human Communication Research* 42, no. 1 (March 17, 2015): 21–44, https://doi.org/10.1111/hcre.12063.

14. Misha (dontcrossagayman), "I Feel Like I'm Not Overreacting," TikTok, November 27, 2023, www.tiktok.com/@dontcrossagayman/video/73062597919 01445409.

15. Sara Lebow, "5 Charts Showing the Creator Economy's Recent Evolution," Insider Intelligence, October 9, 2023, www.insiderintelligence.com /content/5-charts-showing-creator-economy-s-recent-evolution.

16. "Influencer Marketing Trends Report," n.d., www.creatoriq.com/white -papers/influencer-marketing-trends-report-2023.

17. Werner Geyser, "The State of Influencer Marketing 2023: Benchmark Report," Influencer Marketing Hub, October 30, 2023, https://influencermarket inghub.com/influencer-marketing-benchmark-report/.

18. "ANA Influencer Marketing Measurement Guidelines," ANA, n.d., www .ana.net/miccontent/show/id/rr-2022-06-ana-influencer-marketing-measurement.

19. Jack Neff, "Gen Z Favors Social Media over TV for CPG Purchases and Accepts Personalized Ads More Than Other Groups," *Advertising Age*, August 24, 2023, https://adage.com/article/marketing-news-strategy/gen-zs-cpg-buying -habits-and-ad-preferences-revealed-tinuiti-study/2512616.

20. Pew Research Center, "For Shopping, Americans Turn to Mobile Phones while Influencers Become a Factor," November 21, 2022, www.pewresearch .org/short-reads/2022/11/21/for-shopping-phones-are-common-and-influencers -have-become-a-factor-especially-for-young-adults/.

21. Mara Einstein, *Black Ops Advertising: Native Ads, Content Marketing and the Covert World of the Digital Sell*, 2016.

22. Alexander J. Martin, "Staying off Social Media Is Not Enough to Protect Your Privacy, Study Says," *Sky News*, January 21, 2019, https://news.sky.com /story/staying-off-social-media-is-not-enough-to-protect-your-privacy-study -says-11613216.

23. "What Is the Average Conversion Rate for Influencer Marketing Campaigns?" LinkedIn, December 18, 2023, www.linkedin.com/advice/0/what-average-conversion-rate-influencer-marketing-bx3ce#:~:text=Generally%20speaking%2C%20Instagram%20micro%2Dinfluencers,mega%2Dinfluencers%20have%20 0.2%25.

24. Evan Bailyn, "Digital Marketing Conversion Rates: 2024 Report," First Page Sage, December 28, 2023, https://firstpagesage.com/reports/digital-marketing-conversion-rate/#.

25. The Influencer Marketing Factory, "TikTok's Influence w/ Adrienne Lahens & Sofia Hernandez," September 13, 2023, www.youtube.com/watch?v=V-bzLfy Reg0.

26. "11 TikTok Influencer Marketing Examples to Inspire You," n.d., www.mo dash.io/blog/tiktok-influencer-marketing-examples.

27. "16 Influencer Marketing Campaign Examples [+ Key Takeaways]," n.d., www.modash.io/blog/influencer-marketing-campaign-examples#:~:text =images%20from%20customers.-,Campaign%20statistics,million%20timepieces %20in%20annual%20sales.

28. Gillian Follett, "TikTok Shop Launches for All Users—What Brands and Creators Should Know," *Advertising Age*, September 12, 2023, https://adage.com /article/digital-marketing-ad-tech-news/tiktok-shop-launches-all-us-users-what -brands-and-creators-should-know/2515556.

29. Gillian Follett, "Inside Influencer Storefronts and How They're Driving Brand Sales," *Advertising Age*, October 17, 2022, https://adage.com/article/digital -marketing-ad-tech-news/influencer-recommendations-and-storefronts-shape -what-consumers-buy/2442746.; Pew Research Center, "For Shopping, Americans Turn to Mobile Phones while Influencers Become a Factor," November 21, 2022, www.pewresearch.org/short-reads/2022/11/21/for-shopping-phones-are -common-and-influencers-have-become-a-factor-especially-for-young-adults/.

30. "McDonald's Head of Social Media Was as Shocked as We Were about the Grimace Shake Trend," *Today*, July 13, 2023, www.today.com/food/trends /mcdonalds-head-of-social-media-on-grimace-shake-trend-rcna94159; Fraz (the-frazmaz), "RIP Grimace (and me)," TikTok, June 13, 2023, www.tiktok.com/@the frazmaz/video/7244325864169590058?lang=en.

31. Danielle (danimarielettering), "Thirsty after You Catch on Fire?" TikTok, November 15, 2023, www.tiktok.com/@danimarielettering/video/73017 24587488759070?_r=1&_t=8hllC0GT9tH.

32. Ashwinn (shwinnabego), "This Is How Brands Need to Respond and Move on Social," TikTok, November 17, 2023, www.tiktok.com/@shwinnabego/ video/7302488803460304174?_r=1&_t=8hllHks17Zn.

33. Sara Lebow, "What the 'Death' of Social Media Means for Advertisers, According to Our Forecast," Insider Intelligence, September 5, 2023, www .insiderintelligence.com/content/what-death-of-social-media-means-advertisers -according-our-forecast.

34. Cory Doctorow, "The 'Enshittification' of TikTok," *WIRED*, January 23, 2023, www.wired.com/story/tiktok-platforms-cory-doctorow/.

35. Clay Shirky, "Power Laws, Weblogs, and Inequality," Clay Shirky's Writings about the Internet, 2003, www.shirky.com/writings/powerlaw_weblog.html.

36. Sara Fischer, "The Creator Economy Is Failing to Spread the Wealth," Axios, n.d., www.axios.com/2021/10/11/creator-economy-revenue-content.

CHAPTER 9: FROM SKINCARE TO COACHING TO CRYPTOCURRENCY

1. Chris Norlund, "How Social Media Influencers Fed Bankman-Fried's Cult of Personality," CoinDesk, January 18, 2023, www.coindesk.com/consensus-magazine/2023/01/18/how-social-media-influencers-fed-bankman-frieds-cult-of-personality/.

2. Michelle Singletary, "Americans View Crypto Investing as Unreliable. They're Right," *Washington Post*, April 21, 2023, www.washingtonpost.com/business/2023/04/21/americans-view-cryptocurrency-unreliable/.

3. WeGrow, Instagram, November 2018.

4. Michael Bass, "Community as a Service: The Commodification of the Social Commons," (master's thesis, December 2018).

5. Lydia Ramsey Pflanzer, "How Elizabeth Holmes Convinced Powerful Men like Henry Kissinger, James Mattis, and George Shultz to Sit on the Board of Theranos," *Business Insider*, June 2, 2023, www.businessinsider.com/theranos-former-board-members-henry-kissinger-george-shultz-james-mattis-2019-3.

6. Urban Dictionary, s.v. "brofluencer," n.d., www.urbandictionary.com/define.php?term=Brofluencer.

7. Shanti Das, "Andrew Tate: Money-Making Scheme for Fans of 'Extreme Misogynist' Closes," *Guardian*, February 1, 2023, www.theguardian.com/media/2022/aug/20/andrew-tate-money-making-scheme-for-fans-of-extreme-misogynist-closes.

8. Coffeezilla, "I Joined Andrew Tate's Cult and It Was Worse Than I Thought," August 1, 2022, www.youtube.com/watch?v=BijOF8I2t_4.

9. Amanda Holpuch, "Why Andrew Tate's Social Media Accounts Are Being Removed," *New York Times*, August 24, 2022, https://nytimes.com/2022/08/24/technology/andrew-tate-banned-tiktok-instagram.html.

10. Coffeezilla, "I Joined Andrew Tate's Cult."

11. Coffeezilla, "The Cult of Dan Lok—Brainwashed Student Lost $26,000 Testimonial," November 30, 2019, www.youtube.com/watch?v=4VDiM_PMmZA.

12. Richard Shotton, *The Choice Factory: 25 Behavioural Biases That Influence What We Buy* (Petersfield, Hampshire, UK: Harriman House, 2018), 15–16.

13. Michael Serazio, *The Authenticity Industries: Keeping It "Real" in Media, Culture, and Politics* (Stanford, CA: Stanford University Press, 2023), 133.

14. Paul Wedding, "North Texas Fitness Influencer Ordered to Pay $400,000 as Part of Settlement," WFAA, June 8, 2023, www.wfaa.com/article/news/local/north-texas-fitness-influencer-pay-more-than-500000-part-settlement/287-3d410af8-7508-4ecc-a780-ad87016e3f44.

15. Sydney Lima, "I Went to A-Fest, the $3,000 Wellness Festival for Millionaires," *Vice*, November 28, 2022, https://vice.com/en/article/v7vnb9/a-fest-review-vishen-lakhiani.

16. Vishen Lakhiani, *The Code of the Extraordinary Mind* (Emmaus, PA: Rodale, 2019), 194.

17. "Transform Lives, Starting with Yours: The Mindvalley Certified Life Coach Journey," Mindvalley, n.d., www.mindvalley.com/certs/life/masterclass.

18. Mindvalley Coach, "Breaking the Myth: Are There Too Many Coaches in the World?" YouTube, December 7, 2023, www.youtube.com/watch?v=NKsV_Cv2UL0.

19. See @DanielleRyan on YouTube.

20. Rebecca Jennings, "Michelle Phan, Dan Howell, and Why YouTubers Never Log Off," *Vox*, May 10, 2022, www.vox.com/the-goods/23064266/dan-howell-michelle-phan-youtuber-brain; Taylor Lorenz, "Young Creators Are Burning Out and Breaking Down," *New York Times*, September 17, 2021, https://nytimes.com/2021/06/08/style/creator-burnout-social-media.html.

21. Madeline Howard, "The Influencers Are Not Alright," *Women's Health*, December 15, 2022, www.womenshealthmag.com/health/a41946590/influencer-content-creation-hurting-mental-health/.

22. Alex Williams, "Heather Armstrong, 'Queen of the Mommy Bloggers,' Is Dead at 47," *New York Times*, May 11, 2023, https://nytimes.com/2023/05/10/us/heather-armstrong-dead.html.

23. "When a Business Offer or Coaching Program Is a Scam," Consumer Advice, January 9, 2023, https://consumer.ftc.gov/articles/when-business-offer-or-coaching-program-scam.; "FTC Acts to Stop Online Business Coaching Scheme LURN from Deceiving Consumers about Money-Making Potential," Federal Trade Commission, September 28, 2023, www.ftc.gov/news-events/news/press-releases/2023/09/ftc-acts-stop-online-business-coaching-scheme-lurn-deceiving-consumers-about-money-making-potential.

24. ICF numbers (from CNBC) vs IBIS: Sam Rega, "What Is Life Coaching? It's Not Therapy, but It's a Nearly $3 Billion Business," *CNBC*, March 26, 2021, https://cnbc.com/2021/03/26/what-is-a-life-coach.html.; IBISWorld, "Business Coaching in the US," n.d., www.ibisworld.com/industry-statistics/market-size/business-coaching-united-states/.

25. "Rise Together: Couple's Conference 2018," n.d., www.facebook.com/thechicsite/videos/10156254037316259/.

26. Stephanie McNeal, "Rachel and Dave Hollis Played Themselves," *BuzzFeed News*, November 5, 2021, www.buzzfeednews.com/article/stephaniemcneal/rachel-hollis-dave-hollis-instagram-rant.

27. Alyse Parker, "Goodbye Raw Alignment. HELLO Alyse Parker," August 8, 2019, www.youtube.com/watch?v=gzpyOGWG1RM.

28. "Here's an Inside Look at the Unregulated Life Coach Industry," March 23, 2021, https://cnbc.com/video/2021/03/23/the-truth-about-the-unregulated-life-coach-industry.html.

29. Homepage, Institute for Integrative Nutrition, November 27, 2023, www.integrativenutrition.com/.

30. Alyse Parker, "Things Are Finally Changing," November 30, 2023, www.youtube.com/watch?v=inFWbcujRMs.; Danielle Ryan, "Fitness Coach Turned Business Coach Sales Webinar #livereaction," February 24, 2023, www.youtube.com/watch?v=E2L4AEM97pE.

31. Instagram, n.d., www.instagram.com/marieewold/.

32. "Inside the MLM to Life Coach Pipeline," *Slate*, n.d., https://slate.com/transcripts/K2pkWDAyUC92Y1AxcUIxZkhhNXZYWkJ3czZhdkU2WkZyRVBoN2Q1OFJVcz0=; Jennifer Rajala, "The MLM Mindset: A Former MLM Coach & Top-Tier Earner Blows the Whistle," episode 57, Apple Podcasts, May 24, 2023, https://podcasts.apple.com/us/podcast/57-the-mlm-mindset-a-former-mlm-coach-top-tier/id1556669396?i=1000614271551.

33. Mattie Kahn, "For Lee Tilghman, There Is Life after Influencing," *New York Times*, April 14, 2023, https://nytimes.com/2023/04/11/style/lee-tilghman-influencer.html?smid=nytcore-ios-share&referringSource=articleShare.

34. Danielle Ryan, "Welcome to My Channel: Here's What to Expect," YouTube. April 28, 2023, www.youtube.com/watch?v=lW2WnLytXz8.

CHAPTER 10: ALGORITHMS AND "ANGER" FUEL INFLUENCER EXTREMISM

1. Werner Geyser, "How Does the YouTube Algorithm Work: A Peek into Its Changes in 2024," Influencer Marketing Hub, November 14, 2023, https://influencermarketinghub.com/how-does-the-youtube-algorithm-work/.

2. Mark Bartholomew, "The Law of Advertising Outrage," *Advertising & Society Quarterly* 19, no. 3 (January 1, 2018), https://doi.org/10.1353/asr.2018.0023.

3. Jeff Horwitz and Deepa Seetharaman, "Facebook Executives Shut Down Efforts to Make the Site Less Divisive," *WSJ*, May 26, 2020, https://wsj.com/articles/facebook-knows-it-encourages-division-top-executives-nixed-solutions-11590507499; Matthew Rozsa, "Facebook Could Have Stopped 10 Billion Impressions from 'Repeat Misinformers,' but Didn't: Report," *Salon*, April 12, 2021, www.salon.com/2021/04/12/facebook-could-have-stopped-10-billion-impressions-from-repeat-misinformers-but-didnt-report/.

4. Cristiano Lima-Strong and Naomi Nix, "41 States Sue Meta, Claiming Instagram, Facebook Are Addictive, Harm Kids," *Washington Post*, October 25, 2023,

https://washingtonpost.com/technology/2023/10/24/meta-lawsuit-facebook-ins
tagram-children-mental-health/.

5. Julia Carrie Wong, "How Facebook and YouTube Help Spread Anti-Vaxxer Propaganda," *Guardian*, February 1, 2019, www.theguardian.com/media/2019/feb/01/facebook-youtube-anti-vaccination-misinformation-social-media.

6. By the end of third quarter 2023, Google made slightly less than $300 billion, and Meta made close to $127 billion. Meta makes 97 percent of its revenue from advertising. Google makes most of its money from ad sales, but 58 percent is from search ads and 11.35 percent is from YouTube ad sales. Amazon made $512 billion in 2022, with $37.7 billion coming from advertising sales.

7. Patience Haggin, "Google and Meta's Advertising Dominance Fades as TikTok, Streamers Emerge," *WSJ*, January 4, 2023, www.wsj.com/articles/google-and-metas-advertising-dominance-fades-as-tiktok-netflix-emerge-11672711107.

8. Jonathan Vanian, "Meta Lets Amazon Shoppers Buy Products on Facebook and Instagram without Leaving the Apps," *CNBC*, November 9, 2023, https://cnbc.com/2023/11/09/meta-lets-amazon-users-buy-on-facebook-instagram-without-leaving-apps.html.

9. Ethan Cramer-Flood, "Meta's Ad Revenue Share Vastly Exceeds Its Share of Consumer Time," Insider Intelligence, July 28, 2023, https://insiderintelligence.com/content/meta-s-ad-revenue-share-vastly-exceeds-its-share-of-consumer-time.

10. Nick Srnicek, *Platform Capitalism* (New York: John Wiley & Sons, 2017), 46.

11. Max Fisher, *The Chaos Machine: The Inside Story of How Social Media Rewired Our Minds and Our World* (Hachette UK, 2022), 27.

12. Tobias Rose-Stockwell, *Outrage Machine: How Tech Amplifies Discontent, Disrupts Democracy—and What We Can Do about It* (Hachette UK, 2023), 44.

13. BBC, "Seriously . . . Paul Mason and the Kids Who Decide What All the Other Kids Talk About," December 15, 2016, www.bbc.co.uk/programmes/articles/2dLg30714lSN1xmbNYM7129/paul-mason-and-the-kids-who-decide-what-all-the-other-kids-talk-about.

14. Mara Einstein, *Black Ops Advertising: Native Ads, Content Marketing, and the Covert World of the Digital Sell* (New York: OR Books, 2016).

15. Marian Friestad and Peter Wright, "The Persuasion Knowledge Model: How People Cope with Persuasion Attempts," *Journal of Consumer Research* 21, no. 1 (June 1994), 1–31.

16. VICE News, "Startup Social Chain Takes Social-Media Marketing to a New Level (HBO)," March 2, 2017, www.youtube.com/watch?v=J_EPO2lwgpQ.

17. Brendan I. Koerner, "Watch This Guy Work, and You'll Finally Understand the TikTok Era," *WIRED*, October 19, 2023, www.wired.com/story/tiktok-talent-factory-ursus-magana-creator-economy/.

18. Makena Kelly, "Turning Point Is Quietly Building the Next Generation of Conservative Influencers," *The Verge*, January 5, 2022, www.theverge.com/2022/1/5/22868483/turning-point-charlie-kirk-republican-influencers-instagram-today-is-america.

19. MSNBC, Deadline: White House, December 19, 2023.

20. Isaac Stanley-Becker, "Pro-Trump Youth Group Enlists Teens in Secretive Campaign Likened to a 'Troll Farm,' Prompting Rebuke by Facebook and Twitter," *Washington Post*, September 16, 2020, www.washingtonpost.com/politics/turning-point-teens-disinformation-trump/2020/09/15/c84091ae-f20a-11ea-b796-2dd09962649c_story.html.

21. Natalie Weiner, "Candy Brand Sour Patch Kids Providing a Free Home-Away-from-Home for Emerging Artists," *Billboard*, August 3, 2015, www.billboard.com/music/features/candy-brand-sour-patch-kids-patch-houses-interview-6649171/.

22. Taylor Lorenz, "Is the Hype House Era Officially Over?" *Los Angeles Magazine*, October 4, 2023, https://lamag.com/real-estate/hype-house-content-creators-era-officially-over.

23. Alice Hearing, "TikTok Houses: Hype House Members, Clubhouse, More," *Dexerto*, July 2, 2021, www.dexerto.com/entertainment/whos-in-most-popular-tiktok-houses-hype-house-clubhouse-more-1382965/.

24. Tanya Chen, "Virtual TikTok House Works to Boost Biden Gen Z Vote," *BuzzFeed News*, October 19, 2020, www.buzzfeednews.com/article/tanyachen/biden-harris-pac-tiktok-house.

25. "A TikTok Video Told Democrats to Vote after Election Day, Violating the Platform's Rules," Media Matters for America, August 5, 2020, www.mediamatters.org/tiktok/tiktok-video-told-democrats-vote-after-election-day-violating-platforms-rules.

26. Michael Barkun, *A Culture of Conspiracy: Apocalyptic Visions in Contemporary America* (Berkeley: University of California Press, 2003).

27. Boston College Center for Christian-Jewish Learning, "Jonathan D. Sarna, 'White Supremacy and Anti-Semitism: Lessons from the Capitol Attack,'" January 14, 2021, www.youtube.com/watch?v=SC_ZHXCqpb4.

28. Dannagal Goldthwaite Young, *Wrong: How Media, Politics, and Identity Drive Our Appetite for Misinformation* (Baltimore: Johns Hopkins University Press, 2023), 49.

29. Michael F. Schein, *The Hype Handbook: 12 Indispensable Success Secrets from the World's Greatest Propagandists, Self-Promoters, Cult Leaders, Mischief Makers, and Boundary Breakers* (New York: McGraw Hill Professional, 2021), xiii.

30. Schein, *The Hype Handbook*, xx.

31. Hayley Clark-Braverman, "Marketing Insider: Loyalty's Next Frontier: Identity Loyalty," n.d., www.mediapost.com/publications/article/391130/loyaltys-next-frontier-identity-loyalty.html.

32. Schein, *The Hype Handbook*, 102.

33. Gregor Aisch, Jon Huang, and Cecilia Kang, "Dissecting the #PizzaGate Conspiracy Theories," *New York Times*, December 10, 2016, https://nytimes.com/interactive/2016/12/10/business/media/pizzagate.html.

34. Christopher Robbins, homepage, Type Investigations, December 18, 2023, www.typeinvestigations.org/.

35. The Center for Investigative Reporting, "About Us," *Reveal*, May 16, 2023, https://revealnews.org/about-us/.

36. Amanda Robb, "Anatomy of a Fake News Scandal," *Rolling Stone*, July 20, 2020, www.rollingstone.com/feature/anatomy-of-a-fake-news-scandal-125877/.

37. Robb, "Anatomy of a Fake News Scandal."

38. Robb, "Anatomy of a Fake News Scandal."

39. Robb, "Anatomy of a Fake News Scandal."

40. Aaron Katersky, "Alex Jones Still Must Pay $1B Judgment: Judge," *ABC News*, October 20, 2023, https://abcnews.go.com/US/alex-jones-ordered-pay-1-billion-judgment-sandy/story?id=104175574.

41. *Frontline*, "United States of Conspiracy," PBS, January 19, 2023, www.pbs.org/wgbh/frontline/documentary/united-states-of-conspiracy/transcript/.

42. Tiffany Hsu, "What the Trial of Alex Jones Revealed about His Finances," *New York Times*, September 22, 2022, https://nytimes.com/2022/08/05/us/alex-jones-finances.html.

43. Seth Brown, "Alex Jones's Media Empire Is a Machine Built to Sell Snake-Oil Diet Supplements," *Intelligencer*, May 4, 2017, https://nymag.com/intelligencer/2017/05/how-does-alex-jones-make-money.html.

44. "Challenge Validation," n.d., www.similarweb.com/website/infowars.com/#demographics.

45. Lisa Hagen, "Alex Jones' Defamation Trials Show the Limits of De-platforming for a Select Few," *NPR*, September 16, 2022, www.npr.org/2022/09/16/1123249309/alex-jones-defamation-trials-show-the-limits-of-deplatforming-for-a-select-few.

46. Rabbit Rabbit, "A Game Designer's Analysis of QAnon," *Medium*, December 16, 2021, https://medium.com/curiouserinstitute/a-game-designers-analysis-of-qanon-580972548be5.

47. "A Breeding Ground for Conspiracies: How QAnon Helped Bring about the U.S. Capitol Assault," American University, January 7, 2021, www.american.edu/sis/centers/security-technology/how-qanon-helped-bring-about-the-us-capitol-assault.cfm#_ftnref6.

48. HBO, *Q: Into the Storm*, 2021; Anna North, "#SaveTheChildren Is Pulling American Moms into QAnon," *Vox*, September 18, 2020, www.vox.com/21436671/save-our-children-hashtag-qanon-pizzagate.

49. Kaitlyn Tiffany, "Why Multilevel Marketing and QAnon Go Hand in Hand," *The Atlantic*, December 15, 2020, https://theatlantic.com/technology/archive/2020/10/why-multilevel-marketing-and-qanon-go-hand-hand/616885/.

CHAPTER 11: RELIGION MEETS ONLINE EXTREMISM

1. Jessie Lee Ward (@imbosslee), Instagram, May 9, 2023, www.instagram.com/p/CsCH45LJGhP/?hl=en.

2. Blanca Perdomo (blanca_perdomo), "I've Seen MLM Leaders Do Some Pretty Awful Things," TikTok, February 1, 2023, www.tiktok.com/@blanca_perdomo/video/7195207339446652206; The Dream (podcast), season 3, episode 1, "Becoming a #Boss," September 13, 2023, www.pushkin.fm/podcasts/the-dream/s3-e1-becoming-a-boss.

3. Jessie Lee Ward (@imbosslee), Instagram, January 22, 2003, www.instagram.com/p/CnuSIlcLGtq/?utm_source=ig_embed&ig_rid=bbb12363-d9b6-4686-b866-a328bc901dea.

4. Decca Muldowney, "MLM Seller Jessie 'Boss Lee' Ward Dies after Trying to Cure Her Cancer Naturally," The Daily Beast, September 19, 2023, www.thedailybeast.com/mlm-seller-jessie-boss-lee-ward-dies-after-trying-to-cure-her-cancer-naturally.

5. Jessie Lee Ward (@imbosslee), Instagram, September 18, 2023, www.instagram.com/p/CxVdXehM1he/?img_index=1.

6. Melissa Davey, "Jessica Ainscough, Australia's 'Wellness Warrior,' Dies of Cancer Aged 30," Guardian, September 20, 2017, www.theguardian.com/australia-news/2015/mar/01/jessica-ainscough-australia-wellness-warrior-dies-cancer-aged-30.

7. Mara Einstein, "Religious Influencers: Faith in the World of Marketing," in Produsing Theory in a Digital World 3.0, ed. Rebecca Ann Lind (New York: Peter Lang, 2020), 121–38.

8. The categories I developed were traditional religious leaders, religious innovators, religious social celebrities, faith-filled celebrities and industrialists, evangelicals/televangelists, and false profits.

9. Muslim Travel Girl, November 19, 2023, https://muslimtravelgirl.com/.

10. Morgan Baila, "Teal Swan & The Craziest Wellness Cult Conspiracy You've Never Heard Of," Refinery29, August 31, 2018, www.refinery29.com/en-us/2018/08/205915/the-gateway-teal-swan-youtube-cult-jennings-brown.

11. Lebo Diseko, "Teal Swan: The Woman Encouraging Her Followers to Visualise Death," BBC News, November 23, 2019, www.bbc.com/news/world-us-canada-50478821.

12. Teal Swan, Facebook, October 4, 2019, https://facebook.com/tealswanofficial/posts/hello-everyone-as-many-of-you-have-noticed-my-video-on-vaccines-was-removed-from/2913487975346290/?locale=es_LA.

13. Stephanie Alice Baker, "Alt. Health Influencers: How Wellness Culture and Web Culture Have Been Weaponised to Promote Conspiracy Theories and Far-Right Extremism during the COVID-19 Pandemic," European Journal of Cultural Studies 25, no. 1 (2022): 3–24.

14. Centrum für Religionswissenschaftliche Studien, "ISMRC 2023 Keynote Lecture by Stephanie Baker," YouTube, August 3, 2023, www.youtube.com/watch?v=2m8Oi70H43U.

15. Russell Chandler, *Understanding the New Age* (Grand Rapids, MI: Zondervan, 1993), 17.

16. Mara Einstein, *Brands of Faith* (London, Routledge, 2008), 199.

17. Timothy Caulfield, "Misinformation, Alternative Medicine and the Coronavirus," *Policy Options*, April 12, 2021, https://policyoptions.irpp.org/magazines/march-2020/misinformation-alternative-medicine-and-the-coronavirus/.

18. CBS News, "Conspirituality: How Wellness Became a Gateway for Misinformation," September 30, 2021, www.youtube.com/watch?v=yqvGU9o2bGI.

19. Charlotte Ward and David Voas, "The Emergence of Conspirituality," *Journal of Contemporary Religion* 26, no. 1 (January 1, 2011): 103–21, https://doi.org/10.1080/13537903.2011.539846.

20. Einstein, *Brands of Faith*, 198.

21. Krystal Tini (@krystaltini), Instagram, March 30, 2020, www.instagram.com/p/B-WBqe_J6bH/?hl=en&img_index=1.

22. Krystal Tini (@krystaltini), Instagram, April 4, 2020, www.instagram.com/p/B-kwZjaJAyC/.

23. Krystal Tini (@krystaltini), Instagram, October 31, 2020, www.instagram.com/p/CHBNGI7J9Qq/.

24. Krystal Tini (@krystaltini), Instagram, August 28, 2022, www.instagram.com/p/ChzqsX2vnlI/?hl=en.

25. Mara Einstein, *Compassion, Inc.* (Berkeley: University of California Press, 2012), https://doi.org/10.1525/9780520951631.

26. Charles Kriel and Katharina Gellein Viken, directors, *People You May Know* (Metrotone Media, 2020); Anne Nelson, *Shadow Network: Media, Money, and the Secret Hub of the Radical Right* (New York: Bloomsbury Publishing, 2021).

27. Kriel and Gellein Viken, *People You May Know.*

28. CBS News, "Conspirituality: How Wellness Became a Gateway for Misinformation," September 30, 2021, www.youtube.com/watch?v=yqvGU9o2bGI.

29. Madison Malone Kircher, "Is Instagram Strategically Withholding My Likes?" *Intelligencer*, January 19, 2018, https://nymag.com/intelligencer/2018/01/does-instagram-withhold-likes-to-get-users-to-open-app.html.

30. Anderson Cooper, "What Is 'Brain Hacking'? Tech Insiders on Why You Should Care," *60 Minutes*, April 9, 2017, www.cbsnews.com/news/brain-hacking-tech-insiders-60-minutes/.

31. Judson Brewer, *Unwinding Anxiety: New Science Shows How to Break the Cycles of Worry and Fear to Heal Your Mind* (New York: Penguin, 2022), 38.

32. Donie O'Sullivan, "Her Son Was an Accused Cult Leader. She Says He Was a Victim, Too," CNN, September 23, 2023, www.cnn.com/2023/09/23/us/qanon-trump-kennedy-protzman-cult-invs/index.html.

CHAPTER 12: CLIMBING OUT OF THE ONLINE RABBIT HOLE

1. "Stefan Molyneux," Southern Poverty Law Center, n.d., www.splcenter.org/ fighting-hate/extremist-files/individual/stefan-molyneux.

2. Susan Wright, "A Year of 'Permacrisis,'" *Collins Language Lovers Blog*, October 28, 2022, https://blog.collinsdictionary.com/language-lovers/a-year-of -permacrisis/.

3. Kevin Roose, "The Making of a YouTube Radical," *New York Times*, September 3, 2020, https://nytimes.com/interactive/2019/06/08/technology/youtube -radical.html.

4. "Here's Every Word from the Seventh Jan. 6 Committee Hearing on Its Investigation," *NPR*, July 12, 2022, www.npr.org/2022/07/12/1111123258/jan -6-committee-hearing-transcript.

5. Peter Sagal, "The End Will Come for the Cult of MAGA," *The Atlantic*, September 12, 2023, www.theatlantic.com/ideas/archive/2023/08/trumpism -maga-cult-republican-voters-indoctrination/675173/?utm_source=pocket_saves.

6. Sander van der Linden, *Foolproof: Why Misinformation Infects Our Minds and How to Build Immunity* (New York: W. W. Norton, 2023), 23.

7. Abbie has posted several TikToks in which she discusses the pyramid in detail in late 2021.

8. Sinan Aral, *The Hype Machine: How Social Media Disrupts Our Elections, Our Economy, and Our Health—and How We Must Adapt* (New York: Currency, 2020), 51.

9. "Steven Hassan's BITE Model of Authoritarian Control," Freedom of Mind Resource Center, November 9, 2023, https://freedomofmind.com/cult-mind -control/bite-model/.

10. TEDxMidAtlantic, "Dismantling QANon," YouTube, October 22, 2020, www.youtube.com/watch?v=1QbEcG8O-L8.

11. Morgane Rousselet, O. Duretetec, Jean-Benoit Hardouin, and Marie Grall-Bronnec, "Cult Membership: What Factors Contribute to Joining or Leaving?" *Psychiatry Research* 257 (November 1, 2017): 27–33, https://doi.org/10.1016/ j.psychres.2017.07.018.

12. "TikTok's Algorithm Leads Users from Transphobic Videos to Far-Right Rabbit Holes," Media Matters for America, October 5, 2021, www.mediamat ters.org/tiktok/tiktoks-algorithm-leads-users-transphobic-videos-far-right-rabbit -holes; Anna Beahm, "Meet the TikTok Influencers Spreading Christian Nation-alism to a New Generation," *Reckon*, November 29, 2023, https://reckon.news/ news/2023/11/meet-the-tiktok-influencers-spreading-christian-nationalism-to-a -new-generation.html.

13. Julia Conley, "New Massachusetts 'Tax the Rich' Law Raises $1.5 Billion for Free School Lunch and More," *Common Dreams*, January 12, 2024, www.com mondreams.org/news/tax-rich-massachusetts.

14. Rupert Neate, "UK Millionaires Group Projects 'Tax Our Wealth' on to Treasury and Bank of England," *Guardian*, November 21, 2023, www.theguardian .com/uk-news/2023/nov/21/uk-millionaires-tax-wealth-treasury-jeremy-hunt -patriotic-millionaires-uk.

15. Patriotic Millionaires, January 3, 2024, https://patrioticmillionaires.org/; Sophie Charara, "Millionaires Are Begging Governments to Tax Them More," *WIRED*, June 23, 2023, www.wired.com/story/millionaires-begging-govern ments-tax-wealth/.

EPILOGUE

1. Eduardo Morales, "Is Instagram Dying? (Yes, but Not for Everyone)," August 2, 2021, www.publicist.co/the-spin/the-inside-scoop/is-instagram-dying.

2. Ellis Hamburger, "Social Media Is Doomed to Die," *The Verge*, April 18, 2023, www.theverge.com/2023/4/18/23672769/social-media-inevitable-death -monetization-growth-hacks; Ian Bogost, "The Age of Social Media Is Ending," *The Atlantic*, March 10, 2023, www.theatlantic.com/technology/archive/2022/11/ twitter-facebook-social-media-decline/672074/.

3. Cordilia James, "We Aren't Posting on Social Media as Much Anymore. Will We Ever?" *WSJ*, December 24, 2023, https://wsj.com/tech/personal-tech/social -media-nobody-posting-f6c2fd3e?page=1.

4. John Dempsey and Dom Tunon, "Social Media Is Dead. Welcome to the Swipe Era," *Adweek*, July 17, 2023, www.adweek.com/social-marketing/social -media-is-dead/; Toby Shorin, "Life after Lifestyle," September 14, 2022, https:// subpixel.space/entries/life-after-lifestyle/.

5. "Gartner Predicts 50% of Consumers Will Significantly Limit Their Interactions with Social Media by 2025," Gartner, December 14, 2023, www .gartner.com/en/newsroom/press-releases/2023-12-14-gartner-predicts-fifty -percent-of-consumers-will-significantly-limit-their-interactions-with-social -media-by-2025.

BIBLIOGRAPHY

"11 TikTok Influencer Marketing Examples to Inspire You." Modash. January 9, 2023, www.modash.io/blog/tiktok-influencer-marketing-examples.

"16 Influencer Marketing Campaign Examples [+ Key Takeaways]." Modash. February 20, 2024, www.modash.io/blog/influencer-marketing-campaign-examples#:~:text=images%20from%20customers.-,Campaign%20statistics,million%20timepieces%20in%20annual%20sales.

Adams, Chris. "What Is Persuasive Design?" Modern Analyst, n.d. www.modern analyst.com/Careers/InterviewQuestions/tabid/128/ID/4925/What-is-Persuasive-Design.aspx.

Aguilar, Jorge A. "MrBeast's Fans Believe He Has Misled Them into a Refinable Crypto Scam." Gfinity Esports, May 24, 2021. www.gfinityesports.com/gaming-news/MrBeasts-fans-believe-he-has-misled-them-into-a-Refinable-crypto-scam/.

Aisch, Gregor, Larry Buchanan, Amanda Cox, and Kevin Quealy. "Some Colleges Have More Students from the Top 1 Percent Than the Bottom 60. Find Yours." *New York Times*, January 18, 2017. www.nytimes.com/interactive/2017/01/18/upshot/some-colleges-have-more-students-from-the-top-1-percent-than-the-bottom-60.html#:~:text=At%2038%20colleges%20in%20America,the%20entire%20bottom%2060%20percent.

Aisch, Gregor, Jon Huang, and Cecilia Kang. "Dissecting the #PizzaGate Conspiracy Theories." *New York Times*, December 10, 2016. https://nytimes.com/interactive/2016/12/10/business/media/pizzagate.html.

Alexander, Julia. "MrBeast Changed YouTube and Launched an Entire Genre of Expensive Stunt Content." *The Verge*, October 25, 2019. www.theverge.com/2019/10/25/20924718/mrbeast-youtube-stunts-challenges-money-philanthropy-creators-morgz.

Alizadeh, Nader. "McDonald's 'Trick.Treat.Win!' Campaign." Linqia, October 25, 2022. www.linqia.com/customers/mcdonalds/.

Amazeen, M. A. "The Rise of the Influencer Election." Truth in Advertising. March 2, 2020. www.truthinadvertising.org/campaign-2020-the-rise-of-the-influencer-election/.

American University. "A Breeding Ground for Conspiracies: How QAnon Helped Bring about the U.S. Capitol Assault." January 7, 2021. www.american.edu/sis/centers/security-technology/how-qanon-helped-bring-about-the-us-capitol-assault.cfm#_ftnref6.

"ANA Influencer Marketing Measurement Guidelines." ANA. n.d. www.ana.net/miccontent/show/id/rr-2022-06-ana-influencer-marketing-measurement.

"Anne Coughlan Is Wrong on Herbalife." Fraud Files Blog, January 12, 2013. www.sequenceinc.com/fraudfiles/2013/01/anne-coughlan-is-wrong-on-herbalife/.

Aral, Sinan. *The Hype Machine: How Social Media Disrupts Our Elections, Our Economy, and Our Health—and How We Must Adapt.* New York: Currency, 2020.

Ashwinn (shwinnabego). "This Is How Brands Need to Respond and Move on Social." TikTok. November 17, 2023. www.tiktok.com/@shwinnabego/video/7302488803460304174?_r=1&_t=8hllHks17Zn.

Atkin, Douglas. *The Culting of Brands: When Customers Become True Believers.* New York: Portfolio Trade, 2004.

Ault, Susanne. "Survey: YouTube Stars More Popular Than Mainstream Celebs among U.S. Teens." *Variety*, August 5, 2014. https://variety.com/2014/digital/news/survey-youtube-stars-more-popular-than-mainstream-celebs-among-u-s-teens-1201275245/.

Baila, Morgan. "Teal Swan & the Craziest Wellness Cult Conspiracy You've Never Heard Of." *Refinery29*, August 31, 2018. www.refinery29.com/en-us/2018/08/205915/the-gateway-teal-swan-youtube-cult-jennings-brown.

Bailyn, Evan. "Digital Marketing Conversion Rates: 2024 Report." First Page Sage, December 28, 2023. https://firstpagesage.com/reports/digital-marketing-conversion-rate/#.

Bain, Iona. "Is TikTok's 'Shoppertainment' Sales Model Pushing Gen Z into Debt? Just Look at the Numbers." *Guardian*, March 18, 2023. www.theguardian.com/commentisfree/2023/mar/16/tiktoks-shoppertainment-model-gen-z-debt.

Baker, Stephanie Alice. "Alt. Health Influencers: How Wellness Culture and Web Culture Have Been Weaponised to Promote Conspiracy Theories and Far-Right Extremism during the COVID-19 Pandemic." *European Journal of Cultural Studies* 25, no. 1 (2022): 3–24.

"Barbie and Nikki Discuss Racism." YouTube. October 7, 2020. www.youtube.com/watch?v=RCzwoMDgF_I.

Barkun, Michael. *A Culture of Conspiracy: Apocalyptic Visions in Contemporary America.* Berkeley: University of California Press, 2003.

Bartholomew, Mark. "The Law of Advertising Outrage." *Advertising & Society Quarterly* 19, no. 3 (January 1, 2018). https://doi.org/10.1353/asr.2018.0023.

Bass, Michael. "Community as a Service: The Commodification of the Social Commons." Master's thesis, December 2018.

BBC. "Paul Mason and the Kids Who Decide What All the Other Kids Talk About." December 15, 2016. www.bbc.co.uk/programmes/articles/2dLg30714 lSN1xmbNYM7129/paul-mason-and-the-kids-who-decide-what-all-the-other -kids-talk-about.

"Beachbody Sees Gains." *Los Angeles Business Journal*, May 17, 2020. https://labusi nessjournal.com/news/weekly-news/beachbody-sees-gains/.

Beahm, Anna. "Meet the TikTok Influencers Spreading Christian Nationalism to a New Generation." *Reckon*, November 29, 2023. https://reckon.news/news/ 2023/11/meet-the-tiktok-influencers-spreading-christian-nationalism-to-a -new-generation.html.

Beast Philanthropy. "Beast Philanthropy Official Site—Help End Hunger." n.d. www.beastphilanthropy.org/.

"Becoming a #Boss." Season 3, episode 1. *The Dream*. September 13, 2023. www .pushkin.fm/podcasts/the-dream/s3-e1-becoming-a-boss.

Belkin, Douglas. "Who's at the Door? College Officials Delivering Your Accep-tance in Person (Sometimes with a Dog)." *Wall Street Journal*, February 13, 2018. www.wsj.com/articles/whos-at-the-door-college-officials-delivering-your -acceptance-in-person-sometimes-with-a-dog-1518375304.

Berger, John. *Ways of Seeing*. London: Penguin UK, 2008.

Bixby, Scott. "Mike Bloomberg Is Paying 'Influencers' to Make Him Seem Cool." *The Daily Beast*, February 18, 2020. www.thedailybeast.com/mike-bloomberg -is-paying-influencers-to-make-him-seem-cool-9?ref=author.

Blevins, Roberta. "The EMAIL heard round AntiMLM! Life After MLM Pod-cast: Episode 96." YouTube. April 3, 2022. www.youtube.com/watch?v =GnVfBRg0qJI.

Bogost, Ian. "The Age of Social Media Is Ending." *The Atlantic*, March 10, 2023. www.theatlantic.com/technology/archive/2022/11/twitter-facebook-social -media-decline/672074/.

Boston College Center for Christian-Jewish Learning. "White Supremacy and Anti-Semitism: Lessons from the Capitol Attack." January 14, 2021. www.you tube.com/watch?v=SC_ZHXCqpb4.

Bouchard, Nicholas. "TikTok Creativity Program: How to Join the New Creator Fund." The Leap, November 10, 2023. www.theleap.co/blog/tiktok-creativity -program-beta/.

Brewer, Judson. *Unwinding Anxiety: New Science Shows How to Break the Cycles of Worry and Fear to Heal Your Mind*. New York: Penguin, 2022.

Brodesser-Akner, Taffy. "How Goop's Haters Made Gwyneth Paltrow's Company Worth $250 Million." *New York Times*, July 30, 2018. www.nytimes.com/ 2018/07/25/magazine/big-business-gwyneth-paltrow-wellness.html.

"Brofluencer." *Urban Dictionary*, February 9, 2023. www.urbandictionary.com/ define.php?term=Brofluencer.

Brown, Seth. "Alex Jones's Media Empire Is a Machine Built to Sell Snake-Oil Diet Supplements." *Intelligencer*, May 4, 2017. https://nymag.com/intelligencer/2017/05/how-does-alex-jones-make-money.html.

Business for Home. "Hall of Fame MLM Celebrities—How to Handle the Pyramid Myth Objection." September 11, 2014. www.businessforhome.org/2014/09/hall-of-fame-mlm-celebrities/.

Caulfield, Timothy. "Misinformation, Alternative Medicine and the Coronavirus." *Policy Options*, April 12, 2021. https://policyoptions.irpp.org/magazines/march-2020/misinformation-alternative-medicine-and-the-coronavirus/.

CBS News. "Conspirituality: How Wellness Became a Gateway for Misinformation." YouTube. September 30, 2021. www.youtube.com/watch?v=yqvGU9o2bGI.

Center for Investigative Reporting. "About Us." Reveal. May 16, 2023. https://revealnews.org/about-us/.

Centrum für Religionswissenschaftliche Studien. "ISMRC 2023 Keynote Lecture by Stephanie Baker." YouTube. August 3, 2023. www.youtube.com/watch?v=2m8Oi70H43U.

"Challenge Validation." SimilarWeb. n.d. www.similarweb.com/website/infowars.com/#demographics.

Chandler, Russell. *Understanding the New Age*. Grand Rapids, MI: Zondervan, 1993.

Chang, K. S. "Pyramid Schemes and Ponzi Schemes: Koscot Test and Howey Test." The Crime Wire, November 14, 2023. https://thecrimewire.com/money/How-Pyramid-Schemes-and-Ponzi-Schemes-are-Prosecuted-in-the-US.

Charara, Sophie. "Millionaires Are Begging Governments to Tax Them More." *WIRED*, June 23, 2023. www.wired.com/story/millionaires-begging-governments-tax-wealth/.

Chen, Chiung Hwang. "Marketing Religion Online: The LDS Church's SEO Efforts." *Journal of Media and Religion* 10, no. 4 (2011): 185–205. https://doi.org/10.1080/15348423.2011.625265.

Chen, Tanya. "Virtual TikTok House Works to Boost Biden Gen Z Vote." *BuzzFeed News*, October 19, 2020. www.buzzfeednews.com/article/tanyachen/biden-harris-pac-tiktok-house.

Chung, Jaeyeon, Yulong Ding, and Ajay Kalra. "I Really Know You: How Influencers Can Increase Audience Engagement by Referencing Their Close Social Ties." *Journal of Consumer Research* 50, no. 4 (March 14, 2023): 683–703. https://doi.org/10.1093/jcr/ucad019.

Clark-Braverman, Hayley. "Marketing Insider: Loyalty's Next Frontier: Identity Loyalty." MediaPost. November 15, 2023. www.mediapost.com/publications/article/391130/loyaltys-next-frontier-identity-loyalty.html.

CNBC. "Here's an Inside Look at the Unregulated Life Coach Industry." March 23, 2021. https://cnbc.com/video/2021/03/23/the-truth-about-the-unregulated-life-coach-industry.html.

Coffeezilla. "The Cult of Dan Lok—Brainwashed Student Lost $26,000 Testimonial." YouTube. November 30, 2019. www.youtube.com/watch?v=4VDiM_PMmZA.

———. "I Joined Andrew Tate's Cult and It Was Worse Than I Thought." YouTube. August 1, 2022. www.youtube.com/watch?v=BijOF8I2t_4.

Conley, Julia. "New Massachusetts 'Tax the Rich' Law Raises $1.5 Billion for Free School Lunch and More." *Common Dreams*, January 12, 2024. www.common dreams.org/news/tax-rich-massachusetts.

Cooper, Anderson. "What Is 'Brain Hacking'? Tech Insiders on Why You Should Care." *60 Minutes*, April 9, 2017. www.cbsnews.com/news/brain-hacking-tech -insiders-60-minutes/.

Coyne, Sarah M., Adam A. Rogers, Jessica D. Zurcher, Laura Stockdale, and McCall Booth. "Does Time Spent Using Social Media Impact Mental Health? An Eight Year Longitudinal Study." *Computers in Human Behavior* 104 (March 2020). https://doi.org/10.1016/j.chb.2019.106160.

Cramer-Flood, Ethan. "Meta's Ad Revenue Share Vastly Exceeds Its Share of Consumer Time." *Insider Intelligence*, July 28, 2023. https://insiderintelligence.com/content/meta-s-ad-revenue-share-vastly-exceeds-its-share-of-consumer-time.

Cresci, Elena. "Lonelygirl15: How One Mysterious Vlogger Changed the Internet." *Guardian*, February 21, 2017. www.theguardian.com/technology/2016/jun/16/lonelygirl15-bree-video-blog-youtube.

Cruel World Happy Mind. "Tyra Banks Had Her Own MLM Makeup Line?! (It Failed)." YouTube. April 23, 2020. www.youtube.com/watch?v=6zXYHBCj4LQ&amp%3Bt=451s.

Curiosity Stream. "The Origin and Rise of MrBeast." YouTube. March 19, 2022. www.youtube.com/watch?v=_Qq6sCvz4Z0.

Danielle (danimarielettering). "Thirsty after You Catch on Fire?" TikTok. November 15, 2023. www.tiktok.com/@danimarielettering/video/73017245874887 59070?_r=1&_t=8hllC0GT9tH.

Das, Shanti. "Andrew Tate: Money-Making Scheme for Fans of 'Extreme Misogynist' Closes." *Guardian*, February 1, 2023. www.theguardian.com/media/2022/aug/20/andrew-tate-money-making-scheme-for-fans-of-extreme-misogynist -closes.

Davey, Melissa. "Jessica Ainscough, Australia's 'Wellness Warrior,' Dies of Cancer Aged 30." *Guardian*, September 20, 2017. www.theguardian.com/australia-news/2015/mar/01/jessica-ainscough-australia-wellness-warrior-dies-cancer-aged-30.

Dawson, Lorne L. *Comprehending Cults: The Sociology of New Religious Movements.* Oxford: Oxford University Press, 2013.

Deadline: White House. MSNBC. December 19, 2023.

DeLiema, Marguerite, Stacie Bosley, and Doug Shadel. "Multi-Level Marketing as 'Gig' Work: Worker Motivations, Characteristics, and Outcomes in the U.S." *Journal of Labor and Society* 25, no. 1 (2021): 83–121. https://doi.org/10.1163/24714607-bja10029.

DeLiema, Marguerite, Doug Shadel, Amy Nofziger, and Karla Pak. *AARP Study of Multilevel Marketing: Profiling Participants and Their Experiences in Direct Sales.* AARP Foundation, 2018.

Dempsey, John, and Dom Tunon. "Social Media Is Dead. Welcome to the Swipe Era." *Adweek*, July 17, 2023. www.adweek.com/social-marketing/social-media -is-dead/.

Denizet-Lewis, Benoit. "Why Are More American Teenagers Than Ever Suffering from Severe Anxiety?" *New York Times*, October 11, 2017. www.nytimes.com/ 2017/10/11/magazine/why-are-more-american-teenagers-than-ever-suffering -from-severe-anxiety.html.

Deslippe, Philip. "Past the Pejorative: Understanding the Word 'Cult' through Its Use in American Newspapers during the Nineties." *Implicit Religion* 24, no. 2 (2021): 195–217.

Dibble, Jayson L., Tilo Hartmann, and Sarah F. Rosaen. "Parasocial Interaction and Parasocial Relationship: Conceptual Clarification and a Critical Assessment of Measures." *Human Communication Research* 42, no. 1 (March 17, 2015): 21–44. https://doi.org/10.1111/hcre.12063.

Diep, Francie. "Multilevel Marketing Has a 'Goodwill Ambassador' in the Class-room." *Chronicle of Higher Education*, September 19, 2022. www.chronicle.com/ article/multilevel-marketing-has-a-goodwill-ambassador-in-the-classroom.

Direct Selling Fact Sheet. December 20, 2016. www.dsa.org/docs/default-source/ advocacy/direct-selling-fact-sheet.pdf.

Direct Selling in the United States: 2017 Facts and Data. Direct Selling Association, 2018.

Direct Selling in the United States: 2021 Industry Overview. Direct Selling Asso-ciation, 2022. www.dsa.org/docs/default-source/industry-fact-sheets/dsa-2021g -ofactsheetv3.pdf?sfvrsn=51c6d6a5_3%27.

Diseko, Lebo. "Teal Swan: The Woman Encouraging Her Followers to Visualise Death." *BBC News*, November 23, 2019. www.bbc.com/news/world-us-canada -50478821.

Doctorow, Cory. "The 'Enshittification' of TikTok." *WIRED*, January 23, 2023. www.wired.com/story/tiktok-platforms-cory-doctorow/.

Dowd, Katie. "The Awesome Implosion of Bay Area's Biggest Pyramid Scheme." *SFGate*, December 15, 2022. www.sfgate.com/sfhistory/article/The-incredible -implosion-of-Holiday-Magic-16785971.php.

DSA. "Code of Ethics." n.d. www.dsa.org/consumerprotection/code-of-ethics.

Einstein, Mara. "From Cause Marketing to Activist Branding." In *The Routledge Companion to Advertising and Promotional Culture*, edited by Matthew P. Mc-Allister and Emily West, 211–23. New York: Routledge, 2023. https://doi .org/10.4324/9781003124870-23.

———. *Black Ops Advertising: Native Ads, Content Marketing, and the Covert World of the Digital Sell.* New York: OR Books, 2016.

———. *Compassion, Inc.: How Corporate America Blurs the Line between What We Buy, Who We Are, and Those We Help*. Berkeley: University of California Press, 2012.

———. *Brands of Faith: Marketing Religion in a Commercial Age*. London: Routledge, 2008.

———. "Pride Is Not Just about Marketing: Support for LGBTQ Rights and Equality Goes Far beyond Brands." *New York Daily News*, June 25, 2023. www.nydailynews.com/2023/06/25/pride-is-not-just-about-marketing-support-for-lgbtq-rights-and-equality-goes-far-beyond-brands/.

———. "Religious Influencers: Faith in the World of Marketing." In *Produsing Theory in a Digital World 3.0*, Rebecca Ann Lind, 121–38. New York: Peter Lang, 2020.

Einstein, Mara, and Sarah McFarland Taylor, eds. *Selling the Sacred: From Crossfit to QAnon*. Abingdon, Oxon: Routledge, 2024.

Elberse, Anita, and Oliver Band. "MrBeast: Building a YouTube Empire." Harvard Business School Case 523-103, March 2023. www.hbs.edu/faculty/Pages/item.aspx?num=63941.

Emmons, William R., Ana H. Kent, and Lowell R. Ricketts. "Is College Still Worth It? The New Calculus of Falling Returns." Federal Reserve Bank of St. Louis *Review*, 2019. https://research.stlouisfed.org/publications/review/2019/10/15/is-college-still-worth-it-the-new-calculus-of-falling-returns.

ESPN. "The Dream Drew Brees—and AdvoCare—Is Trying to Sell." March 15, 2016. www.espn.com/espn/feature/story/_/id/14972197/questions-surround-advocare-nutrition-empire-endorsed-saints-qb-drew-brees.

Federal Trade Commission. "FTC Acts to Stop Online Business Coaching Scheme LURN from Deceiving Consumers about Money-Making Potential." September 28, 2023. www.ftc.gov/news-events/news/press-releases/2023/09/ftc-acts-stop-online-business-coaching-scheme-lurn-deceiving-consumers-about-money-making-potential.

———. "FTC Puts Businesses on Notice That False Money-Making Claims Could Lead to Big Penalties." March 16, 2022. www.ftc.gov/news-events/news/press-releases/2021/10/ftc-puts-businesses-notice-false-money-making-claims-could-lead-big-penalties.

———. "Penalty Offenses Concerning Money-Making Opportunities." March 17, 2023. www.ftc.gov/enforcement/notices-penalty-offenses/penalty-offenses-concerning-money-making-opportunities.

———. "When a Business Offer or Coaching Program Is a Scam." Federal Trade Commission. January 9, 2023. https://consumer.ftc.gov/articles/when-business-offer-or-coaching-program-scam.

Federal Trade Commission. "Business Guidance Concerning Multi-Level Marketing." January 4, 2018. https://hbw.citeline.com/-/media/supporting-documents/rose-sheet/2018/01/180104-ftc-mlm-guidance.pdf.

Fischer, Sara. "The Creator Economy Is Failing to Spread the Wealth." *Axios*, October 12, 2021. www.axios.com/2021/10/11/creator-economy-revenue -content.

Fisher, Max. *The Chaos Machine: The Inside Story of How Social Media Rewired Our Minds and Our World*. London: Hachette UK, 2022.

———. "Disinformation for Hire, a Shadow Industry, Is Quietly Booming." *New York Times*, July 25, 2021. www.nytimes.com/2021/07/25/world/europe/disin formation-social-media.html.

FitzPatrick, Robert L. *Ponzinomics: The Untold Story of Multi-Level Marketing*. Charlotte, NC: FitzPatrick Management, 2022.

Follett, Gillian. "Inside Influencer Storefronts and How They're Driving Brand Sales." *AdAge*, October 17, 2022. https://adage.com/article/digital-marketing -ad-tech-news/influencer-recommendations-and-storefronts-shape-what-con sumers-buy/2442746.

———. "TikTok Shop Launches for All US Users—What Brands and Creators Should Know." *AdAge*, September 12, 2023. https://adage.com/article/digital -marketing-ad-tech-news/tiktok-shop-launches-all-us-users-what-brands-and -creators-should-know/2515556.

Fraz (thefrazmaz). "RIP Grimace (and me)." TikTok. June 13, 2023. www.tiktok .com/@thefrazmaz/video/7244325864169590058?lang=en.

Freedom of Mind Resource Center. "Steven Hassan's BITE Model of Authoritarian Control." November 9, 2023. https://freedomofmind.com/cult-mind -control/bite-model/.

Friestad, Marian, and Peter Wright, 1994. "The Persuasion Knowledge Model: How People Cope with Persuasion Attempts." *Journal of Consumer Research* 21, no. 1 (June 1994): 1–31.

Frontline. "United States of Conspiracy." PBS. January 19, 2023. www.pbs.org/ wgbh/frontline/documentary/united-states-of-conspiracy/transcript/.

Gartner. "Gartner Predicts 50% of Consumers Will Significantly Limit Their Interactions with Social Media by 2025." December 14, 2023. www.gart ner.com/en/newsroom/press-releases/2023-12-14-gartner-predicts-fifty-per cent-of-consumers-will-significantly-limit-their-interactions-with-social -media-by-2025.

Gathering, The. "The Gathering of Cult Brands." YouTube. October 7, 2014. www.youtube.com/watch?v=SeoB2qJpNyA.

"Gen Z & Millennials' Top 17 Favorite Celebrity List Reveals a Generation Gap." YPulse, September 11, 2019. www.ypulse.com/article/2019/09/11/gen-z-mill ennials-top-17-favorite-celebrity-list-reveals-a-generation-gap/.

Geyser, Werner. "How Does the YouTube Algorithm Work: A Peek into Its Changes in 2024." Influencer Marketing Hub, November 14, 2023. https:// influencermarketinghub.com/how-does-the-youtube-algorithm-work/.

————. "Influencer Rates: How Much Do Influencers Really Cost in 2024?" Influencer Marketing Hub, November 9, 2023. https://influencermarketinghub.com/influencer-rates/.

————. "The State of Influencer Marketing 2023: Benchmark Report." Influencer Marketing Hub, October 30, 2023. https://influencermarketinghub.com/influencer-marketing-benchmark-report/#toc-10.

————. "TikTok Money Calculator [Influencer Engagement & Earnings Estimator]." Influencer Marketing Hub, November 24, 2023. https://influencermarketinghub.com/tiktok-money-calculator/.

————. "What Are MCNs for YouTube Creators (+ Top Multi-Channel Networks)." Influencer Marketing Hub, May 30, 2022. https://influencermarketinghub.com/mcn-youtube-creators/#toc-5.

Gill, Brian. "Brian Gill Unveils Marketing Initiatives at Younique Convention 2015." YouTube. August 11, 2015. www.youtube.com/watch?v=3JIW5BMJSY8.

Gleason, Tracy R., Sally A. Theran, and Emily M. Newberg. "Parasocial Interactions and Relationships in Early Adolescence." *Frontiers in Psychology* 8 (February 23, 2017). https://doi.org/10.3389/fpsyg.2017.00255.

Go, Alison. "Baylor Pays Freshmen to Retake SAT." *U.S. News and World Report*, October 15, 2008. www.usnews.com/education/blogs/paper-trail/2008/10/15/baylor-pays-freshmen-to-retake-sat.

Goodwin, A. M., K. Joseff, and S. C. Woolley. "Social Media Influencers and the 2020 U.S. Election: Paying 'Regular People' for Digital Campaign Communication." Center for Media Engagement. October 2020. https://mediaengagement.org/research/social-media-influencers-and-the-2020-election.

Grothaus, Michael. "96.5% of YouTube Creators Don't Make above the U.S. Poverty Line." FastCompany.com. www.fastcompany.com/40537244/96-5-of-youtube-creators-dont-make-above-the-u-s-poverty-line.

Hagen, Lisa. "Alex Jones' Defamation Trials Show the Limits of Deplatforming for a Select Few." NPR, September 16, 2022. www.npr.org/2022/09/16/1123249309/alex-jones-defamation-trials-show-the-limits-of-deplatforming-for-a-select-few.

Haggin, Patience. "Google and Meta's Advertising Dominance Fades as TikTok, Streamers Emerge." *WSJ*, January 4, 2023. www.wsj.com/articles/google-and-metas-advertising-dominance-fades-as-tiktok-netflix-emerge-11672711107.

Hamburger, Ellis. "Social Media Is Doomed to Die." *The Verge*, April 18, 2023. www.theverge.com/2023/4/18/23672769/social-media-inevitable-death-monetization-growth-hacks.

Harris, Matthew. "Nick Sarnicola Co Founder of Visalus: Master MLM Recruiting Training—MIM Episode #32." YouTube. April 18, 2013. www.youtube.com/watch?v=bei86CyN3yI.

Haupt, Angela. "In Defense of Parasocial Relationships." *TIME*, July 13, 2023. https://time.com/6294226/parasocial-relationships-benefits/.

Hearing, Alice. "TikTok Houses: Hype House Members, Clubhouse, More." *Dexerto*, July 2, 2021. www.dexerto.com/entertainment/whos-in-most-popular-tiktok-houses-hype-house-clubhouse-more-1382965/.

Heras, Gema de las, Colleen Tressler, Lesley Fair, and Alvaro Puig. "Multi-Level Marketing Businesses and Pyramid Schemes." Federal Trade Commission Consumer Advice, November 25, 2022. https://consumer.ftc.gov/articles/multi-level-marketing-businesses-pyramid-schemes#pyramid.

Hesse-Biber, Sharlene. *The Cult of Thinness*. New York: Oxford University Press, 2007.

Holiday, Ryan. *Trust Me, I'm Lying: Confessions of a Media Manipulator*. New York: Profile Books, 2018.

Hollis, Rachel. "Rise Together—Couple's Conference 2018." Facebook. June 21, 2018. www.facebook.com/thechicsite/videos/10156254037316259/.

Holman, Jordyn, and Sapna Maheshwari. "Shein Flew Influencers to China to Help Its Image. A Backlash Ensued." *New York Times*, June 30, 2023. www.nytimes.com/2023/06/29/business/shein-influencers-backlash.html.

Holpuch, Amanda. "Why Andrew Tate's Social Media Accounts Are Being Removed." *New York Times*, August 24, 2022. https://nytimes.com/2022/08/24/technology/andrew-tate-banned-tiktok-instagram.html.

Hoover, Eric. "Application Inflation: When Is Enough Enough?" *New York Times*, November 5, 2010. www.nytimes.com/2010/11/07/education/edlife/07HOOVER-t.html.

Horton, Donald, and Robert Wohl. "Mass Communication and Para-Social Interaction." *Psychiatry MMC* 19, no. 3 (August 1, 1956): 215–29. https://doi.org/10.1080/00332747.1956.11023049.

Horwitz, Jeff, and Deepa Seetharaman. "Facebook Executives Shut Down Efforts to Make the Site Less Divisive." *WSJ*, May 26, 2020. https://wsj.com/articles/facebook-knows-it-encourages-division-top-executives-nixed-solutions-11590507499.

Howard, Madeline. "The Influencers Are Not Alright." *Women's Health*, December 15, 2022. www.womenshealthmag.com/health/a41946590/influencer-content-creation-hurting-mental-health/.

Hsu, Tiffany. "What the Trial of Alex Jones Revealed about His Finances." *New York Times*, September 22, 2022. https://nytimes.com/2022/08/05/us/alex-jones-finances.html.

Hussar, Bill, Jijun Zhang, Ke Wang, Ashley Roberts, Jiashan Cui, Mary Smith, Farrah Bullock Mann, Amy Barmer, Rita Dilig, and Stephen Purcell. *The Condition of Education*, edited by Thomas Nachazel and Megan Barnett. Washington, DC: National Center for Education Statistics, 2020. https://nces.ed.gov/programs/coe/pdf/coe_cha.pdf.

IBISWorld. "Business Coaching in the US—Market Size (2005–2031)." June 1, 2024. www.ibisworld.com/industry-statistics/market-size/business-coaching-united-states/.

———. "Online Vitamin & Supplement Sales in the US—Market Size, Industry Analysis, Trends and Forecasts (2024–2029)." September 2023. www.ibisworld.com/united-states/market-research-reports/online-vitamin-supplement-sales-industry/#IndustryStatisticsAndTrends.

"Income Disclosure Statement—Monat Global." Monat Global. June 16, 2023. https://monatglobal.com/income-disclosure-statement/.

"Income Disclosure." Forever Living Products. https://foreverliving.com/usa/en-us/income-disclosurev. Accessed January 16, 2024.

Influencer Marketing Factory, The. "TikTok's Influence w/ Adrienne Lahens & Sofia Hernandez." YouTube. September 13, 2023. www.youtube.com/watch?v=V-bzLfyReg0.

"Influencer Marketing Trends Report." CreatorIQ. n.d. www.creatoriq.com/white-papers/influencer-marketing-trends-report-2023.

Institute for Integrative Nutrition. Homepage. November 27, 2023. www.integrativenutrition.com/.

James, Cordilia. "We Aren't Posting on Social Media as Much Anymore. Will We Ever?" WSJ, December 24, 2023. https://wsj.com/tech/personal-tech/social-media-nobody-posting-f6c2fd3e?page=1.

Jenkins, Ryan. "Generation Z versus Millennials: The 8 Differences You Need to Know." Inc., July 19, 2017. www.inc.com/ryan-jenkins/generation-z-vs-millennials-the-8-differences-you-.html.

Jennings, Rebecca. "Michelle Phan, Dan Howell, and Why YouTubers Never Log Off." Vox, May 10, 2022. www.vox.com/the-goods/23064266/dan-howell-michelle-phan-youtuber-brain.

Joseph, Seb. "The Rundown: Google, Meta and Amazon Are on Track to Absorb More Than 50% of All Ad Money in 2022." Digiday. February 4, 2022. https://responsema.org/digital-marketing/the-rundown-google-meta-and-amazon-are-on-track-to-absorb-more-than-50-of-all-ad-money-in-2022/.

Kahn, Mattie. "For Lee Tilghman, There Is Life after Influencing." New York Times, April 14, 2023. https://nytimes.com/2023/04/11/style/lee-tilghman-influencer.html?smid=nytcore-ios-share&referringSource=articleShare.

Kaplan, Alex. "A TikTok Video Told Democrats to Vote after Election Day, Violating the Platform's Rules." Media Matters for America. August 5, 2020. www.mediamatters.org/tiktok/tiktok-video-told-democrats-vote-after-election-day-violating-platforms-rules.

Karimi, Faith. "Forget the Influencers. Here Come the 'Deinfluencers.'" CNN. June 1, 2023. www.cnn.com/2023/06/11/us/deinfluencing-tiktok-trend-explained-cec/index.html.

Katersky, Aaron. "Alex Jones Still Must Pay $1B Judgment: Judge." ABC News. October 20, 2023. https://abcnews.go.com/US/alex-jones-ordered-pay-1-billion-judgment-sandy/story?id=104175574.

Keegan, Rebecca, and Nicole Sperling. "Shakespeare in Love and Harvey Weinstein's Dark Oscar Victory." Vanity Fair, December 8, 2017. www.vanityfair

.com/hollywood/2017/12/shakespeare-in-love-and-harvey-weinsteins-dark
-oscar-victory.

Kelly, Makena. "Turning Point Is Quietly Building the Next Generation of
Conservative Influencers." *The Verge*, January 5, 2022. www.theverge.com/
2022/1/5/22868483/turning-point-charlie-kirk-republican-influencers-insta
gram-today-is-america.

"Key Information about Being an Herbalife Independent Distributor." Herbalife.
September 8, 2023. https://iamherbalifenutrition.com/wp-content/uploads/
2023/09/Typical-Herbalife-Independent-Distributor-Earnings_USEN.pdf.

Kircher, Madison Malone. "Is Instagram Strategically Withholding My Likes?"
Intelligencer, January 19, 2018. https://nymag.com/intelligencer/2018/01/does
-instagram-withhold-likes-to-get-users-to-open-app.html.

Koerner, Brendan I. "Watch This Guy Work, and You'll Finally Understand
the TikTok Era." *WIRED*, October 19, 2023. www.wired.com/story/tiktok
-talent-factory-ursus-magana-creator-economy/.

Korn, Melissa. "Some Elite Colleges Review an Application in 8 Minutes (or
Less)." *Wall Street Journal*, January 31, 2018. www.wsj.com/articles/some-elite
-colleges-review-an-application-in-8-minutes-or-less-1517400001.

Kriel, Charles, and Katharina Gellein Viken, directors. *People You May Know*.
Metrotone Media, 2020.

Lai, Stephanie. "Campaigns Skirt Political Ad Rules by Paying Influencers." *New
York Times*, November 2, 2022. www.nytimes.com/2022/11/02/us/elections/
influencers-political-ads-tiktok-instagram.html.

Lakhiani, Vishen. *The Code of the Extraordinary Mind: Ten Unconventional Laws to
Redefine Your Life & Succeed on Your Own Terms*. Emmaus, PA: Rodale, 2019.

Lalich, Janja. "Why Do People Join Cults?" TED. June 2017. www.ted.com/talks/
janja_lalich_why_do_people_join_cults#t-174.

"Lazy, Stupid, Greedy or Dead." Season 1, episode 7. *The Dream*. October 29,
2018.

Lears, T. J. Jackson. "From Salvation to Self-Realization: Advertising and the
Therapeutic Roots of the Consumer Culture, 1880–1930." *Advertising & Society
Review* 1 (2000).

Lebow, Sara. "5 Charts Showing the Creator Economy's Recent Evolution."
Insider Intelligence. October 9, 2023. www.insiderintelligence.com/content/5
-charts-showing-creator-economy-s-recent-evolution.

———. "Facebook Still Generates Most of Meta's Ad Revenues, as Instagram
Drives Growth." Insider Intelligence, December 21, 2022. www.insiderintelli
gence.com/content/facebook-still-generates-most-meta-ad-revenues-instagram
-drives-growth.

———. "What the 'Death' of Social Media Means for Advertisers, According
to Our Forecast." Insider Intelligence, September 5, 2023. www.insiderintelli
gence.com/content/what-death-of-social-media-means-advertisers-according
-our-forecast.

Lima, Sydney. "I Went to A-Fest, the $3,000 Wellness Festival for Millionaires." *Vice*, November 28, 2022. https://vice.com/en/article/v7vnb9/a-fest-review-vish en-lakhiani.

Lima-Strong, Cristiano, and Naomi Nix. "41 States Sue Meta, Claiming Instagram, Facebook Are Addictive, Harm Kids." *Washington Post*, October 25, 2023. https://washingtonpost.com/technology/2023/10/24/meta-lawsuit-facebook -instagram-children-mental-health/.

Little, Olivia, and Abbie Richards. "TikTok's Algorithm Leads Users from Transphobic Videos to Far-Right Rabbit Holes." Media Matters for America. October 5, 2021. www.mediamatters.org/tiktok/tiktoks-algorithm-leads-users -transphobic-videos-far-right-rabbit-holes.

Littler, Jo. *Against Meritocracy: Culture, Power and Myths of Mobility*. London: Routledge, 2018.

Lorenz, Taylor. "Is the Hype House Era Officially Over?" *Los Angeles Magazine*, October 4, 2023. https://lamag.com/real-estate/hype-house-content-creators -era-officially-over.

———. "Young Creators Are Burning Out and Breaking Down." *New York Times*, September 17, 2021. https://nytimes.com/2021/06/08/style/creator -burnout-social-media.html.

Maheshwari, Sapna. "Are You Ready for the Nanoinfluencers?" *New York Times*, November 12, 2018. www.nytimes.com/2018/11/11/business/media/nanoin fluencers-instagram-influencers.html.

Martin, Alexander J. "Staying Off Social Media Is Not Enough to Protect Your Privacy, Study Says." *Sky News*, January 21, 2019. https://news.sky.com/ story/staying-off-social-media-is-not-enough-to-protect-your-privacy-study -says-11613216.

Martin, Hannah. "Thinking of Joining an MLM? Read the Truth behind the 'Income Opportunity.'" Talented Ladies Club, February 5, 2023. www.talented ladiesclub.com/articles/thinking-of-joining-a-mlm-read-the-truth-behind-the -income-opportunity/.

"McDonald's Head of Social Media Was as Shocked as We Were about the Grimace Shake Trend." *Today*. July 13, 2023. www.today.com/food/trends/ mcdonalds-head-of-social-media-on-grimace-shake-trend-rcna94159.

McGee, Jon. *Breakpoint: The Changing Marketplace for Higher Education*. Baltimore: Johns Hopkins University Press, 2015.

McIntire, Mike. "Tax Records Reveal How Fame Gave Trump a $427 Million Lifeline." *New York Times*, September 29, 2020. www.nytimes.com/interactive/ 2020/09/28/us/donald-trump-taxes-apprentice.html.

McNeal, Stephanie. "Anastasia Beverly Hills Will No Longer Work with Rodan + Fields after a Ton of Fan Backlash." *BuzzFeed News*, February 7, 2020. www .buzzfeednews.com/article/stephaniemcneal/anastasia-beverly-hills-rodan -fields-mlm-backlash.

———. "Rachel and Dave Hollis Played Themselves." *BuzzFeed News*, November 5, 2021. www.buzzfeednews.com/article/stephaniemcneal/rachel-hollis-dave-hollis-instagram-rant.

Megan. "15 Ways to Use Sensory Marketing in 2023." Brandastic, November 17, 2022. https://brandastic.com/blog/sensory-marketing/.

Meyer, Robinson. "Everything We Know about Facebook's Secret Mood-Manipulation Experiment." *The Atlantic*, August 5, 2021. www.theatlantic.com/technology/archive/2014/06/everything-we-know-about-facebooks-secret-mood-manipulation-experiment/373648/.

Mindvalley. "Transform Lives, Starting with Yours: The Mindvalley Certified Life Coach Journey." n.d. www.mindvalley.com/certs/life/masterclass.

Mindvalley Coach. "Breaking the Myth: Are There Too Many Coaches in the World?" YouTube. December 7, 2023. www.youtube.com/watch?v=NKsV_Cv2UL0.

Misha (dontcrossagayman). "I Feel Like I'm Not Overreacting." TikTok. November 27, 2023. www.tiktok.com/@dontcrossagayman/video/7306259791901445409.

Moen, Matt. "MrBeast Asks Fans to Clean up His Chocolate Bar Store Display." *Paper Magazine*, March 8, 2023. www.papermag.com/mrbeast-chocolate-bar#rebelltitem13.

MONAT Global. "MONATions 2022 Recap." YouTube. September 15, 2022. www.youtube.com/watch?v=f-a3m0HwW34.

Morales, Eduardo. "Is Instagram Dying? (Yes, but Not for Everyone)." Publicist. August 2, 2021. www.publicist.co/the-spin/the-inside-scoop/is-instagram-dying.

Muldowney, Decca. "MLM Seller Jessie 'Boss Lee' Ward Dies after Trying to Cure Her Cancer Naturally." *The Daily Beast*, September 19, 2023. www.thedailybeast.com/mlm-seller-jessie-boss-lee-ward-dies-after-trying-to-cure-her-cancer-naturally.

"Multilevel Marketing: Last Week Tonight with John Oliver." YouTube. November 7, 2016. www.youtube.com/watch?v=s6MwGeOm8iI.

Muniz, Albert M., and Thomas C. O'Guinn. "Brand Community." *Journal of Consumer Research* 27, no. 4 (2001): 412–32. https://doi.org/10.1086/319618.

Muslim Travel Girl. Homepage. November 19, 2023. https://muslimtravelgirl.com/.

"National Park Foundation." Tupperware US. n.d. https://web.archive.org/web/20230314174002/https://www.tupperware.com/pages/national-park-foundation.

NBC News. "Influencers Warned by FTC over 'Inadequate' Disclosures of Artificial Sweetener Promotions." November 15, 2023. www.nbcnews.com/news/us-news/ftc-influencer-warning-disclosures-artificial-sweetener-promos-rcna125396.

Neate, Rupert. "UK Millionaires Group Projects 'Tax Our Wealth' on to Treasury and Bank of England." *Guardian*, November 21, 2023. www.theguardian

.com/uk-news/2023/nov/21/uk-millionaires-tax-wealth-treasury-jeremy
-hunt-patriotic-millionaires-uk.

Neff, Jack. "Gen Z Favors Social Media over TV for CPG Purchases and Accepts
Personalized Ads More Than Other Groups." *AdAge.* August 24, 2023. https://
adage.com/article/marketing-news-strategy/gen-zs-cpg-buying-habits-and-ad
-preferences-revealed-tinuiti-study/2512616.

Nelson, Anne. *Shadow Network: Media, Money, and the Secret Hub of the Radical
Right.* New York: Bloomsbury, 2021.

Norlund, Chris. "How Social Media Influencers Fed Bankman-Fried's Cult of
Personality." Coindesk. January 18, 2023. www.coindesk.com/consensus-maga
zine/2023/01/18/how-social-media-influencers-fed-bankman-frieds-cult-of
-personality/.

North, Anna. "#SaveTheChildren Is Pulling American Moms into QAnon."
Vox, September 18, 2020. www.vox.com/21436671/save-our-children-hashtag
-qanon-pizzagate.

Not the Good Girl. "Why I Quit the MLM Industry at the Top—Anti-MLM
Horror Story." May 21, 2020. www.youtube.com/watch?v=xzOt_Hmjcbo.

NPR. "Here's Every Word from the Seventh Jan. 6 Committee Hearing on Its
Investigation." July 12, 2022. www.npr.org/2022/07/12/1111123258/jan
-6-committee-hearing-transcript.

Nutrition for Zero Hunger." Herbalife. March 14, 2023. https://iamherbalife
nutrition.com/global-responsibility/nutrition-for-zero-hunger/.

Offline with Jon Favreau. Episode 96. "The Truth about TikTok's Spin on Israel-
Gaza." November 11, 2023. https://crooked.com/podcast/the-truth-about-tik
toks-spin-on-israel-gaza.

O'Neil, Cathy. *Weapons of Math Destruction: How Big Data Increases Inequality and
Threatens Democracy.* New York: Crown Books, 2016.

O'Sullivan, Donie. "Her Son Was an Accused Cult Leader. She Says He Was a
Victim, Too." CNN. September 23, 2023. www.cnn.com/2023/09/23/us/
qanon-trump-kennedy-protzman-cult-invs/index.html.

Pariser, Eli. *The Filter Bubble: What the Internet Is Hiding from You.* New York:
Penguin, 2011.

Parker, Alyse. "Goodbye Raw Alignment. HELLO Alyse Parker." YouTube.
August 8, 2019. www.youtube.com/watch?v=gzpyOGWG1RM.

———. "Things Are Finally Changing." YouTube. November 30, 2023. www
.youtube.com/watch?v=inFWbcujRMs.

Patch, Will. "Social Media for College Search in 2022." Niche. August 24, 2022.
www.niche.com/about/enrollment-insights/social-media-for-college-search
-in-2022/.

Patel, Neil. "12 Genius Ways to Apply Emotional Marketing to Facebook Ads."
2017. https://neilpatel.com/blog/emotional-marketing-to-facebook-ads/.

Patriotic Millionaires. Homepage. January 3, 2024. https://patrioticmillionaires
.org/.

Patten, Bonnie. "Self-Regulation in the Direct Selling Industry: Can It Ever Be More Than Symbolic?" (2022 keynote address, Multilevel Marketing: The Consumer Protection Challenge, June 10, 2022). www.mlmconference.com/conference-videos-copy.

Peoplehood. Homepage. n.d. www.peoplehood.com/.

Perdomo, Blanca (blanca_perdomo). "I've Seen MLM Leaders Do Some Pretty Awful Things." TikTok. February 1, 2023. www.tiktok.com/@blanca_perdomo/video/7195207339446652206.

Pérez-Peña, Richard, and Daniel E. E. Slotnik. "Gaming the College Rankings." *New York Times*, January 31, 2012. www.nytimes.com/2012/02/01/education/gaming-the-college-rankings.html.

Perry, Nick. "10 MLM Statistics You Need to Know." Fundera. January 23, 2023. www.fundera.com/resources/mlm-statistics.

Pew Research Center. "For Shopping, Americans Turn to Mobile Phones while Influencers Become a Factor." November 21, 2022. www.pewresearch.org/short-reads/2022/11/21/for-shopping-phones-are-common-and-influencers-have-become-a-factor-especially-for-young-adults/.

Pflanzer, Lydia Ramsey. "How Elizabeth Holmes Convinced Powerful Men Like Henry Kissinger, James Mattis, and George Shultz to Sit on the Board of Theranos." *Business Insider*, June 2, 2023. www.businessinsider.com/theranos-former-board-members-henry-kissinger-george-shultz-james-mattis-2019-3.

Pine II, B. J., and J. H. Gilmore. *The Experience Economy*. Boston: Harvard Business School Press, 2011.

Prins, Kai, and Mariah L. Wellman. "Dodging Negativity Like It's My Freaking Job: Marketing Postfeminist Positivity through Beachbody Fitness on Instagram." *Feminist Media Studies* 23, no. 3 (2021): 1292–1308. https://doi.org/10.1080/14680777.2021.1992645.

Purser, Ronald E. *McMindfulness: How Mindfulness Became the New Capitalist Spirituality*. London: Repeater, 2019.

Pyramid Schemes. New York State Attorney General. Accessed January 17, 2024. https://ag.ny.gov/pyramid-schemes.

Q: Into the Storm. HBO, 2021.

Quart, Alissa. *Squeezed: Why Our Families Can't Afford America*. New York: Ecco, 2019.

Quinterno, John. *The Great Cost Shift: How Higher Education Cuts Undermine the Future Middle Class*. Demos, 2012.

Rabbit, Rabbit. "A Game Designer's Analysis of QAnon." *Medium*, December 16, 2021. https://medium.com/curiouserinstitute/a-game-designers-analysis-of-qanon-580972548be5.

Ragas, Matthew W., and Bolivar Bueno. *Power of Cult Branding*. New York: Random House, 2002.

Rao, Pallavi. "How Much the Most Followed Instagram Accounts Earn on Posts." Visual Capitalist. July 20, 2023. www.visualcapitalist.com/cp/most-followed -instagram-accounts-earn-posts/.

Rega, Sam. "What Is Life Coaching? It's Not Therapy, but It's a Nearly $3 Billion Business." CNBC. March 26, 2021. https://cnbc.com/2021/03/26/what-is-a -life-coach.html.

Robb, Amanda. "Anatomy of a Fake News Scandal." *Rolling Stone*, July 20, 2020. www.rollingstone.com/feature/anatomy-of-a-fake-news-scandal-125877/.

Robbins, Christopher. Homepage. Type Investigations. December 18, 2023. www.typeinvestigations.org/.

Rogers, Gil. *The Maturation of Mobile and Social: The 2017 Social Admissions Report.* Digital Marketing Solutions for Education Institutions, 2017.

Roose, Kevin. "The Making of a YouTube Radical." *New York Times*, September 3, 2020. www.nytimes.com/interactive/2019/06/08/technology/youtube -radical.html.

Rose-Stockwell, Tobias. *Outrage Machine: How Tech Amplifies Discontent, Disrupts Democracy—and What We Can Do about It.* London: Hachette UK, 2023.

Rossen, Jake. "Sell-Shocked: The Pyramid Schemer Who Convinced His Targets to Climb into Coffins." Mental Floss. May 19, 2022. www.mentalfloss.com/ posts/holiday-magic-pyramid-scheme.

Rousselet, Morgane, Olivier Duretete, Jean-Benoît Hardouin, and Marie Grall-Bronnec. "Cult Membership: What Factors Contribute to Joining or Leaving?" *Psychiatry Research* 257 (November 1, 2017): 27–33. https://doi.org/10.1016/ j.psychres.2017.07.018.

Rozsa, Matthew. "Facebook Could Have Stopped 10 Billion Impressions from 'Repeat Misinformers,' but Didn't: Report." *Salon*, April 12, 2021. www.salon .com/2021/04/12/facebook-could-have-stopped-10-billion-impressions-from -repeat-misinformers-but-didnt-report/.

Russakoff, Dale, and Juan Williams. "Rearranging 'Amway Event' for Reagan." *Washington Post*, January 22, 1984. www.washingtonpost.com/archive/politics/ 1984/01/22/rearranging-amway-event-for-reagan/b3e74482-5ce0-4d20-9f98 -ebdc9b4d4918/.

Russell, Dominic, Alan Smith, and Carrie Sloan. *The Financialization of Higher Education.* Roosevelt Institute, 2016.

Ryan, Danielle. "Fitness Coach Turned Business Coach Sales Webinar." YouTube. February 24, 2023. www.youtube.com/watch?v=E2L4AEM97pE.

———. "Welcome to My Channel: Here's What to Expect." YouTube. April 28, 2023. www.youtube.com/watch?v=lW2WnLytXz8.

Sagal, Peter. "The End Will Come for the Cult of MAGA." *The Atlantic*, September 12, 2023. www.theatlantic.com/ideas/archive/2023/08/trumpism-maga -cult-republican-voters-indoctrination/675173/?utm_source=pocket_saves.

"Scents Make Sense: Using Smell in Marketing and Retail." ANA. May 13, 2022. www.ana.net/miccontent/show/id/aa-2022-05-scent-in-marketing.

Schein, Michael F. *The Hype Handbook: 12 Indispensable Success Secrets from the World's Greatest Propagandists, Self-Promoters, Cult Leaders, Mischief Makers, and Boundary Breakers*. New York: McGraw Hill Professional, 2021.

Schutter, Candice. The Deeper Pulse with Candice Schutter. Episode 57. "The MLM Mindset: A Former MLM Coach & Top-Tier Earner Blows the Whistle—Jennifer Rajala, Part 1 of 2." May 24, 2023. https://podcasts .apple.com/us/podcast/57-the-mlm-mindset-a-former-mlm-coach-top-tier/ id1556669396?i=1000614271551.

"The Science of Sensory Marketing." *Harvard Business Review*, February 17, 2015. https://hbr.org/2015/03/the-science-of-sensory-marketing.

Selingo, Jeffrey. "Colleges' Endless Pursuit of Students." *The Atlantic*, April 10, 2017. www.theatlantic.com/education/archive/2017/04/the-business-of-col lege-marketing/522399/.

"Sensory Marketing: The Power of the 5 Senses in Retail." Kendu. June 1, 2021. www.kendu.com/retail-news-trends/sensory-marketing/#:~:text=Due%20 to%20the%20constant%20need,point%20of%20difference%20among%20stores.

Serazio, Michael. *The Authenticity Industries: Keeping It "Real" in Media, Culture, and Politics*. Stanford, CA: Stanford University Press, 2023.

Shaw, Norman, Brenda Eschenbrenner, and Daniel Baier. "Online Shopping Continuance after COVID-19: A Comparison of Canada, Germany and the United States." *Journal of Retailing and Consumer Services* 69 (November 1, 2022): 103100. https://doi.org/10.1016/j.jretconser.2022.103100.

Shellnutt, Kate, and Hannah Anderson. "The Divine Rise of Multilevel Marketing." *Christianity Today*, November 23, 2015. www.christianitytoday.com/ ct/2015/december/divine-rise-of-multilevel-marketing-christians-mlm.html.

Shirky, Clay. "Power Laws, Weblogs, and Inequality." Clay Shirky's Writings about the Internet. 2003. www.shirky.com/writings/powerlaw_weblog.html.

Shorin, Toby. "Life after Lifestyle." Subpixel Space. September 14, 2022. https:// subpixel.space/entries/life-after-lifestyle/.

Shotton, Richard. *The Choice Factory: 25 Behavioural Biases That Influence What We Buy*. Petersfield, Hampshire, UK: Harriman House, 2018.

Simply Kelly Noelle. "Why I Quit My MLM from the Top .4%." YouTube. September 19, 2022. www.youtube.com/watch?v=RP4vwEVphQI.

Singletary, Michelle. "Americans View Crypto Investing as Unreliable. They're Right." *Washington Post*, April 21, 2023. www.washingtonpost.com/business/ 2023/04/21/americans-view-cryptocurrency-unreliable/.

Slate. "Inside the MLM to Life Coach Pipeline." September 20, 2023. https:// slate.com/transcripts/K2pkWDAyUC92Y1AxcUIxZkhhNXZYWkJ3czZhd kU2WkZyRVBoN2Q1OFJVcz0=.

Southern Poverty Law Center. "Stefan Molyneux." n.d. www.splcenter.org/ fighting-hate/extremist-files/individual/stefan-molyneux.

Srnicek, Nick. *Platform Capitalism*. New York: John Wiley & Sons, 2017.

Stam, Aleda. "Stagwell Acquires Movers+Shakers." *AdAge*. November 2, 2023. https://adage.com/article/agency-news/stagwell-acquires-moversshakers/2526506.

Stanley-Becker, Isaac. "Pro-Trump Youth Group Enlists Teens in Secretive Campaign Likened to a 'Troll Farm,' Prompting Rebuke by Facebook and Twitter." *Washington Post*, September 16, 2020. www.washingtonpost.com/politics/turning-point-teens-disinformation-trump/2020/09/15/c84091ae-f20a-11ea-b796-2dd09962649c_story.html.

Startup Grind. "How to Build Habit-Forming Products." YouTube. March 10, 2017. www.youtube.com/watch?v=-jXM4NymIcA.

Stolzenberg, Ellen Bara, Kevin Eagan, Edgar Romo, Elaine Jessica Tamargo, Melissa C. Aragon, Madeline Luedke, and Nathaniel Kang. *The American Freshman: National Norms Fall 2018*. Los Angeles, CA: Higher Education Research Institute, 2019.

Sumar, Alexandra, and Colleen Christison. "The History of Social Media in 33 Key Moments." Hootsuite. April 6, 2023. https://blog.hootsuite.com/history-social-media/

"Survey Finds Disordered Eating Behaviors among Three out of Four American Women (Fall, 2008)." UNC Gillings School of Global Public Health, February 11, 2015. https://sph.unc.edu/cphm/carolina-public-health-magazine-accelerate-fall-2008/survey-finds-disordered-eating-behaviors-among-three-out-of-four-american-women-fall-2008/.

Swan, Teal. Facebook. October 4, 2019. https://facebook.com/tealswanofficial/posts/hello-everyone-as-many-of-you-have-noticed-my-video-on-vaccines-was-removed-from/2913487975346290/?locale=es_LA.

Taibbi, Matt. "The Great College Loan Swindle." *Rolling Stone*, June 25, 2018. www.rollingstone.com/politics/politics-features/the-great-college-loan-swindle-124484/.

Taylor, Jon M. *The Case (for and) against Multi-Level Marketing*. Consumer Awareness Institute, 2011.

"TechCrunch Is Part of the Yahoo Family of Brands." July 12, 2022. https://techcrunch.com/2022/07/12/google-exec-suggests-instagram-and-tiktok-are-eating-into-googles-core-products-search-and-maps/.

TEDxMidAtlantic. "Dismantling QANon." YouTube. October 22, 2020. www.youtube.com/watch?v=1QbEcG8O-L8.

Thompson, Caroline. "How to Get a Friend Out of an MLM." *Vice*, October 22, 2018. www.vice.com/en/article/43e573/how-to-get-a-friend-out-of-an-mlm-herbalife-amway-younique-?__twitter_impression=true.

Tiffany, Kaitlyn. "Why Multilevel Marketing and QAnon Go Hand in Hand." *The Atlantic*, December 15, 2020. https://theatlantic.com/technology/archive/2020/10/why-multilevel-marketing-and-qanon-go-hand-hand/616885/.

Timberg, Craig, and Isaac Stanley-Becker. "Cambridge Analytica and the RNC Suppressed Black Voters in 2016." *Washington Post*, September 28, 2020. www

.washingtonpost.com/technology/2020/09/28/trump-2016-cambridge-analy
tica-suppression/.

Tini, Krystal. Instagram. March 30, 2020. www.instagram.com/p/B-WBqe_J6bH/
?hl=en&img_index=1.

———. Instagram. August 28, 2022. www.instagram.com/p/ChzqsX2vnlI/?hl=en.

Tough, Paul. "Americans Are Losing Faith in the Value of College. Whose Fault
Is That?" *New York Times*, September 5, 2023. www.nytimes.com/2023/09/05/
magazine/college-worth-price.html.

Truth in Advertising. "Enagic Income Claims Database." December 11, 2021.
https://truthinadvertising.org/evidence/enagic-income-claims-database/.

———. "Trial Court Rules Neora Is Not a Pyramid Scheme." September 28, 2023.
https://truthinadvertising.org/articles/trial-court-rules-neora-not-a-pyramid
-scheme/.

"Tupperware!" *American Experience*, February 9, 2004. www.pbs.org/wgbh/american
experience/films/tupperware/#transcript.

Twenge, Jean M. "What We Know Now about Screen Time for Kids." *Deseret
News*, March 8, 2022. www.deseret.com/2022/3/7/22965534/what-we-know
-now-about-screen-time-for-kids-jean-twenge-igen-social-media.

Van der Linden, Sander. *Foolproof: Why Misinformation Infects Our Minds and How to
Build Immunity*. New York: W. W. Norton, 2023.

Vanian, Jonathan. "Meta Lets Amazon Shoppers Buy Products on Facebook and
Instagram without Leaving the Apps." CNBC. November 9, 2023. https://
cnbc.com/2023/11/09/meta-lets-amazon-users-buy-on-facebook-instagram
-without-leaving-apps.html.

Vesoulis, Abby, and Eliana Dockterman. "How MLM Distributors Are Using
Coronavirus to Grow." *Time*, July 9, 2020. https://time.com/5864712/multi
level-marketing-schemes-coronavirus/.

VICE News. "Startup Social Chain Takes Social-Media Marketing to a New Level
(HBO)." YouTube. March 2, 2017. www.youtube.com/watch?v=J_EPO2lw
gpQ.

Volpe, Allie. "What Happened When the MLMs Found Tinder." *Bustle*, January
10, 2022. www.bustle.com/wellness/mlm-recruitment-dating-social-apps.

Von Abrams, Karin. "Global Ecommerce Forecast 2021." Insider Intelligence.
July 7, 2021. www.insiderintelligence.com/content/global-ecommerce-forecast
-2021.

Waite, Amanda. "A New Way to Apply to College Simplifies the Process, Promotes Equity & Access." Coalition for College. August 1, 2022. www.coalition
forcollegeaccess.org/news-announcements/apply-coalition-on-scoir-launch.

Ward, Charlotte, and David Voas. "The Emergence of Conspirituality." *Journal of
Contemporary Religion* 26, no. 1 (January 1, 2011): 103–21. https://doi.org/10.1
080/13537903.2011.539846.

Ward, Jessie Lee. Instagram. January 22, 2023. www.instagram.com/p/CnuSIl cLGtq/?utm_source=ig_embed&ig_rid=bbb12363-d9b6-4686-b866-a328bc 901dea.

———. Instagram. May 9, 2023. www.instagram.com/p/CsCH45LJGhP/?hl=en.

———. Instagram. September 18, 2023. www.instagram.com/p/CxVdXeh M1he/?img_index=1.

Ware, Asia Milia. "Everything We Know about the Lash Drama on TikTok." *The Cut*, January 27, 2023. www.thecut.com/2023/01/everything-we-know-about -the-lash-drama-on-tiktok.html.

Wedding, Paul. "North Texas Fitness Influencer Ordered to Pay $400,000 as Part of Settlement." WFAA. June 8, 2023. www.wfaa.com/article/news/local/ north-texas-fitness-influencer-pay-more-than-500000-part-settlement/287 -3d410af8-7508-4ecc-a780-ad87016e3f44.

Weiner, Natalie. "Candy Brand Sour Patch Kids Providing a Free Home-Away-from-Home for Emerging Artists." *Billboard*, August 3, 2015. www.billboard .com/music/features/candy-brand-sour-patch-kids-patch-houses-interview -6649171/.

Wells, Georgia, Jeff Horwitz, and Deepa Seetharaman. "Facebook Knows Insta-gram Is Toxic for Teen Girls, Company Documents Show." *Wall Street Journal*, September 14, 2021. www.wsj.com/articles/facebook-knows-instagram-is-toxic -for-teen-girls-company-documents-show-11631620739.

What Americans Think about College: Government Funding and Assistance. APM Re-search Lab, 2019.

"What Happened to ViSalus? (Explained)." BehindMLM. November 23, 2020. https://behindmlm.com/companies/visalus/what-happened-to-visalus -explained/.

"What Is the Average Conversion Rate for Influencer Marketing Campaigns?" LinkedIn. December 18, 2023. www.linkedin.com/advice/0/what-average -conversion-rate-influencer-marketing-bx3ce#:~:text=Generally%20 speaking%2C%20Instagram%20micro%2Dinfluencers,mega%2Dinfluencers%20 have%200.2%25.

Williams, Alex. "Heather Armstrong, 'Queen of the Mommy Bloggers,' Is Dead at 47." *New York Times*, May 11, 2023. https://nytimes.com/2023/05/10/us/ heather-armstrong-dead.html.

Wilson, Jeff. *Mindful America: The Mutual Transformation of Buddhist Meditation and American Culture*. New York: Oxford University Press, 2014.

Wofford, Benjamin. "Meet the Lobbyist next Door." *WIRED*, July 14, 2022. www.wired.com/story/meet-the-lobbyist-next-door/.

Wold, Marie. Instagram. n.d. www.instagram.com/marieewold/.

Wong, Julia Carrie. "How Facebook and YouTube Help Spread Anti-Vaxxer Propaganda." *Guardian*, February 1, 2019. www.theguardian.com/media/2019/ feb/01/facebook-youtube-anti-vaccination-misinformation-social-media.

Wright, George. "NXIVM: 'Why I Joined a Cult—and How I Left.'" BBC News. April 13, 2019. www.bbc.com/news/world-47900242?ocid=socialflow_twitter.

Wright, Susan. "A Year of 'Permacrisis.'" *Collins Language Lovers Blog*, October 28, 2022. https://blog.collinsdictionary.com/language-lovers/a-year-of-permacrisis/.

Young, Dannagal Goldthwaite. *Wrong: How Media, Politics, and Identity Drive Our Appetite for Misinformation*. Baltimore: Johns Hopkins University Press, 2023.

INDEX